AN INTRODUCTION TO
AIRLINE ECONOMICS

AN INTRODUCTION TO AIRLINE ECONOMICS
Sixth Edition

WILLIAM E. O'CONNOR

Westport, Connecticut
London

Library of Congress Cataloging-in-Publication Data

O'Connor, William E.
   An introduction to airline economics / William E. O'Connor.—6th ed.
     p. cm.
   Includes bibliographical references and index.
   ISBN 0–275–96911–8 (alk. paper)
    1. Airlines—United States. 2. Airlines—United States—Management. I. Title.
   HE9803.A4026 2001
   387.7'1'0973—dc21   00–032620

British Library Cataloguing in Publication Data is available.

Library of Congress Catalog Card Number: 00–032620
ISBN: 0–275–96911–8

First published in 2001

Praeger Publishers, 88 Post Road West, Westport, CT 06881
An imprint of Greenwood Publishing Group, Inc.
www.praeger.com

Printed in the United States of America

The paper used in this book complies with the
Permanent Paper Standard issued by the National
Information Standards Organization (Z39.48–1984).

10 9 8 7 6 5 4 3 2 1

Contents

Tables

Preface

This book is an introduction to the economics of the airline service of
the United States, both domestic and international, for the reader whose
need is for a relatively simple, yet college-level, text. It is intended as a
textbook for one-semester courses of the type becoming common in U.S.
colleges today and bearing such titles as "Aviation Administration," "Air
Transportation," or "Economics of Air Transportation."

Since the appearance of the fifth edition in 1995, there has been a
continuation of the remarkable changes in the fabric of the airline industry that have characterized the years since the rise of the deregulation
movement in the mid-1970s. The gradual relaxation of government economic regulation of the airlines, especially with respect to their domestic
services, was completed by 1985. Since then, the industry has seen a
series of mergers and a general trend toward consolidation into fewer
but larger airlines. Route patterns have been reconstructed about hub
cities. The early 1990s saw unprecedented operating deficits, with two
major carriers going out of existence, but the late 1990s, by contrast, have
seen a swing to highly profitable operations. The late 1990s have also
been characterized by the forming of "alliances" among United States
and foreign airlines, often involving the buying of equity shares in one
another. The sixth edition contains substantial revisions consistent with
these changes, including complete rewriting of many portions.

As with previous editions, the sixth continues to emphasize plain En-
glish and to avoid the more obscure reaches of economics that can
frighten away, or be downright unintelligible to, a student who has not

done advanced work in economics. Although an elementary college-level course in economics is helpful, it is not essential in order for a student to be at ease with this text.

For each chapter there are self-testing questions so that students can check their progress. In this respect the book is adaptable to the self-paced teaching method. These questions are of the essay type, and would be suitable for take-home examinations and for selective use in classroom tests such as comprehensive finals. They may also serve as a guide to an instructor in the preparation of more specific questions for examinations of the objective type.

Certain portions of the basic transportation statute—the former Federal Aviation Act, as amended by the deregulation acts—that are pertinent to the text are reproduced or summarized in an appendix.

Although the reform legislation greatly reduced the degree of governmental economic regulation of the airlines, some regulation continues with respect to service to small communities and to all international services. Thus, the legal and political framework within which the industry operates continues to be important and is carefully covered. The international arena is given great attention in light of the extreme importance of the airline, with the virtual demise of the scheduled passenger ocean liner, as the primary form of passenger transportation between the United States and foreign countries. As for the air cargo sector, it has a chapter of its own in recognition of its unique problems and growing importance.

In addition to a substantial bibliography at the end of the book, there is at the end of each chapter a short list of selected references pertinent to the subject matter of that chapter. Not all of these are easy reading for a student, and it is suggested that an instructor survey these references in advance to determine how many of them are appropriate for assignment as supplementary reading for a particular class. Material in these selected references might also lend itself to the preparation of term papers.

In as lively and changing a field as airline economics, it is essential that both students and instructors follow the current scene. Of the periodicals listed in the bibliography, four should be made available in the college library, and instructors would be well advised to have their own personal subscriptions. These are *Air Cargo World*, *Air Transport World*, *Aviation Week and Space Technology*, and the *Journal of Air Law and Commerce*. An excellent source of data on the U.S. airline industry is the Annual Report of the Air Transport Association. Another good source is the Department of Transportation's Office of Aviation Analysis.

The general format of this sixth edition is similar to that of previous editions. Chapters 1 and 2 are introductory, the first giving an overall view of the airline industry, the second a look at the many ways in which the airlines serve the public interest and assist in the achievement of various individual and governmental goals. Chapter 2 includes a glimpse of the objectives of foreign countries as they may impinge on U.S. international airline service. Moving into the basic economics of the industry, Chapter 3 covers entry of airlines into and exit from markets (managerial policies, governmental restrictions, the impact of regulatory reform, mergers, and arrangements with foreign governments for entry on international routes). Chapter 4 analyzes airline costs; Chapter 5 deals with the demand for airline services. Chapter 6 is an extensive treatment of airline rates; Chapter 7 concerns air cargo; and Chapter 8 analyzes current problem areas such as airports, fuel prices, and the trend toward concentration. A bibliography and a detailed index complete the book.

Although oriented to the needs of a one-semester college course, this text is intended to be useful to many persons: students of all modes of transportation who need a simple, basic treatment of the air mode; students majoring in economics or business administration who need an introduction to this essential and growing industry; airline employees who wish a better knowledge of their company's problems; traffic managers of manufacturing or retail firms that send cargo by air; consumer representatives; attorneys and public officials who may be called upon to deal with airline problems; and anyone else desiring a primary understanding of airline economics. Professional and business readers in particular should find the selected references and the bibliography useful as a starting point for pursuing specific topics in greater depth.

Recent years have seen a searching national examination of the economics of our airline service that has had dramatic consequences for this young industry, which, in its short life, has so altered the quality of our lives. The years ahead promise to be a time of continuing experimentation and change.

Acknowledgment is gratefully made to the many sources drawn upon for this and previous editions—especially to Frank Hausman for his valuable help in monitoring the press for significant articles; to Professors Alan Bender, Rudolph Knabe, and Robert A. Kuropkat of Embry-Riddle Aeronautical University; and to Carole A. Bridges, Patricia T. Thomas, and their many co-workers in the Department of Transportation.

Abbreviations

ACI	Air Cargo, Inc.
ACMI	aircraft, crew, maintenance, insurance
ADA	Airline Deregulation Act
AGV	automatic guided vehicle
ATC	Air Traffic Conference
ATPCO	Airline Tariff Publishing Company
CAB	Civil Aeronautics Board
COFC	container on flatcar
CRAF	Civil Reserve Air Fleet
CRS	computer reservations system
DOC	direct operating cost
DOJ	Department of Justice
DOT	Department of Transportation
DPFI	Domestic Passenger Fare Investigation
EDI	electronic data interchange
ESOP	employee stock ownership plan
EU	European Union
FAA	Federal Aviation Administration
IATA	International Air Transport Association
IATCA	International Air Transportation Competition Act

ICAO	International Civil Aviation Organization
ICC	Interstate Commerce Commission
JIT	just-in-time concept
LASH	lighter aboard ship
LTL	less than truckload
NAFTA	North American Free Trade Agreement
NMB	National Mediation Board
OAG	Official Airline Guide
REA	Railway Express Agency
SFFL	standard foreign fare level
SFRL	standard foreign rate level
SIFL	standard industry fare level
SST	supersonic transport aircraft
TOFC	trailer on flatcar
ULD	unit load device
WTO	World Trade Organization

1

An Overall Look at the Structure of Air Transportation

This book will concern itself primarily with the common carrier system of air transportation—that is, with air services offered to the public for hire. It will include services from the tiniest air taxi to the largest of airlines, will cover charter as well as scheduled services, and will deal with the transport of cargo and mail as well as of passengers.

There are, of course, many aircraft in the skies that do not fall under this common carrier designation, for example, military planes and the broad category called "general aviation," such as private aircraft for pleasure flying and planes owned by corporations and used to fly executives to scattered plants. We shall deal with these noncommon carriage operations only to the extent that they impinge upon common carrier systems. We shall also consider problems of airports, airways, and aircraft manufacturing to the extent that they affect common carrier services.

Our focus will be on the United States but will include the services of both U.S. and foreign airlines that connect the United States with the rest of the world.

In 1938 the economic aspects of airline service were placed under control by the federal government in a manner resembling the historic control of surface carriers by the Interstate Commerce Commission (ICC) and of public utilities such as electric power companies by state public utility commissions. The agency established to govern the economic regulation of airlines was the Civil Aeronautics Board (CAB). It consisted of five members, appointed for six-year terms by the president with the consent of the Senate, assisted by a staff that averaged about 750 employees.

Then, on October 24, 1978, the Airline Deregulation Act of 1978 (ADA) became law and with it was launched a new era in the history of our airlines. Despite its name, this act did not eliminate all economic regulation. Rather, it reduced the extent of this regulation by steps over a period of several years through the end of 1984, at which time the CAB was abolished. Pursuant to the Civil Aeronautics Board Sunset Act (P.L. 98–443), enacted October 4, 1984—referred to hereinafter as the Sunset Act—all the CAB's remaining functions were transferred to the Department of Transportation (DOT).

ECONOMIC REGULATION DEFINED

What do we mean by economic regulation? Formerly it involved having the CAB decide how many airlines and which airlines were going to operate in a particular market (the term *market* here meaning a pair of cities). Entry by an airline into a market was controlled by requiring that every airline obtain a certificate from the CAB specifying the routes that must be followed. Exit was controlled by requiring an airline to receive CAB approval before dropping service to a city. Prior governmental approval of mergers and acquisitions was another aspect of entry and exit control. This topic will be examined more fully in Chapter 3. Suffice it to say here that entry and exit control for domestic airline service has largely terminated except for minimal essential services at certain small points, regulation of which is exercised by DOT. Control with respect to international services still exists and is exercised by DOT. (For simplicity's sake, in this book we will use the word "domestic" for what the current transportation statute calls "interstate," which it defines as including service to and within U.S. possessions as well as among the fifty states of the United States.)[1]

Another form of economic regulation in the CAB era was control by that board over airline rates. Today, regulation of domestic airline rates has been virtually eliminated, while regulation of international rates is a function of DOT. The topic of rates will be covered in Chapter 6.

REGULATORY REFORM

Later chapters will examine the details of the deregulation process and the economic thinking that gave rise to the deregulation movement. Let us note here, however, the timing of the steps by which it occurred.

Even before enactment of the Airline Deregulation Act of 1978, a majority of the five members of the CAB had begun to make decisions in accordance with the philosophy behind the deregulation movement.

They gradually liberalized policy toward the entry of airlines into new markets and their exit from markets that were no longer profitable. With respect to rates, they granted broader latitude to the airlines.

On December 31, 1981, in accordance with the timetable in the ADA, control over domestic entry largely ceased. A year later, most control over domestic passenger fares was terminated. Most of the control over domestic cargo rates had been removed by legislation enacted November 9, 1977, as will be described in Chapter 3. At the end of 1984, the CAB's authority over foreign air transportation was transferred to DOT. (As defined in the transportation statute, foreign air transportation means services to and from the United States by both U.S. and foreign airlines.) Also, as of the end of 1984, the job of protecting and subsidizing minimal essential services at small points went over to DOT, along with several other CAB functions to be described later.

In consequence of the deregulation legislation, the airlines have faced, in the ensuing years, such radical changes as the appearance of many new small airlines, the expansion of existing airlines into new markets, many mergers and bankruptcies, and a sharpening of rate competition— all to a degree previously unheard of in the airline industry.

The term *regulatory reform* more accurately describes this whole process than does the term *deregulation*, since it leaves intact certain aspects of economic regulation, especially over international services. Moreover, the changes in no way reduce governmental regulation of airline safety and navigation, the province of the Federal Aviation Administration (FAA).

Originally the regulatory reform movement was largely a U.S. phenomenon and its philosophy was not generally shared by other countries. By the mid-1980s, however, the trend was toward relaxation of economic controls on airline services in Canada and Western Europe; by the mid-1990s the trend was worldwide, though not without firm resistance by many governments and foreign airlines. In the international arena, where the U.S. government is only one of many sovereign governments, many of which desire a government-directed air transport industry, it is difficult to see how this country can completely deregulate its foreign air transportation. For example, if the U.S. government desires to have, say, five U.S. airlines flying between San Francisco and Tokyo, but the Japanese government is determined to limit this to two, then all five cannot begin service regardless of what the U.S. government may have authorized. However, in recent years the United States has rather effectively bargained with other countries to obtain agreements permitting an increased number of its airlines to foreign points and more competitive international airline rates.

The very complex subject of international airline service will be considered later. We will also discuss the International Air Transportation

Competition Act (IATCA), enacted on February 15, 1980. This act alters procedures and guidelines for the regulation of foreign air transportation, with the objective of having such regulation promote maximum managerial flexibility over routes and rates.

THE TRANSPORTATION STATUTE

The law that we will be most concerned with was called the Federal Aviation Act from its enactment in 1958 (as an amended version of the Civil Aeronautics Act of 1938) to July 5, 1994. On that date, P.L. 103–272 made modifications of language, but not substance, in the act, dropped the name of the act, and recodified the material so that it is now properly described as "Title 49 United States Code: 40101–49105." It remains the basic law governing economic regulation of common carrier air services of the United States. We will refer to it simply as "the transportation statute." It also imposes extensive safety and navigation regulations on *all* aircraft, not merely those of the common carriers, but we will be concerned with these regulations only as they may affect airline economics.

The regulatory reform legislation, such as the ADA, the IATCA, and the Sunset Act, consisted of a series of amendments to the Federal Aviation Act; thus, they are all contained in the 1994 statute. (See the Appendix for a digest of certain portions of the statute that apply to those aspects of airline economics that are still regulated.)

The statute contains a lengthy set of definitions. It defines *air transportation*, in a peculiarly restricted sense, as any *common carrier* transportation of passengers or cargo by air within the United States, or to or from the United States, or any carriage of U.S. mail by aircraft. The term *air carrier* is defined in a similarly restricted sense; it means only those carriers that are engaging in "air transportation" and is limited to U.S. carriers. A foreign airline that engages in "air transportation" by serving the United States is defined as a *foreign air carrier*.

The statute then subjects the "air transportation" branch of aviation to a degree (though now a greatly diminished degree) of governmental regulation over its economic affairs. This would all be very well if the statute defined *common carrier*, but it does not. Actually the common carrier has a legal background going back to stagecoach days in England and chugging into modern times with the steam railroad. It can be defined, for practical purposes, as any person (including a corporation) that not only offers transportation service for hire but also offers it to the general public. Thus, the term applies even to an air taxi operator with one small aircraft that limits itself to charter service.

Since the Federal Aviation Act did not extend economic regulation to purely intrastate airlines, there were several carriers in the pre-deregulation era that escaped CAB controls altogether by confining their services within one state. Outstanding examples were Pacific Southwest Airlines within California and Southwest Airlines within Texas. However, with the relaxation of entry controls under deregulation, these operators extended their services well beyond their home states.

SPECIAL ECONOMIC CHARACTERISTICS

Apart from, or in addition to, the headaches of governmental controls, the airlines have the normal headaches of any business: controlling costs, negotiating with labor unions, seeking rates that accurately reflect the various elasticities of demand, obtaining financing, and making the kind of profits that will keep stockholders happy and will attract capital. In addition, they must live with certain special economic characteristics. We will discuss some of these characteristics briefly in this chapter, but leave more detailed discussion of their complexities for later chapters.

An Undifferentiated Product

Airline service tends to be what economists call an undifferentiated product—that is, to many passengers the service of one airline is rather hard to differentiate from the service of another. Modern aircraft are very much alike, at least within any given size range. The speed, comfort, and safety aspects of a journey are likely to be much the same, whichever airline a passenger selects. Airlines frequently have concentrated their advertising on desperate attempts to differentiate their product by emphasizing steak dinners aloft, friendly smiles, and similar minor benefits. Yet probably a flight is chosen not by reason of favoring one airline over another but simply by the most convenient times of departure and arrival. In a sense, flight scheduling is a form of product differentiation, and it would appear to be the most important one.

In the days of CAB regulation, the similarity of product resulted in competing airlines' tending to charge the same fare for the same service, so that passengers usually took it for granted that they would pay the same fare regardless of which airline they picked. The CAB did not ordinarily require that fares be identical, though it often set a maximum or minimum; the identity resulted from a belief by airline management that it had to meet the competition. This is still largely true today even in the absence of domestic rate regulation. Typically a fare in a market will be the lowest fare that any one of the competing carriers wishes to charge, although in the deregulated marketplace today there are often exceptions, as we shall later see.

Proponents of regulatory reform contend that greater product differentiation exists than has been realized. They point, for example, to various experiments with no-frill service and with flights that serve convenient downtown airports such as Love Field in Dallas and Midway Airport in Chicago. And their contention that unregulated entry and unregulated rates would open the way to experimentation with a variety of services and prices has now been demonstrated in some markets.

A Highly Perishable Product

An airline deals in a highly perishable product in the sense that an unfilled seat on a flight is immediately perishable—that is to say, it cannot be stored for future sale in the way manufactured goods can be stored. As with motel rooms and theater seats, empties are a dead loss. As we will see in Chapter 6, the airlines have developed highly complex rate structures to cope with this problem.

Ease of Entry

It is relatively easy to enter the airline business and easier still for an existing airline to expand into a new market. (Remember that we are using the word *market* to mean a pair of cities.) Unlike a railroad, which must buy a right-of-way and lay miles of track before it can make a nickel, an airline need own only the vehicle. It does not own the "road" over which its vehicles travel or the terminals (that is, the airports). And even the vehicle can be leased or bought on credit, aircraft typically being sold with a mortgage (often called an equipment trust) on them. The economic barrier seems small indeed, compared with almost any manufacturing industry. Here there are no factories to be built, no assembly lines to equip. It is relatively easy for anyone to buy a plane and jump into the business or easier still for an existing airline to move into a new market—to the extent that remaining governmental barriers, as in international service, will permit.

All this, of course, oversimplifies the problem. Modern aircraft are expensive, and monthly payments on them are huge. Various taxes, charges, and rentals must be paid for the use of airports and the airways. There are the costs of getting any business started—hiring and training personnel, advertising one's entrance into the new market. Then there is the question of the need to operate on a particular scale in order to realize cost savings. On this point there is much disagreement. Some economists will hold that the largest airline, if well managed, will have the lowest costs. Others will point to the experience of smaller airlines that often have been more profitable than the larger ones. Perhaps shrewd adapting of the size of one's operations to the peculiar economics of one's routes is of greater cost significance than mere size alone. (This question will be examined in more detail in Chapters 3 and 4.)

Tendency to Monopoly or Oligopoly

Another characteristic of airline service may seem somewhat contradictory to the one just mentioned. It is that airlines may have an inherent tendency toward gradual elimination of competitors, with a resultant oligopoly, or even monopoly, in a market. This is a controversial point, but a belief in such a tendency has been one basis for the existence of governmental economic regulation of the industry. Is it contradictory to say that this is a field that competitors can enter with ease, yet at the same time a field where only the strongest will survive? It is not contradictory if we distinguish between the short run and the long run. It is one thing for a small company to enter the airline business, and quite another for it to survive. The relaxation of entry controls that came with deregulation has been followed, as we will later see, by the entry of many new small airlines but the survival of very few.

Economists who favor deregulation argue that to the extent that monopolistic tendencies exist, they are largely counteracted by competitive forces in a deregulated system. And, to the extent that such forces fail to maintain a competitive system, the regular antitrust laws that apply to other industries will come into play.

The ADA, however, was cautious on the question of monopolistic tendencies; it provided that prior approval still had to be obtained for airline mergers, acquisitions, and other control relationships. The Sunset Act in October 1984 transferred this power from the expiring CAB to DOT, but also provided that the power would terminate at the end of 1988, which it did. The airlines now fall under the regular antitrust laws, administered by the Department of Justice (DOJ), that apply to other industries.

OTHER ECONOMIC CHARACTERISTICS

There are various other characteristics of airline service. For instance, airlines have experienced a long-term growth rate well in excess of that of most other industries. Table 1 shows the astonishing growth of passenger service by decade from 1940 to 1970 and the somewhat more moderate, but still remarkable, growth for the two following decades. Between 1990 and 1998, however, growth slowed, totaling only about 35 percent.

Another characteristic is that the long-run tendency (at least until recent years) to larger, faster aircraft served to make the airlines more capital-intensive and less labor-intensive, although this trend can give way to a fuel-intensive period when there are sharp hikes in fuel price levels. Still another characteristic has been that, as new technology brings new models of aircraft on the market, the airlines may go through years of financial problems as they receive earlier-ordered aircraft that cause

Table 1
Passenger Traffic, Domestic and International, U.S. Scheduled Airlines, 1940–90, by Decade, and 1998

Year	Revenue Passenger Miles (in millions)	Percent Increase
1940	1,262	—
1950	10,688	747
1960	38,873	264
1970	131,710	239
1980	254,180	93
1990	457,915	80
1998	619,456	35

Source: Air Transport Association.

their capacity to grow faster than their traffic. (Break-in costs of crews and aircraft may add to their woes.)

Airlines are particularly sensitive to business cycles, especially with respect to the demand for pleasure travel. They also tend to have high debt/equity ratios—that is, the total debt in the form of bonds, aircraft equipment trusts, and so forth is high relative to the stockholders' equity. A business enterprise in such a situation is not in a good position to survive an extended period of economic recession. We will examine these and other characteristics in later chapters.

CHARACTERISTICS OF INTERNATIONAL SERVICE

By law, air traffic between one U.S. point and another U.S. point (the legal term for which is cabotage traffic) can be carried only by U.S. carriers, except that in certain emergencies foreign airlines may be authorized to participate temporarily in such service. Foreign airlines, however, have major scheduled services between the United States and foreign points, in competition with U.S. carriers, and carry about half of this international traffic.

Any international service by any airline can operate only with the consent of the governments at both ends of the trip, as we have previously noted. Any airline wishing to carry traffic between New York and London, for example, must serve two masters—the United States and Great Britain—whether the airline's nationality be U.S., British, or that of a third country. In this situation who decides questions of entry, routes, and rates?

Entry—International

Entry into international markets is determined through an elaborate series of bilateral agreements between governments. If a U.S. airline wishes to fly across the Atlantic to several points in Europe and then continue through the Middle East to India, the U.S. government must have a separate agreement with *each* of the governments along the way that grants one or more U.S. airlines the right to conduct transportation business at specified cities in its territory along a route described in the agreement. In turn, the United States grants similar rights to airlines of the foreign country to serve a point or points in the United States.

Chapter 3 will cover in more detail the complex and often fascinating subject of international cooperation in the economic regulation of airlines and of recent efforts by the United States to bring about a relaxation of governmental controls on international services. As we will see, a type of bilateral agreement described as "open skies" has been negotiated with several countries which allows airlines of each country to serve whichever points they choose in the other country.

Rate Regulation—International

The regulation of international airline rates used to fall largely to an association of airlines known as the International Air Transport Association (IATA), to which most, but not all, of the major airlines of the world belong. Although today much international ratemaking is accomplished outside its system, the IATA mechanism still applies over many routes. The rate agreements of IATA must receive the approval of every government, but to the extent that the airlines and governments wish to have an agreed set of rates, there is a built-in pressure to give ground in order to arrive at an agreement.

The regulatory reform movement in the United States has taken a particularly dim view of the whole IATA ratemaking procedure. The question of complete U.S. withdrawal from the system has been raised, but it now seems likely that a conditional, limited participation by the United States will continue, although the United States now considers these IATA rate agreements advisory rather than binding. Meanwhile the United States has made various arrangements that completely circumvent the IATA system and give airline management great pricing freedom in many international markets. (International rates will be examined in detail in Chapter 6.)

STRUCTURE OF THE U.S. AIRLINE INDUSTRY

Before entering into a more detailed study of airline economics, a student ought to have a general picture of the structure of the U.S. airline

Table 2
U.S. Major Airlines, Ranked by 1998 Operating Revenues

Airline	1998 Revenues (in millions)
United Airlines	$17,518
American Airlines	16,299
Delta Air Lines	14,630
Federal Express	13,666
Northwest Airlines	8,707
US Airways	8,556
Continental Airlines	7,299
Southwest Airlines	4,164
Trans World Airlines	3,259
United Parcel Service	1,997
America West Airlines	1,983
Alaska Airlines	1,581
DHL Airways	1,349

Source: Air Transport Association, Annual Report—1998.

industry. In past years airlines were rigidly classified by the CAB according to their particular mission—trunk lines (primarily serving larger cities over medium and long distances), local service carriers (primarily serving smaller points over short distances), all-cargo carriers, charter carriers, and so on. However, as a consequence of regulatory reform legislation, the distinctions lost much of their significance, and in 1981 the CAB dropped these classifications when publishing airline data and instead began using new categories based simply on the size of the carrier's revenues. DOT currently uses this system.

Under this system, airlines with annual operating revenues of over $1 billion are described as *majors*. They are shown in Table 2, ranked by their 1998 operating revenues. Six of the thirteen are former trunk lines. Three, Federal Express, United Parcel Service, and DHL Airways, are all-cargo carriers whose services will be described in Chapter 7.

Airlines with operating revenues between $100 million and $1 billion are described as *nationals*. There were 34 of these in 1998, including five all-cargo carriers. Airlines with annual operating revenues below $100 million are described as *regionals*; there were 51 of these in 1998. They may use large aircraft, but their operations are on a relatively small scale. They should not be confused with the *commuter air carriers*, which operate small aircraft (not over 60 seats or 18,000 pounds payload) and are not included in these DOT reporting categories. In a sense, they can be considered scheduled air taxis, though they are seldom referred to as such. They operate under a general exemption, found in Section 40109 of the transportation statute, from certification requirements. (The distinction between certification and exemption will be clarified in Chapter 3.)

The terminology for the DOT categories may be confusing, since a national carrier is in no way obliged to have a nationwide service, nor are the regionals limited to serve only one region. Also, it should be emphasized that this terminology is DOT's, designed for data classification, and may not be the prevailing usage elsewhere. In fact, the terms *regional airline* and *regional carrier* are commonly used to include the commuter air carriers.

Since deregulation, the traffic volume of the commuter air carriers has grown greatly, as has their significance to society. Many communities now depend entirely on them for scheduled air service. They have moved well beyond the business-day-trip traffic that gave them their name and have become important feeders of traffic to the major airlines. Similarly, the regional airlines, with aircraft larger than those of the commuters but generally smaller than those of the majors, are often the only service at some communities and serve as connections to the major airline networks.

As for the nonscheduled air taxis, as of 1999 there were about 2,400 of them registered with DOT. Subject to the same aircraft size limitations as the commuters and operating under the same exemption, they limit their service to on-demand charters, often with very small aircraft.

Airlines with authority to carry passengers also have authority to carry cargo. However, it is possible to obtain a certificate for domestic all-cargo service only, pursuant to Section 41103, as will be explained further in Chapter 3.

It should be emphasized that, although there are many air carriers of one category or another, the industry continues to be dominated by a few giants. The ten passenger majors accounted for 93 percent of the total revenue passenger miles of the U.S. scheduled airline industry in 1998.[2]

Airlines have become overwhelmingly dominant in intercity common carrier passenger travel in the United States. Precise figures are elusive because of difficulties with defining, especially for bus and train, what is "intercity," what is "commuter," and what is "local." However, one source gives data for 1993, measured by revenue passenger miles, as air 90.6 percent, bus 6.3 percent, and rail 3.1 percent of intercity travel.[3] But keep in mind that these are figures for common carrier travel; the private automobile, it is estimated, carries about 80 percent of all intercity travel.

So much for structure. The following chapter explores the more philosophical area of how airlines serve the interests of the public.

NOTES

1. Transportation Statute, Section 40102 (a)(25).
2. Author's calculations from Air Transport Association, *Annual Report—1999*, pp. 4 and 17.
3. Author's calculations from U.S. Bureau of the Census, *Statistical Abstract of the United States*, 117th ed., 1997, p. 619, Table 992.

SELECTED REFERENCES

The structure and characteristics of the airline industry, both in the United States and worldwide, are described in Paul S. Dempsey and Laurence E. Gesell, *Airline Management: Strategies for the 21st Century* (Chandler, Ariz.: Coast Aire Publications, 1997), pp. 2–21.

A good statistical picture of the U.S. airline industry may be found in the *Annual Report* of the Air Transport Association, Washington, D.C.

2

How Airlines Serve the Public Interest

U.S. PUBLIC INTEREST OBJECTIVES

The transportation statute, in Section 40101 (a)(7) of its declaration of policy, in language taken from the former Federal Aviation Act, speaks of an air transportation system adapted "to the present and future needs of (A) the commerce of the United States; (B) the United States Postal Service; and (C) the national defense." This three-way division of the public interest into commerce, postal, and defense is useful enough, though it by no means exhausts the goals that the public and its government seek from airline services, even if we define the word *commerce* very broadly to cover the social desirability of being able to travel swiftly from one end of the nation to the other and the national cohesiveness, both political and social, that derives in part from ease of travel.

The Postal Service wants good air transportation, not only for its first class and other priority mail but also for the large and increasing proportion of other categories of mail that it now often sends by air on a "space available" basis.

The Defense Department wants airline service for its normal needs to transport personnel and cargo beyond what is carried by military transport aircraft. But it has a larger, long-range interest in having a substantial commercial airline fleet available as a standby facility for a military emergency.

The term *commerce* includes the flow of air freight, business travel, tourist travel, and, indeed, the travel of anyone for any purpose. This much is obvious. What may be less obvious is that members of the public who may seldom, if ever, have occasion to fly have a major stake in having adequate airline service. They include persons connected directly or indirectly with the tourist industry, all residents of areas heavily dependent on tourist travel, and the owners and employees of industries whose executives depend on air travel or whose operations may rely on air freight. It includes the stockholders and employees of the aircraft manufacturing industries, since the manufacture of civil transport aircraft—that is, aircraft specifically designed for use by airlines—depends on airlines as customers.

The entire economies of regions where aircraft manufacturing is a major industry (the Seattle area with respect to the Boeing Company, for example) thus become indirectly dependent on the health and development of airline service. And, since components for aircraft—and this includes the engines—are frequently manufactured by companies other than the designated aircraft manufacturers, the ramifications spread. General Electric, for example, makes aircraft engines.

The process of ramification can also be illustrated by tourist travel. Important enough to the economies of such cities as Miami and San Francisco, airline service becomes even more critical to Hawaii, where geographical isolation and the slow speed of ocean vessels effectively prevented the two-week vacationer from visiting the islands before the advent of airline service.

Indeed, as the airline economist Melvin Brenner has put it, "transportation is a basic part of the economic/social/cultural infrastructure, which affects the efficiency of all other business activities in a community and the quality of life of its residents."[1]

But we have been taking a rather commercial view of the term *commerce*. The ability to travel is prized by most people. A few clichés may demonstrate the point. We want to see the world, or we say that travel broadens a person in one sense or another. And few of us are immune to the romance of far-off places as an advertising ploy. There is travel to get away from it all, whether by fleeing to the beach or the mountains or by fleeing the quiet life for a place of excitement. Almost anyone would like to see one's children have a chance to visit foreign countries as part of their education, to experience the languages and cultures and try to appreciate the different values of societies other than our own. "See America First" is yet another cliché whose message leads U.S. travelers to overcrowd Disneyland, Yellowstone Park, and so on.

And, for at least some of us, the process of traveling itself may be an enjoyable and rewarding experience. Yet another cliché—getting there is half the fun—was used a few years ago by the transatlantic ocean transport companies in a losing battle with the airlines for passenger traffic. The airlines, of course, put much effort into persuading passengers that they are extremely happy just to be on board an aircraft, though this writer has never noticed any great number of passengers who appear filled with regret when the trip ends.

The point to be emphasized here is that although this book will dwell largely on economic matters, the ultimate objectives of the economic effort go far beyond the fields of economics or business administration and touch questions concerning the very nature of humanity.

If the foregoing discussion seems to paint a wholly rosy picture of what airlines do for us, let it be noted here that airline service can be injurious as well as helpful to the public. Obvious examples are the environmental problems of noise and air pollution in the vicinity of airports, airline accidents, and injury to competing industries. The latter category includes motor carriers losing freight to airlines and the major inroads into long-distance railroad passenger service that the airlines have made. And it is possible that not all residents of a tourist mecca are delighted with the air-delivered seasonal swarms of people who crowd and overtax their facilities.

Moreover, there are those who would say that, in a world of rapidly growing population, countries with high per capita drain on the earth's finite resources, such as the United States, should seek to level off the seemingly endless rise in such consumption activities as airline service. Travel by air in the United States continues to increase at a rate far beyond the increase in our population or wealth, with attendant drain on the world's petroleum resources and aggravation of the environmental impact of airports, two topics we will consider in later chapters. Yet much business travel, and perhaps even some family travel, could be foregone in favor of such devices as computer links, conference telephone calls, and/or videotelephones. One must expect the airlines to promote their service, and the travel industry to promote vacation trips, but national policy and public opinion may some day have to lean in the opposite direction.

The Public Importance of Airlines

The great importance of airline service was undoubtedly one factor causing Congress in 1938 to establish a regime of regulation similar to what had been established for the railroads (1887) and for the motor carriers (1935). But although these transportation modes have been regulated much as electric power and telephone companies are regulated by public utilities commissions, it can be misleading to describe them as "public utilities," since this term is reserved by most economists for enterprises that not only are part of the essential framework of the economy but also have strong "natural monopoly" characteristics. An example of the latter is the electric power industry. It would be tremendously costly to the public to have two electric power companies running their lines side by side about a city, and the virtues of having competition would be more than canceled out by the very high cost of the duplication of the facilities.

Among transportation companies, the railroads seem the most likely example of the natural monopoly with their heavy investment in right-of-way and track. Yet there are pairs of cities served by more than one railroad, and the term *natural monopoly* must be applied with some caution. Neither the trucking industry nor the airlines would appear to fit this natural monopoly concept. Federal economic regulation for them has meant regulating the degree of competition in each market, which can be a more complex task than the job faced by a public utilities commission regulating a monopoly electric power company. The relaxation of the economic regulation of airlines has had its counterpart in similar relaxation for the motor carriers and, to a lesser extent, for the railroads. But while proponents of this deregulation questioned the usefulness of regulating these carriers, they in no way disputed the high degree of their importance to society.

In fact, the ADA and later the IATCA made some revisions in the Federal Aviation Act's declaration of policy that expand its description of goals. The language, now continued as Section 40101(a) of the transportation statute, includes emphasis on the "availability of a variety of adequate, economic, efficient, and low-priced services." And, as means to these ends, it advocates such approaches as maximum reliance on competitive forces, prevention of unfair or anticompetitive practices, encouraging the entry of new carriers, and encouraging existing carriers to enter new markets.

OBJECTIVES OF INTERNATIONAL AIRLINE SERVICE

It is one thing to consider the air transport goals and policies of the United States within the borders of the United States, where we are dealing with one national economy and with the jurisdiction of one government. It is quite another thing to consider U.S. goals and policies toward the airline services between the United States and the rest of the world, where the United States must deal with a multiplicity of airlines and governments of countries with differing cultures, political systems, economic problems, and levels of technological development. Our government can determine what policies it would like to see applied to world airline service, but the implementation of such policies requires the consent of foreign governments and their airlines. We must do more than merely seek out U.S. objectives; we must also try to identify and understand the objectives and motives of other governments in establishing and promoting their world airline services.

In general, governments have the same objectives with respect to their international services that they have with respect to domestic services, plus some additional ones. The "commerce, postal, and defense" trio mentioned above applies to the services between one's country and the rest of the world as well as within the country. Yet conflicts between governments on aviation matters tend to dwell on the promotion by each government of its airlines as against the airlines of other countries.

The basic question then becomes: What goals motivate each government in this promotional climate?

Among the objectives we may single out the following:

1. Having an international airline may win a country prestige in the sense of improving the esteem in which the country is held or perhaps in impressing the world with the country's technological progress. In the earlier days of aviation, much weight was attached to the prestige factor, but today, when airline service has become far less dramatic, it is questionable whether governments should place much emphasis on it. Indeed, with today's trend toward airlines forming "alliances" with airlines of other nationalities and with airlines buying part ownership in airlines of different nationalities (as we will see in Chapter 3), the attaching of national pride to a country's airline becomes less and less logical.

2. Some isolated, underdeveloped countries may feel that improved air links with the world will encourage trade, tourist travel, and investment. Of course, airlines of other countries may be furnishing adequate service, but if not, the development of a national carrier to serve over world routes may seem desirable.

3. A country may wish its airline to serve a particular foreign country as part of a policy of promoting a political linkage with that country. In the period prior to World War II, the European countries with colonial empires promoted and heavily subsidized what for the times were substantial airline services around the earth to their colonies. With the dissolution of the major colonial empires, many of these airline linkages remain, partly because of a continuing policy by the former mother country to maintain what ties it can to its former colony. Another example of the political linkage motivation is the former Soviet Union's air service to Cuba.

4. The earnings of a national airline may be significant in the total economy of a country and may be particularly important in the country's foreign exchange balance. This is especially so when a small country has developed a relatively large world airline. An example is KLM, of Netherlands nationality, most of whose passengers neither originate in nor are destined for the Netherlands. The term *merchant airline* is often used to describe this type of carrier. However, even an airline of a large country that carries much home-country traffic may be a significant item in the country's foreign exchange balance, the British carriers being an example. U.S. airlines also, to some extent, help to alleviate the U.S. balance-of-payments problem, but a far more important factor in the balance for the United States is the sale abroad of U.S. transport aircraft.

5. For a poor and technologically backward country, establishing an international airline may contribute to a desired psychological effect on people, impelling them away from a traditional apathetic approach and toward a setting of new goals. To this may be added the concept of "technological density," meaning that one element in developing a backward economy is to increase the number of persons trained in skilled occupations, professions, and administration.

6. Development of a country's airlines along international routes may promote the home manufacture of transport aircraft. Clearly this will apply only to the few countries with such manufacturing. The United States, Great Britain, and Russia are three outstanding examples.

7. A country's standby fleet for a military emergency will be augmented if its airlines expand their fleets to accommodate expanding international services. The expansion of a pool of fully trained flight crews is also of interest as a military standby. The United States has a Civil Reserve Air Fleet program (CRAF) under which the Department of Defense has access in an emergency to about 500 passenger and cargo aircraft of U.S. airlines, with flight crews. CRAF was activated during the Persian Gulf War and transported 25 percent of the airborne cargo and 63 percent of the airborne passengers in that operation.[2]

8. There are some situations where the desire of a government to curry favor with (or refrain from giving offense to) another government is a factor in making a bilateral exchange of rights. A similar situation arises where two governments establish airline service for the specific purpose of making a friendly gesture intended to lessen tensions. The obvious case here was the U.S.-USSR bilateral agreement under which service between New York and Moscow by a Soviet and a U.S. airline was instituted for the first time in 1968. It had been possible for a number of years to travel between the two cities via a simple change of planes in Western Europe, and in light of the thin traffic there was little economic justification for the service.

9. Civic leaders may feel that with the economy becoming more globalized, a city or metropolitan area without good air links to the world will be left behind. In this sense, a parallel can be drawn with the rise of seaports in an earlier era.

This discussion does not exhaust every objective and every factor entering into governmental policies concerning international airlines, but it should give a picture of the major considerations.

A closing thought: perhaps governments devote too much attention to political and psychological considerations and not enough to the more mundane concepts of an airline as a device for moving passengers, cargo, and mail from one place to another.

NOTES

1. Melvin Brenner, "Airline Deregulation—A Case Study in Public Policy Failure," *Transportation Law Journal* 16 (1988): 189.

2. U.S. General Accounting Office, *Airline Competition: Impact of Changing Foreign Investment and Control Limits on U.S. Airlines*, 1992, p. 15.

SELECTED REFERENCES

Detailed discussions of the objectives of governments in their airline policies can be found in Mahlon R. Straszheim, *The International Airline Industry* (Washington, D.C.: Brookings Institution, 1969), pp. 8–18: William E. O'Connor, *Economic Regulation of the World's Airlines* (New York: Praeger, 1971), chap. 4; George W. James, ed., *Airline Economics* (Lexington, Mass.: D.C. Health, 1982), pp. xxiv–xxx; and Ramon de Murias, *The Economic Regulation of International Air Transport* (Jefferson, N.C.: McFarland, 1989), pp. 10–13, 25, 28.

The CRAF program is described and analyzed in U.S. General Accounting Office, *Airline Competition: Impact of Changing Foreign Investment and Control Limits on U.S. Airlines*, 1992, pp. 15 and 50–59.

The attitudes of some developing countries toward their airlines is described in Assad Kotaite, "Investment and Training Needs among Key Challenges Facing Developing Countries," *ICAO Journal* 48 (March 1993): 24–26.

A detailed analysis of the extensive ramifications of aviation through the whole U.S. economy can be found in Robert J. Zuelsdorf and Eric B. McClellan, "The Economic Impact of Civil Aviation on the U.S. Economy," in *Handbook of Airline Economics*, ed. Darryl Jenkins (Washington, D.C.: McGraw-Hill, 1995), pp. 267–84.

The impact of airlines on the environment and proposed remedial measures are discussed in Pablo M. J. Mendes de Leon and Steven A. Mirmina, "Protecting the Environment by use of Fiscal Measures: Legality and Propriety," *Journal of Air Law and Commerce* 62 (February-March 1997): 791–821; and Paul S. Dempsey and Laurence E. Gesell, *Air Transportation: Foundations for the 21st Century* (Chandler, Ariz.: Coast Aire Publications, 1997), pp. 465–99.

3

Entry and Exit

Entry can mean that an existing airline institutes service in a market or in a series of markets along a route. It may also mean that a brand new enterprise enters the airline business; as a result of deregulation, there have recently been many of these. Exit means an airline's discontinuing service in a market either by its own decision or by governmental action.

This chapter addresses the question of what motivates an airline to wish to enter or leave a market. We will also consider the nature of governmental involvement in the entry and exit process over the years, how it has changed under deregulation, and the effects of these changes on the economics of the airline industry.

We will consider mergers as involving both entry and exit, and ask why an airline may want to merge with or acquire another airline.

With respect to international service, this chapter will look at the remaining governmental controls, exercised by DOT, and will also show how foreign governments have a say in the entry of U.S. airlines into international markets. This includes limitations on the *degree* of entry, such as restrictions on the frequency of international flights.

AIRLINE ENTRY AND EXIT POLICIES

Why does an airline wish to enter a market? There is the obvious business reason of perceiving a profit to be made, but this can be broken down into many elements. An airline with a strong summer peaking in its system may desire to fly to Miami, where the peak season is winter.

Or, if it has idle capacity on weekends and holidays because of a preponderance of business travel on its system, it may wish to add tourist markets. An airline may have aircraft that operate at lowest cost on long hauls and thus will be motivated to seek new routes with widely separated major cities. In some cases an airline may simply have too much capacity (aircraft, personnel, terminal facilities, computerized reservations systems, and so on) for its volume of business and may feel the solution is to enlarge the size of its route system.

The precise nature of the existing route system can be an important factor. How well would the additional point or route tie in with the airline's scheduling pattern? The planning of an airline's schedules and the allocation of its operating personnel are extremely complex problems, and compatibility of proposed new points or routes with the existing pattern is critical. If the carrier already has terminal facilities at one or more of the points along the proposed new route, that fact will weigh in its favor. In other instances an airline's expansion plans will be tied to the concept of back-up or feeder traffic; for example, if an airline has a route from New York to San Francisco, it will be painful to see one's passengers transferring to another airline for onward flights to Hawaii when acquiring a San Francisco–Hawaii route would make it possible to offer the complete haul.

Attention will also be given to the density of the market—that is, to the quantity of traffic already flowing in it—and to indicators of future growth, such as population and income trends for the areas in question. And, of course, the number and strength of the airlines already in each market will be a major consideration, as will an estimate of what others may be planning to enter. This has become far more difficult to predict with the relaxation of governmental controls over entry.

To these sound motivations perhaps we should add that, since airline managers are human beings, there may at times be an impulse to favor growth as inherently good, to feel pride as additional dots are placed on the company's map.

Economies of Scale, Scope, and Density

Economists make a distinction among economies of scale, economies of scope, and economies of density. An airline that expands its total operations may realize economies of *scale*, but whether any major airline is likely to realize economies by simply getting bigger is a matter of much controversy. However, an airline adding a route branching out from its existing network may well realize economies of *scope*—that is, savings because, for example, its airport facilities and personnel are already in place at the point of origin and their costs can now be spread over more units of output. On the other hand, economies of *density* do not come from adding a new route but from getting better utilization of existing services.[1] "For example, an airline which carries 100 passengers in a single plane to a destination as opposed to carrying 50 passengers in two aircraft to that same destination is making use of economies of density."[2]

Hub-and-Spoke Systems

Since deregulation, the major airlines have increasingly emphasized the development of so-called hub-and-spoke systems, which one authority has defined as follows:

A hub and spoke system consists of a set of "spoke" routes flying to and from minor markets into major "hub" cities. The major airline which creates the hub and spoke system flies some of these spokes itself. Commuter, local, or smaller airlines whom the major airline has co-opted into the system fly other spokes. A set of much longer and heavier regional spokes connects major traffic hubs and are all operated by the creator of the particular system. Indeed, the traffic potential of the regional spokes is the reason behind the creation of the system[3]

Another authority offers this description of how such systems work:

The basic notion of a hub and spoke system is that flights from many different cities converge on a single airport—the hub—at approximately the same time, and after giving the passenger sufficient time to make connections, all then leave the hub airport bound for different cities. Such a convergence of flights on a hub is often called a "connecting complex" or "connecting bank."[4]

Although there were hub-and-spoke systems back in the days of domestic route regulation, such as ones centered at Atlanta by both Delta and Eastern, the emphasis was on the development of long main routes, resulting in so-called linear networks. Since deregulation, the airlines have further developed those hubs they had and have established many new ones. Not all are at the largest cities; in some instances a less crowded secondary point is selected for a major hub.

One motive of an airline in developing hub-and-spoke systems is to increase the average number of passengers on its flights, an obvious critical element in earning a profit. By developing traffic along the feeder spokes, an airline increases its traffic along its longer hauls. Moreover, it controls the flow of the spoke traffic onto its long-haul flights since it controls the arrival times of the feeder flights at the hub airport. Thus, an airline with a strong hub system protects its traffic from being diverted to another airline en route.

From the passenger's standpoint there may be an advantage in increasing the number of flights to and from minor points, but there is the great disadvantage of a reduction in the number of nonstop flights and of flights without a change of planes.

We will consider later in this chapter some problems arising from the strong trend to hub-and-spoke systems, such as the crowding of airport facilities and the power that a strong hub gives to the incumbent major airline in keeping out a new competitor. Let us note here, however, that the trend has gone so far that it has been estimated that as much as 80 percent of all U.S. airline domestic seat miles involve hubbing operations.[5]

Airline Exit Policies

The reasons why an airline wishes to exit from a market are largely the reverse of its reasons for entry. An operation may have proved unprofitable—or less profitable than if the resources were employed elsewhere—and future prospects do not seem bright. Competition from other airlines may have proved severe. Perhaps little feeder effect has occurred, or perhaps a change in the composition of the carrier's fleet has made a short-haul market too expensive to service. (A sharp rise in fuel costs can exacerbate the latter problem.) Or maybe the carrier is in weakened financial condition and must undergo a general retrenchment.

GOVERNMENT REGULATION OF ENTRY

Until 1938 anyone could enter or leave any market with no legal requirement to approach the government at all, except with respect to safety matters. But there was virtually no chance for a profitable service without obtaining an air mail contract from the Post Office Department, which involved a substantial subsidy. Thus, the postmaster general held the practical power to determine which airline or airlines were to enter each market. (Prior to 1925 there had been scattered efforts to establish airline services, and there were a few air mail contracts issued, but most air mail was carried by the Post Office Department in its own aircraft. The Kelly Act of 1925 began the phasing out of the Post Office's own operation and the growth of the air mail-subsidized private airline.)

The 1925–38 period saw the emergence of four major domestic carriers (American, Eastern, TWA, and United), which became known unofficially as the Big Four. In the international area the period saw the rise to dominance of a single airline, Pan American World Airways, on Latin American routes. There was, in 1938, no transatlantic airline service; only a small experimental transpacific service had been launched by Pan American in 1936.

The Civil Aeronautics Act of 1938 made it illegal to operate a common carrier airline service unless the newly established five-member board (given its designation, Civil Aeronautics Board, in 1940) had issued a "certificate of public convenience and necessity" authorizing such service and describing the routes. The act, however, directed that such certificates were to be granted to the airlines then in existence with respect to those points they were then serving. The airline had only to show that it was serving the points continuously and adequately, except for interruptions beyond its control, between May 18, 1938, and the enactment date of the act, August 23, 1938.

The new five-member board promptly ground out these certificates, which became known unofficially as "grandfather" certificates. Since that time the routes of these airlines have greatly expanded, but subsequent growth required their obtaining additional certifications through a much more difficult procedure.

The Certification Procedure

The language of the 1938 act concerning certification was continued in the 1958 Federal Aviation Act and remained substantially unchanged until the regulatory reform legislation of 1977–80. The language directed the board to grant a certificate only if it found that the proposed service was "required by the public convenience and necessity." The board also had to find that the airline was "fit, willing, and able" to perform the service and to obey the act and the board's rules (usually just called the "fitness" requirement), but most airlines could meet this latter test. In practice, the opinion of the board's members as to whether a proposed service was "required by the public convenience and necessity" was the governing factor in permitting or denying entry by an airline into new markets. The declaration of policy (Section 102 of the act) did not, prior to the ADA in 1978, contain the current language emphasizing "maximum reliance on competitive market forces" and "the encouragement of entry into air transportation markets by new air carriers," as well as "the encouragement of entry into additional air transportation markets by existing air carriers." Instead, between 1938 and 1978 there was no mention of the encouragement of entry, and the question of competition was dealt with in the following language, which became the major guiding principle during this 40-year period.

Competition to the extent necessary to assure the sound development of an air-transportation system properly adapted to the needs of the foreign and domestic commerce of the United States, of the Postal Service, and of the national defense.[6]

The important words here were "to the extent necessary"; they implied an in-between position on the subject. Competition was seen as sometimes good and sometimes bad for the public. Determining when competition—or, more precisely, when the number of competitors in a market—should be increased proved to be a complex task that relied heavily on human judgment. The individual economic and political philosophies of board members left an imprint on entry decisions in this era.

The conflicting philosophies were well described in a study prepared by the consulting firm Arthur D. Little, Inc.

The proponents of less competition argue that the reduction in the intensity of competition will result in the ability of carriers to tailor capacity more closely to traffic demand and thus maintain higher load factors and avoid the needless cost of unutilized capacity . . . Proponents of greater competition argue that the only practicable assurance of a continuing high standard of service available to the public when desired, at rates in line with the costs of providing the service, is effective competition that affords the passenger a choice of services and a means of expressing preferences among innovative alternatives.[7]

In general, from 1938 through 1978, CAB followed a "presumption doctrine," which meant "a strong, although not conclusive, presumption in favor of competition on any route which offered sufficient traffic to support competing services without unreasonable increase of total operating cost."[8] As a result there was a trend during these years toward an increased number of competitors in most markets and a greatly expanded route system for each airline. However, there were times when the presumption seemed to run against additional competitors rather than in their favor. For example, in the early 1950s and again in the early 1970s, the airlines were suffering financial problems and had excess capacity; the CAB, in response, certificated additional competitors in very few markets.

When the board decided a case, its job was divided into two main problems: to determine whether there was need for additional service and, if so, to decide which carrier or carriers should be selected to perform it. After elaborate procedural steps required by law and often resulting in delays of several years, the two problems were brought to a decision. The service of existing carriers was examined in regard to its adequacy for current and future traffic, and other prospective public benefits, such as increasing nonstop services, were considered. The position of the carriers already in the markets was also taken into account. The diversionary effects on them from adding a competitor were estimated and the results predicted. Despite the presumption doctrine, the board was unlikely to certificate an additional carrier in a market if it felt that carriers already in the market would suffer severe diversion of traffic.

Once a decision was made that an additional carrier was "required by the public convenience and necessity," the problem of selecting among a number of applicants (and there were usually plenty of applicants) had to be resolved. It was often a disadvantage to be one of the large trunk lines, because the CAB typically sought balanced competition and was reluctant to make the biggest airlines any bigger. More likely it would grant entry to a smaller trunk line. Sometimes it would select the weakest of the applicants for the purpose of strengthening it; this brought criticism for rewarding the weakest and penalizing the most efficient. On the other hand, an airline was sometimes found to be too small or too financially weak to be able to operate the service properly.

One factor in selecting a carrier was how well the new service would tie in with the carrier's system. The board looked at many of the considerations that had caused the airline to apply—a smoothing of its peak loads, better fleet utilization, and feeding of traffic from its existing routes into the new route it sought. It also looked at managerial skill, the past record of management in making innovations, and managerial ability to control costs.

Defenders of a conservative government policy toward entry argue that the consumer may derive little or no benefit from increasing the number of competitors in a market above two. Will three or four airlines have any greater incentive than two to please the passenger? The total number of flights in the market may increase, but unless the number of passengers flying in that market increases proportionately (and there is no reason to assume that this will happen), there will be lower load factors and higher costs, with a long-run result of higher fares. And an increased number of reservations systems, ticket counters, and advertisements adds nothing to the consumer's welfare, while increasing the cost of the service.

Yet it should be noted that during the 40 years of what, by today's standards, may seem tight governmental control over entry, the trend was to increase the number of competitors, so that it was not uncommon by the 1970s to find seven or eight airlines in many major markets, and as many as a dozen in a few. Of course, not all of these were major participants in the traffic; it was unusual to find more than three or four airlines dominant in any market.

Criticism of this system was not confined to matters of policy. It was also levied at the complicated and time-consuming procedures. An evidentiary hearing was required, presided over by an official of the board's staff (an administrative law judge), at which each airline or other interested party presented witnesses and could cross-examine witnesses of the other parties. Voluminous exhibits, largely economic data in support of or in opposition to the applicant airlines, were introduced and became part of the record. An initial decision by the administrative law judge was issued. Then, for the first time, the five board members would become involved, presiding over an oral argument wherein lawyers for the disappointed parties would attack the initial decision. Later, the board would issue its decision, sometimes simply accepting the initial decision, other times reversing part or all of it. Following this there could be petitions for reconsideration and sometimes even appeals to the federal courts. This lengthy procedure may still be used today if the agency (now DOT) elects to do so, which it may in cases such as international entry or controversial fitness decisions.

Since appeals to the federal courts will continue to be possible respecting any decision by DOT, whether arrived at by the formal procedure described above or by less formal means, perhaps a word about them is in order. An airline's appeal of a DOT order may result in the voiding of the order or its temporary suspension combined with a "remand" to the agency—that is, the order is sent back for further work. Appeals from an order are entitled by law to skip the lower level of federal courts, so that they are heard initially by a circuit court of appeals. A final step, sometimes undertaken, is a further appeal to the United States Supreme Court.

The federal courts are not supposed to act as if they were the government's experts on airline entry questions. They are supposed to let an order stand unless there is a specific legal basis for voiding or suspending it. Such grounds include improper procedures in the conduct of the case that infringe on the rights of any party, exceeding by the agency of its authority, and lack of substantial evidence or of a logical development from the evidence to the order's conclusions.

Changes in Certification Procedures

The first change in long-standing entry procedure and policy was with respect to domestic cargo, in the cargo regulatory reform law of November 9, 1977, designated as P.L. 95–163. (This law was given no formal name by Congress, and only certain parts of it deal with regulatory reform. We will refer to it simply as "the cargo regulatory reform law.")

Under this law any airline that had conducted scheduled freighter service anywhere between January 1, 1977, and November 9, 1977, was entitled for the asking to a certificate from the CAB permitting it to perform freighter service between any points of its choosing within the United States. ("Freighter" means an aircraft devoted entirely to cargo.) This included the certificated cargo carriers, the passenger airlines that also operated freighter flights, and many air taxis (including some commuter air carriers) that were operating all-cargo flights or all-mail flights for the Postal Service. There was no showing of public convenience and necessity, or even of fitness, required. The result was the virtual elimination of controls over entry into scheduled domestic all-cargo service.

The new law further provided that after a year's delay (November 9,

1978) these certificates (unofficially called "Section 418 certificates" after a new section in the Federal Aviation Act describing them) would become available to any air carrier even though it had not offered all-cargo flights in the 1977 period. Moreover, they would be available to any "citizen of the United States"—with the word "citizen" meaning a person, partnership, or corporation. However, in these instances the applicant had to show that it was "fit, willing, and able" to provide the service and to comply with CAB (now DOT) regulations. The provisions of Section 418 remain current today under Section 41103 of the transportation statute.

Today, this provision is of diminished importance since under the ADA, after January 1, 1982, a certificate combining authority for passenger and/or cargo service with no limitation on domestic routes can be had on only a fitness showing. Even so, as of September 1999, there were five carriers whose only authorization was for domestic all-cargo service.

A fitness showing for any kind of DOT air carrier certificate is a form of regulation that has survived the deregulation process and has been receiving increased emphasis from the late 1980s through the 1990s. Going all the way back to the 1938 Civil Aeronautics Act, the fitness concept is really a consumer protection device. A negative finding by DOT can result if an applicant has a reputation for managerial incompetence, has shown a pattern of indifference to safety and other regulations, and/or has serious financial problems. A new applicant without a previous record of air service must show reasonable planning as well as adequate financial and managerial resources.

The major piece of regulatory reform legislation, the ADA, came along nearly a year after the cargo act. It made changes with respect to entry into passenger markets that initially were somewhat less sweeping, though more complicated, than those that had been made with respect to domestic cargo service. Certificates of public convenience and necessity continued to be required, but a one-word change in the law made a major difference in the ease with which such certificates could be obtained. The board was no longer to determine whether the proposed service was "required" by the public convenience and necessity, but only whether it would be "consistent" with the public convenience and necessity. (The "required" language was left unchanged by the ADA with respect to international entry, but it, too, was changed to the "consistent" language by the IATCA in 1980.) In effect, this change in language meant that doubts were to be resolved in favor of granting certificates. A finding of fitness continued to be required.

From the standpoint of procedure, a major change also was made. The CAB was no longer required to hold evidentiary hearings but was permitted to grant or deny a certificate on the basis of the material in the application and in any response to the application supporting or opposing it. The board could simply look at the evidence and data filed by the applicant and the other supporting or opposing parties and issue an order. Also, by the revisions in the declaration of policy, which emphasized competition and new entry, the ADA was guiding the CAB into a very liberal interpretation of the new language concerning consistency with the public interest.

These provisions of the ADA became effective at once, as did several transitional provisions designed to ease the system gradually toward the day (January 1, 1982) when even the "consistent" language would be abolished for domestic entry, leaving only the fitness requirement. The transitional programs, however, while used to some extent, were largely superseded by the CAB's new philosophy of trying to go the ADA one better. Applications for entry were processed rapidly under the new, streamlined procedures and were freely granted.

With the arrival of January 1, 1982, all reference to "public convenience and necessity" was removed from consideration of domestic entry and, although certificates continued to be required, only a fitness showing was necessary. Section 401 of the Federal Aviation Act over the long years of CAB regulation had begun: "No carrier shall engage in any air transportation unless there is in force a certificate issued by the Board authorizing such air carrier to engage in such transportation." Now it had, in effect, been so liberalized with respect to domestic passenger service (or domestic flights carrying both passengers and cargo) that certification was on the same basis as had been granted in 1977 to the cargo carriers under Section 418—a certificate was still required but would be issued upon nothing more than a finding of fitness and would no longer specify the points to be served but would leave the selection of points entirely up to the airline. (The ADA did not clearly transfer this fitness certification function—with respect to either Sections 401 or 418—to DOT with the expiration of the CAB, but the Sunset Act in 1984 did just that.)

The fitness requirement began to receive increased attention with the coming of deregulation and the consequent entry into business of many new and small airlines. As of 1984, the CAB reported that, although there had been only a few denials of certificates, the fitness requirement had "served to weed out unsophisticated and potentially unfit applicants, who are deterred from filing applications or who do not prosecute them to completion when questioned on fitness matters."[9] More recently, when major airlines became involved in leveraged financial arrangements and reorganizations under the protection of the bankruptcy laws (so-called Chapter 11 bankruptcies, referring to a chapter of the bankruptcy laws), the fitness concept was applied to large established airlines. In 1993, the new secretary of transportation stated that "in our view, the failure of previous administrations to take prudent steps to maintain airline fitness by challenging overly leveraged deals accounts for some of the current financial difficulties of the U.S. airline industry." [10]

The General Accounting Office has described the fitness procedure as follows:

When an airline first applies for operating authority, requests a change in the type of authority it holds (e.g., a change from nonscheduled service to scheduled service), or undergoes significant changes in its financing, ownership, or management, DOT's Air Carrier Fitness Division conducts a "fitness review." For example, a fitness review could be triggered by an airline's filing for Chapter 11 bankruptcy court protection or by a significant change in the ownership of voting stock.[11]

It should be noted that the fitness procedure we have been discussing is separate from, though it supplements, an evaluation made by the FAA. Every airline, including commuters and air taxis, must obtain from the FAA an air carrier operating certificate premised on technical competence in maintaining and flying aircraft safely.

One result of the drastic reforms in the regulation of domestic entry has been a breaking down of the concept of dividing airlines into categories in accordance with a primary "mission" for each category. The former local service carriers are a case in point. Their mission, since their establishment by the CAB in the 1940s, was to serve small points within a region and to feed traffic from those points into larger cities for connections with long-distance travel on the trunk lines. At the time of the passage of the ADA in late 1978, there were eight local service carriers, six of which were receiving subsidies. Even prior to the ADA, they had been allowed, over the years, gradually to drop many of their smallest points (where subsidy per passenger was greatest), to take on some long-haul services between large cities, and to increase the areas that each one served. They had already developed many aspects of trunk lines, and deregulation simply enabled them to continue the trend without need for government approval.

Moreover, the terms of the ADA tended to push them firmly out of the small-point, short-haul markets by a provision that all subsidy to them was to stop by the end of 1985. Congressional action terminating appropriations for such subsidies as of the end of September 1983 put an even earlier date on their departure from their original mission. Through a series of mergers and acquisitions, the local service carriers had ended up by the late 1980s absorbed by the trunk lines (now called majors), except for US Airways, which evolved into a major in its own right. Many of the services once performed by local service carriers are being performed today by regional airlines or by commuter air carriers with small aircraft, some of it under the essential air service program, which will be discussed shortly.

International services by U.S. airlines require DOT certification not only on a basis of fitness but also on a finding of "consistency with the public convenience and necessity." Moreover, international certificates may specify the routes for which authority is granted. Where bilateral agreements limit the number of U.S. airlines that may serve a route to a foreign country, DOT must select one or a few from many applicants. In applying the language about "consistent with the public convenience and necessity," the agency may look at such factors as the quality and dependability of service an airline has offered on other routes, the possibility that an airline may introduce low-fare operations and thus be an important competitive influence on rates, and the fact that an airline may have a substantial network of domestic routes leading into the U.S. gateway city from which the foreign route is to proceed.

A foreign airline must obtain entry authorization from the U.S. government, but the word *permit* is used rather than *certificate*, and the governing section of the transportation statute is 41302 rather than 41102. Here the principal question in practice is whether the airline has been designated by its government to perform the service under the terms of a bilateral agreement. If it has been so designated, a permit is issued upon a finding of fitness. Even if, for some reason, designation under a bilateral agreement has not been given, DOT is authorized to grant the permit if, in addition to the finding of fitness, it also finds "that such transportation will be in the public interest." As with certificate proceedings, no hearing is required, but DOT must allow opportunity for written objections.

Both foreign air carrier permits (to give them their full name) and certificates for U.S. airlines for international service must be submitted to the White House before being issued, in order to give the president a chance to disapprove them. However, by law, the president may disapprove "only if the reason for disapproval is based on foreign relations or national defense considerations" but not "if the reason is economic or related to carrier selection" (Section 41307). The president has 60 days to act; in the absence of action within that time, the order becomes effective. During the 60 days, the Departments of State and Defense may be consulted.[12]

Prior to the ADA, the president had broader powers that required specific approval of any certificate for international service or foreign air carrier permit and did not limit the grounds for presidential action to foreign relations or national defense. The power was sometimes exercised to reverse CAB decisions on economic grounds or to select a different U.S. carrier than the one the board had picked for certification on an international route.

Limitations on Domestic Entry after Deregulation

The great relaxation of governmental barriers to domestic entry brought about by deregulation seemed, by the late 1980s, to have been succeeded by a nongovernmental, but nonetheless effective, process by which a large, well-established airline can prevent the entry, or limit the scope of entry, of a competitor into its markets, especially if the competitor is a new or small airline.

The process begins with the development of hubs (or "hubbing" as it is now sometimes called), which, as we have seen, results in many inbound flights converging at about the same time in order to connect with outgoing flights. An airline seeking to discourage the entry of others will try to control the "spokes" of the hub, the inbound feeder flights. Some of the feeder flights are its own, but many others are by regional or commuter carriers. These carriers are often owned outright by the major airlines or there are contractual arrangements between them. In either case, feeder flights will be timed to meet the major airline's services and, in most cases, will be described in timetables and computer reservations systems by the identifying code of the major airline.

The timing of flights so as to minimize passenger layover times results, at least at busier airports at busiest times of day, in severe competition for airport counter space, gate space, and operational slots. (A "slot" means a period of time sufficient for one takeoff or one landing.) We will discuss computer reservations systems and airport gates and slots in later chapters. Suffice it to say here that they have become tools by which a major airline entrenched at an airport may effectively limit competition at that point.

One example of the effectiveness of this process can be found at St. Louis, which had service by five major airlines before deregulation, then saw nine new entrants in the first years of deregulation. By mid-1987, however, according to the *Wall Street Journal*,

Now most of the traffic is handled by one carrier: Trans World Airlines. Having driven back or acquired its major rivals, TWA today enjoys a degree of dominance here that any airline would have envied prior to deregulation. Its 317 departures a day dwarf those of its nearest rival, Southwest Airlines, which has 22 . . . In fact, at 15 of the nation's top airports, either half the business is already controlled by one carrier, or two share more than 70%.[13]

More recently, as of 1994, according to Professors Dempsey and Gesell: "Today, dominant airlines control more than half the enplanements at more than half of the nation's 50 largest airports." Examples include American 61 percent at Dallas/Fort Worth, Delta 79 percent at Atlanta,

Northwest 83 percent at Minneapolis, TWA 65 percent at Saint Louis, United 63 percent at Denver, and US Airways 91 percent at Pittsburgh.[14]

These limitations on entry, along with others to be discussed under mergers, are factors in the trend toward the emergence of a new oligopoly (and, indeed, at some points, a near monopoly) after an earlier post-deregulation shakedown period during which numerous small innovative carriers challenged big ones in the manner that deregulation proponents had hoped.

The 1990s have seen a trend among the airlines to reduce the size of their hub-and-spoke systems somewhat by reducing or even eliminating service along some of the shorter hauls and by discontinuing some hubs altogether. American, for example, has discontinued its hubs at Raleigh-Durham, North Carolina, and San Jose, California. There has been some trend back toward point-to-point (also called "linear") service. The airlines may end up trying to strike a balance between hubbing and linear services as they balance the savings from hubbing (especially higher load factors) against its costs. These include lower utilization of aircraft and labor, as well as less efficient fuel consumption. However, since most city pairs do not have enough traffic to justify a nonstop, point-to-point service, the airlines are likely to continue routing most passengers through hubs[15]

The practical limitation on entry caused by hubbing may be alleviated to some extent by a shift to some linear routes, but this does not mean a trend away from one-carrier dominance at each hub point. In fact, the majors seem to withdraw altogether from any hub city that they cannot dominate, leaving each hub with one dominant airline. Entry by new competition is extremely difficult under such circumstances.

In the long term, however, the secular growth in passenger traffic may shift the balance in favor of the linear route pattern. More passengers will make hub congestion even worse and will allow for higher load factors on nonstop linear routes.[16]

Entry into Charter Service

Scheduled airlines have a right to perform charters without need for additional certification. But there are also some carriers that hold certificates designated simply for charter service. They were formerly known as "supplemental air carriers," but the ADA changed the terminology to "charter air carriers."

Prior to regulatory reform legislation, a carrier could not hold one certificate as a supplemental air carrier and another as a scheduled airline. Would-be airlines sought supplemental certificates because they were far easier to obtain than a certificate for scheduled service, and it was better to have charter authority than no authority at all. Often a supplemental certificate could be obtained by an applicant upon showing proper financing, expertise, and equipment, whereas no new entrants were permitted into trunk line scheduled service during the whole 1938–78 period. However, most carriers found it difficult to make a profit when limited to charter service alone, and at the time of the ADA there were only nine of them left.

Today the holder of a charter certificate is not precluded from obtaining a certificate for scheduled service. As of September 1999, there were 28 carriers with charter certificates, 17 of them holding only the charter certificate.

The definition of what constitutes a charter flight was gradually liberalized throughout the 1960s and 1970s. Originally the entire capacity of the aircraft had to be chartered to a single group, but the "split charter" was introduced whereby part of the plane may be chartered to one group and part to another or to several others. Also, the definition of a proper charter group was gradually liberalized. Earlier restrictions designed to protect scheduled services from losing too many passengers to charters—requiring that participants belong to a bona fide organization or that they purchase an inclusive tour along with the charter—have largely been done away with.

In the future it appears that the major restrictions on charters will be in the international area and will be imposed by foreign governments. Even in this case the United States has obtained country-of-origin stipulations concerning charters in some bilateral agreements; this means that charters are governed by the rules of the country of origin (regardless of the nationality of the airline) and not by the country of destination.

Entry by Exemption

An informal procedure is provided by Section 40109 of the transportation statute which allows DOT to exempt airlines, including foreign air carriers, from the certification (and foreign air carrier permit) requirements, and from many other economic regulatory provisions. Prior to the ADA, the exemption power was limited to U.S. air carriers and was intended for limited operations and for short periods of time. Entry by exemption is, of course, entirely discretionary with DOT, and in practice is used for limited or unusual situations. DOT need only find that that the exemption would be "consistent with the public interest."

Air Taxi and Commuter Exemption

The air taxi class (which technically includes the scheduled commuter air carriers) operated, prior to the ADA, under a blanket exemption issued by the CAB under powers granted by Section 416 (b) of the Federal Aviation Act. Originally such operators did not have to approach the CAB at all, so long as their aircraft stayed within the then very small size limit, but had only to deal with the Federal Aviation Administration in regard to its safety requirements. Then, in 1969, the CAB revised its rules to require every air taxi to register with it once a year, pay a fee, and file a certificate attesting to liability insurance coverage. The ADA made the air taxi exemption a matter of law rather than of CAB regulation by giving such service its own subparagraph in Section 416. This provision—continued in effect by Section 40109(f) of the transportation statute—specifies that any air carrier with aircraft having a maximum passenger capacity of not over 55 seats or a cargo payload capacity of not over 18,000 pounds is exempt from the certification requirements. Authority was left with the CAB (and later with DOT) to raise, but not to lower, these limits. The board raised the passenger ceiling to 60 and DOT has left it there.

We noted in Chapter 1 that there are about 2,400 air taxis operating under the exemption. All of them must register with DOT and file evidence of liability insurance. A commuter air carrier must also meet fitness requirements. A commuter air carrier is defined for this purpose as a passenger carrier within the 60-seat limit with a minimum of five round trips a week between any pair of points, with a published schedule.

The Essential Air Service Program

The ADA placed in the Federal Aviation Act a new section (Section 419) which established an essential air service program intended to assure a minimum service at small points even, where necessary, with federal subsidy. The program has the odd distinction of being an instance of intensive governmental regulation created by a "deregulation" act. The ADA set a ten-year termination date, but Congress extended the period for another ten years, through September 30, 1998, and then, by P.L. 104–264, extended it indefinitely. The substance of Section 419 is now to be found in Sections 41731–41742 of the transportation statute.

As of July 1999, there were 106 small communities receiving subsidized service under this program, of which 27 were in Alaska. All were being served by carriers using aircraft with fewer than 60 seats, with 19-seat aircraft the predominant size, except for Alaska Airlines which, although a major carrier, had a subsidized service using Boeing 737 aircraft.[17]

Under the provisions of the statute, DOT has had to determine for each of these points what constitutes "basic essential air service," looking at traffic and service data, as well as views of state and local authorities. However, the minimum service must not be below two daily round trips six days a week between the point and a hub airport that has convenient connecting flights to many destinations. (The term *hub airport* is used in an entirely different sense from the "hub-and-spoke" airline route pattern. It refers to the volume of traffic at an airport, measured in passenger enplanements per year. About 75 U.S. airports meet this standard.) Flights must be at reasonable times, rates must not be excessive, aircraft must have at least 15 seats and two engines, and must use two pilots, although there are some permissible exceptions to these standards. (Within Alaska, where conditions are unique and dependence on the program unusually critical, there are different standards for what constitutes essential service, as well as for other aspects of the program.)

DOT is authorized to pay a subsidy if it finds that essential service will not be furnished without one. In deciding on a fair amount of compensation, the agency looks at representative costs of other air carriers using similar aircraft. A carrier serving under this program must give 90 days notice to drop a point or reduce service there below the "essential" level. DOT then invites applicants and asks each to specify the amount of subsidy they would require. The low bidder will not necessarily be selected since, under the statute, DOT must consider the preferences of users as reflected by local governments, "the contractual and marketing arrangements the applicant has made with a larger carrier to ensure service beyond the hub airport," and "the interline arrangements that the applicant has made with a larger carrier to allow passengers and cargo of the applicant to be transported by the larger carrier through one reservation, ticket, and baggage check-in" (Section 41733).

Clearly, Congress has given its blessing to close ties between a major airline and its stable of commuters when the latter are involved in the essential service program. It has also provided, however, in Section 41739, that when an airline agrees that a commuter air carrier will share its code designator, the airline shares responsibility with the commuter for the quality of the service.

A state or local government, as provided in Section 41735, may ask DOT for "enhanced" essential air service, meaning a service set higher than what DOT has decided is "essential," but with the state or local government "or a person" sharing the additional subsidy equally with the federal government. "Person" as used here can mean a corporation as well as an individual. As of July 1999, there were only two points where a state or local government was contributing to the subsidy.[18]

Subsidies under the transportation statute are administered differently from the old subsidy program of the local service carriers, which, as we have seen, was terminated by Congress in 1983. That program was premised on the overall need of each airline for subsidy to operate its entire system, while the new program is premised on the needs of a particular community.

In 1987, when the first extension of the essential air service program was being considered, DOT told Congress that there were 143 communities being subsidized, of which 41 were in Alaska. By July 1999, the number of communities had dropped to 106, of which 29 were in Alaska. Beginning in Fiscal Year 1998, Congress has been funding the program at $50 million a year. By way of comparison, the total subsidy in 1978, paid to the local service carriers in the last year of that program, came to $75.4 million. That sum, adjusted for inflation, would exceed $200 million. Clearly the essential air service program is a far smaller burden on the taxpayer than the earlier local service carrier subsidy program.

The essential air service program is the one aspect of domestic air service that continues to be subject to intensive economic regulation. Clearly, when DOT authorizes payment of a subsidy out of the public treasury, it must make a variety of determinations. It must select one carrier out of what may be several applicants; it must determine a reasonable amount of subsidy and the minimum level of service to be maintained (if to be above the minimum now set by statute); it may take into account whether the type of aircraft used by a carrier is inappropriate from a cost standpoint and thus unreasonably adds to subsidy; and it may even take into account the reasonableness of the rates being charged.

Regional and Commuter Air Services—Public Reaction

Small communities have not all been happy with regional and commuter services, especially those that were accustomed in pre-deregulation days to service by trunk lines or local service carriers using jet airliners of the DC-9 or 727 variety. They have had to accustom themselves to much smaller aircraft, often not pressurized, which usually are piston or turboprop aircraft rather than jets. There is psychological resistance by many passengers to flying on small aircraft, as well as to flying on airlines other than the large, well-known ones.

On the other hand, some communities have found that business travelers are better accommodated since flight departures and arrivals now tend to correspond with morning and evening rush hours. Previous service by local service and trunk carriers often favored the needs of the larger points on their routes and resulted in departures and arrivals at smaller points at times not connected with the business working day. Pleasure travel may also be accommodated better in the sense that early morning departures to a hub airport may enable good connections for long-distance travel. The growing trend of commuter systems coordinated with a parent major airline at a hub, as we have previously described, may offer a small community improved access to the whole national airline network.

What complaints small communities have are generally met with an unsympathetic response from defenders of deregulation. They tend to hold that a community that sees its service quality drop from large jet to small turboprop aircraft, or that loses air service altogether, is merely having to face economic realities. They tend to be dubious about the essential air service subsidies. Indeed, as of early 1994, the Clinton administration had a recommendation from its own National Performance Review Program that these subsidies be reduced. A contrary view, however, is expressed by those who criticize all or part of the deregulation movement. Professor Laurence E. Gesell, for example, in advocating a selective degree of reregulation, would see air service "up-graded at smaller communities—even if at the expense of society at large, just as there are other welfare considerations beyond the profit margins of corporate structures. . . . [S]ocial responsibilities cannot be separated from the economics of profit-taking or cost allocation."[19]

Complaints by small communities may be alleviated as regionals and some commuters equip themselves with new jet aircraft, being introduced in the late 1990s, with 50 to 70 seats, providing greater speed and comfort. We will refer to these again in Chapter 4.

GOVERNMENT REGULATION OF EXIT

Government regulation of exit may be broken down into those instances where an airline wishes to cease serving a market or markets and those where the airline wishes to continue serving but the government temporarily suspends or permanently revokes its right to do so.

Exit on Airline Initiative

Prior to the regulatory reform legislation, a certificated airline had to get the permission of the CAB to suspend service in any market on its certificate or to have a point or points deleted from its certificate. The theory was that in return for its privileged franchise, the airline had an obligation to furnish service. By implication, an airline was expected to fly in unprofitable markets as part of the price for being allowed a protected franchise to fly in profitable ones. Often proceedings to discontinue service resulted in public hearings at which community representatives appeared before the CAB and fought to keep service.

With the enactment of the ADA in 1978, the CAB began permitting suspensions and abandonments rather liberally. And, under the ADA, as of January 1, 1982, exit became voluntary with the airlines, except for certain advance notice requirements affecting the essential air service program and international routes.

Exit by Governmental Action

The philosophy behind regulatory reform, while aimed at minimizing governmental regulation of airlines, was sufficiently consumer-oriented that the reform legislation continued many of the earlier provisions of the Federal Aviation Act under which the CAB could suspend or revoke a carrier's authority for lack of fitness. DOT now exercises this function. We have already examined the fitness concept as a requirement for entry; but an air carrier (and this includes commuters) must continuously maintain fitness or face a procedure under which DOT may cause it to exit. The fitness concept, as we have seen, includes managerial competence, adequate financing, and a disposition to comply with safety and other regulations.

In the case of international services by U.S. airlines, DOT may suspend or revoke authority either for lack of fitness or simply because the airline is not performing the service. This can be an important function of DOT whenever a foreign government insists on limiting the number of U.S. airlines serving its country. Perforce, DOT will have the burden of deciding which airlines, and, if the ones selected do not offer service or offer and then withdraw the service, there may well be justification for revoking those certificates and selecting other airlines.

All suspension and revocation actions on international certificates must be submitted to the White House. The president has 60 days to disapprove on foreign policy or national defense grounds, in the manner described earlier with respect to the issuance of these certificates.

Similar authority (subject to presidential disapproval) over the suspension or revocation of the foreign air carrier permits of foreign airlines is vested in DOT. In addition, however, that agency may suspend service of a foreign airline if it or its government has engaged in unfair practices or has failed to honor the rights of U.S. airlines under the bilateral agreement. Exercise of this latter power requires specific affirmative approval by the president, not merely the disapproval procedure described above.

Exit by Bankruptcy

An airline may exit by simply going broke, having its assets sold to cover part of its debts, and going out of business. The early 1990s saw this happen to Eastern Air Lines and Pan American World Airways, two of the original trunk lines. A less drastic procedure—reorganization under Chapter 11 of the bankruptcy laws—has enabled several airlines, notably two other former trunk lines, Continental and TWA, to avoid involuntary "exit." They emerged successfully from Chapter 11 reorganizations in 1993.

MERGERS AND ACQUISITIONS

The merger or consolidation of two or more airlines into one company involves the concepts of both entry and exit. It is an action that may have important consequences for the entire airline industry and the public, and it can generate much controversy. When two airlines merge, each route system is added to the other so that a single enlarged system is formed. To the extent that both airlines may have been competing in some markets prior to the merger, there will obviously be a reduction in the number of competitors in those markets—a type of exit. In other instances a major carrier may acquire a small one with the motive of adding the routes of that carrier to its system, for example, the acquisition of Air California by American Airlines. This is, in a sense, a form of entry, and the word *acquisition* is more appropriate than *merger*.

There are many reasons why an airline would wish to merge with another. Perhaps it wishes to increase its overall size, in the hope of realizing economies of scale, although we should note again that the question of the optimal size for an airline is very controversial. It may want to acquire a profitable route or to add points that, taken together with its existing routes, would result in more profitable operations. Still, with domestic entry becoming open as of 1982, a carrier may extend itself into markets within the United States without need for merger. An airline with peak business in the summer may seek to acquire a carrier with a winter-peaking route, but here again the opening up of domestic entry makes it possible for the airline to proceed to enter the winter market without the need to acquire the other carrier. It appears that post-deregulation motives include the acquisition of additional aircraft, trained personnel, airport gates and slots, and customer goodwill, as well as the desire to eliminate a competitor.

In any merger the usual practice is for one of the airlines to be described as the surviving carrier, meaning that its name is the one that survives. When a financially strong carrier acquires a financially weak one, or a large carrier a small one, it will very likely be the name of the stronger or larger that will survive. It is possible, however, for a merger to result in a corporation with a new name altogether; for example, two local service airlines, North Central and Southern, merged in 1979 to form Republic.

The ADA specified that the requirement of advance governmental approval of airline mergers and acquisitions would continue in effect, and that, with the demise of the CAB at the end of 1984, the function would be transferred to the Department of Justice, which is the agency that handles antitrust problems throughout the U.S. industrial system. However, before the transfer could happen, the Sunset Act of 1984 put the function in DOT rather than DOJ but specified that the authority would cease at the end of 1988, which it did. Since then, airline mergers, acquisitions, and other control relationships are treated the same as with other industries under the antitrust laws administered by DOJ.

In the past, under CAB regulation, the board weighed the probable effects on competition in the markets involved to determine whether a merger would be in the public interest. It examined estimates of cost savings and of service improvements (such as more modern aircraft or more nonstop flights) and decided whether the public benefits in such respects would outweigh a possible public detriment from a reduction in the number of competitors. Much as with entry policy, the board was guided by a philosophy favoring competitive balance, and it tended to look dubiously on any proposal that would sharply increase the size of any of the big trunk lines. For example, it refused to permit a merger of American Airlines and Western Airlines in 1972.

In 1978, the ADA amended Section 408 of the Federal Aviation Act to change the emphasis of the guidelines to be followed in merger and similar cases. Consistent with deregulation philosophy, it deleted language that would protect any carrier from being "jeopardized" by the proposed arrangement; instead, there is language emphasizing the public interest in competition. Disapproval was directed for any transaction that would substantially lessen competition, unless "the anticompetitive effects of the proposed transaction are outweighed in the public interest by the probable effect of the transaction in meeting significant transportation conveniences and needs of the public," and there is no "reasonably available alternative having materially less anticompetitive effects." This was the language applicable to DOT in the 1985–88 period, during which time it approved, as we will shortly see, numerous significant mergers. Termination of Section 408 occurred at the end of 1988 and, of course, the guidelines expired with it. However, as we will later see, DOJ since 1988, applying the regular antitrust laws, has been taking a stricter view of airline mergers than did DOT in its period of control over them.

The Wave of Mergers of the Mid-1980s

Between 1985 and 1988, a series of mergers took place, the more significant of which were: American acquired the former intrastate carrier Air California; Delta merged with Western; Northwest acquired Republic; TWA acquired Ozark; Texas Air (originally a small local service carrier which in 1981 had acquired Continental) acquired People Express and Eastern; United acquired the Pacific Division of Pan American; and USAir acquired Piedmont and the former intrastate carrier Pacific Southwest. In addition, during this period several of these major airlines acquired, or bought part ownership in, commuter air carriers.

Of the foregoing, only the United purchase of the Pan American Pacific operation appears motivated by the old-fashioned pre-deregulation motive of acquiring operating rights. Since international operations still require foreign government approvals through bilateral agreements and carrier selection by DOT, United bought itself a transpacific service it otherwise had little chance of obtaining. (To be sure, it also acquired aircraft and personnel already thoroughly broken in; only Pan American's serious financial straits allowed United so good a deal.)

In the other instances, what was acquired involved largely domestic services, and the acquiring carrier, under the free entry of deregulation, could simply have initiated service over the routes it wanted without need for any merger action. But apparently the airlines have found that the practical way to enter new markets effectively is to buy up a carrier already in being, with its aircraft, personnel, airport gates and slots, and public identification in those markets. Other motives, such as scale economies and the control of markets by eliminating a competitor, also entered the picture with many of these mergers. TWA's acquisition of Ozark, for example, served to eliminate a competitor at St. Louis and make TWA the heavily dominant competitor there. Similarly, Northwest's acquisition of Republic gave the merged airline a heavily dominant position at its Minneapolis hub.

Obviously this wave of mergers, which by 1988 had reduced the number of major passenger airlines to eight, has given rise to concern that the airline industry is trending toward an ever-tighter oligopoly where the competition sought by deregulation will be greatly reduced. Yet DOT granted the required approval to all of these mergers, putting a limiting condition on only one—that Texas Air in acquiring Eastern had to assure that Pan American's competing shuttle service in the northeast corridor would have enough slots at the New York and Washington airports. Certainly DOT has recognized the danger of overconcentration. In one merger order, while noting that "the threat of new entry will ordinarily curb the exercise of market power by an incumbent to increase prices or reduce service," it goes on to say:

However . . . factors such as restraints on airport access may insulate an incumbent carrier from competitive forces by making new entry more difficult or time consuming. Likewise, other factors, such as the importance of feed traffic or other efficiencies from hubbing, may make new entry more expensive, or at least more risky. Such factors may also insulate an incumbent carrier from competitive forces and permit the exercise of market power.[20]

But DOT went on to note that a potential entrant may have certain advantages as against an incumbent carrier, such as a lower cost structure, having hubs at the other ends of city pairs, or having access to some local and interline feed traffic. Moreover, the ADA had shifted the burden of proof in merger cases from the applicant airlines to the opponents; in short, in case of doubt as to anticompetitive effects, the merger was supposed to be approved.

In the lexicon of antitrust enforcement, the term *market power* is a familiar one. It has been defined as "the power to raise prices or reduce services profitably while restricting the entry of competitors."[21]

By the time DOJ took over the control of airline mergers in 1989, concern had been expressed in Congress that merger policy had been too lax. The theory of "contestability" had been a basic tenet of the earlier proponents of deregulation. By this theory, deregulation would make entry so easy that an incumbent carrier in a market would always face the threat of a potential entrant if it began monopoly-style pricing. The assumption of contestability appears to have been a guiding principle in DOT's easy attitude toward mergers in the 1985–88 period. DOJ, taking over in 1989, seems to have largely abandoned this concept and instead assumed that contestability was not generally applicable to the airline industry, that competition could not be assumed, and that, left to its own devices, the industry could gravitate toward dominance by a shrinking number of giant carriers.

The early 1990s, however, saw the trend to such dominance continue, but not so much by mergers as by the demise of Eastern and Pan American, and by the continued shrinking of TWA through the sale of some of its routes. American, Delta, and United were acquiring routes of these three carriers and were emerging as the three giants. In 1991, a committee of experts under the auspices of the Transportation Research Board recommended that DOJ should oppose not only mergers but route acquisitions if the carriers shared a hub airport and/or if they competed in many markets. Mergers or route acquisitions might be acceptable, however, if they joined routes end-to-end.[22]

With the advent of the Clinton administration in 1993, the government's policy was tightened further. The new secretary of transportation stated that "in the future, we will insist that mergers, acquisitions and sales of route authority be well-grounded, pro-competitive and financially viable."[23]

The latter 1990s have seen a trend away from mergers toward relationships among U.S. carriers called *domestic partnerships* or *alliances*. These terms have no specific definition. They may include one, more, or all of the following: coordinating schedules, coordinating baggage handling and airport gates, allowing frequent flyer mileage earned on one carrier to be used on the other, joint marketing of one another's flights, and code sharing. (The growing use of such alliances among U.S. and foreign airlines will be covered shortly under international entry.) Arrangements of this general sort have been proposed, for example, between American Airlines and US Airways; Northwest and Continental; Delta and United.

The advantages to an airline of this type of arrangement by contrast to a merger or acquisition have been well described by one authority as follows:

Among the recent major developments in the industry are airlines trying to form alliances instead of implementing mergers and acquisitions. Depending on how they are structured, we estimate that the carriers can obtain anywhere from 30 to 80 percent of the benefits of a merger without incurring most of the risks involved in a merger. In the past, mergers in this industry have caused much disruption and costs as the two carriers integrated fleets, labor, operations, and cultures.[24]

Other Merger Problems

Any government agency with responsibility for merger matters will find it difficult to oppose a merger if one of the parties is in severe financial straits. An airline in weakening financial shape is likely to offer a deteriorating quality of service, perhaps with some safety implications. If bankruptcy results, with the airline actually liquidated (that is, with its aircraft sold and its employees laid off), the public will be deprived of the service, the number of competitors in its markets will be reduced, and there will be the human hardships and political repercussions that follow the collapse of any large firm. It can be argued that in such a case a merger would only recognize a reduction in competition that was going to occur anyway.

There is a legal concept called the "failing business doctrine" which the courts recognize as giving government agencies great latitude in merger cases of this sort, even where it is clear that there may be unfortunate competitive results.

One problem faced in any merger proposal is that the airline unions will wish to participate in the airline negotiations and will press for protective provisions for labor such as fair integration of seniority lists, severance pay for those to be laid off, and moving expenses for those to be transferred. The airlines must consider the probable costs of labor-protective provisions in deciding whether a merger is desirable.

There are certain types of mergers which may pose some questions of national policy in the future. Some examples follow:

1. A major airline and one or more small new entrants that are offering innovative cut-rate services. The latter are part of the dream of regulatory reform proponents, and if they are regularly gobbled up by large old-line competitors, as seems to be happening, we may see opposition develop to their being acquired by those competitors even when they want to be.

2. An airline and a large surface carrier—Greyhound and a major airline, or a cargo airline and a large trucking firm—raising the basic question of whether such multimodal companies enhance or hold back the development of good air service.

3. An airline and a noncarrier such as a conglomerate. It is not unusual for an airline to be engaged in airline-related lines of business such as hotels, credit card companies, or car rental firms. However, if an airline is a subordinate element among many nonaviation activities of a massive corporation—perhaps as a subsidiary of a large holding company—some question might be raised if it were felt that airline needs would be neglected or that airline profits would be siphoned off to support other corporate areas.

As the 1990s ended, however, merger problems seem to have given way to alliance problems as a focus for industry, public, and congressional attention.

INTERNATIONAL ENTRY—BILATERAL AGREEMENTS

To enter an international market—that is, to begin a scheduled service between a point in an airline's home country and a point in another—the airline must have the approval of its own government and the government of the foreign country. The award to a U.S. carrier of an international certificate, even though properly issued by DOT and properly cleared through the White House in the manner earlier described, does not enable the airline to begin the service unless and until the approval of the foreign government is obtained. If the United States has a bilateral agreement with that government (usually called an air transport agreement or an air transport services agreement), the U.S. government simply informs the foreign government that it has "designated" this particular airline to serve in this market. The foreign government then, pursuant to its obligations under the bilateral agreement, will issue whatever authorization its own laws require. In a few instances there may be no bilateral agreement between the two countries. The airline may, nevertheless, be granted permission by the foreign government in some circumstances—for example, when that country has no airline of its own that it wishes to have serve the United States, or where it has been impossible to agree on a bilateral but each government allows the other's airline to enter the market on a tentative basis pending conclusion of a bilateral. (The word *bilateral* in the world of international aviation has come to be used as a noun, meaning, of course, *bilateral agreement*.)

Let us look for a moment at the reverse of the above situation—that is, where a foreign airline wishes to begin service to the United States. It must obtain whatever authorization is required from its own government, and that government then informs the United States that it has designated this particular airline for this service under the bilateral agreement. But the foreign airline has yet another hurdle to clear before it can begin service; it must obtain a document very similar to the certificate received by a U.S. airline, called a foreign air carrier permit. If the airline can show that it is properly designated and that it meets other requirements, such as that it is predominantly owned and controlled by nationals of its home country, the issuance of the foreign air carrier permit is virtually a foregone conclusion. To deny it would mean that the U.S. government was reneging on a commitment it had made in the bilateral agreement.

The requirement that the airline be predominantly owned by nationals of its home country is not a hard and fast rule. In the past, foreign air carrier permits have been issued to airlines with multinational ownership, such as Air Afrique, with 11-nation ownership, and SAS, with 3-nation ownership. Moreover, there is a growing trend for carriers of different nationalities to buy shares in one another, blurring nationality lines. It seems likely that the ownership and control provisions traditionally included in bilateral agreements will often be relaxed in the future.

The United States has bilateral agreements with about 80 governments, reflecting the large number of countries served by U.S. airlines. In them, each government agrees that airlines designated by the other government may establish scheduled service in its territory. In the traditional bilateral agreement, a route is usually described as from any point or points in the home country of the airline to specified points in the foreign country, via intermediate points (which may also be specified) in other countries. Often "beyond rights" are granted—for example, a traditional agreement with France might specify a route from the United States to Paris "and beyond to points in Italy and the Middle East." Conversely, the United States might grant the French a route from France to New York "and beyond to Mexico."

Note that "beyond" and intermediate-point rights do not merely concern traffic to and from the home country of the airline. In the above example, they would allow the U.S. airline to pick up traffic in Paris and take it to Italy, while the French airline could pick up traffic in New York and take it to Mexico.

As a matter of convenience, routes are often described in terms of the flight that originates in the home country of the airline, but it should be clearly understood that the agreements grant the right to operate in both directions.

Beginning in 1992, the United States has been seeking a new liberal type of bilateral agreement called an *open skies agreement*, whereby airlines of each country may serve any point in the other country, any intermediate point en route, and any "beyond" points. After years of negotiating, the United States had, by the end of the 1990s, bilateral agreements of this type with Argentina, France, Germany, Italy, the Netherlands, New Zealand, Peru, most Central American countries, nine smaller Western European countries, and a few small Pacific Rim countries.[25] The precise terms of the individual agreements may, of course, vary—for example, the new (1999) agreement with France is to be phased in slowly over a five-year period.

Whether a bilateral agreement is of the traditional or "open skies" type, it will ordinarily cover passengers, cargo, and mail, including all-cargo flights. Some agreements, however, provide specific routes for all-cargo services. Typically, a bilateral agreement binds the governments for an indefinite period but subject to the right to denounce the agreement on a year's notice. (The word *denounce* in international law does not carry any connotation of severe disapproval, as it does in everyday usage; it merely means to give notice, much as an employee might give two weeks' notice of plans to quit a job.)

Under U.S. law the bilaterals are executive agreements rather than treaties. They are negotiated by the State Department with the assistance of DOT and often with advice from the U.S. airlines. But since they are not treaties, they are not submitted to the Senate for consent to ratification. At times there has been criticism of leaving in the hands of DOT and the State Department the power to bind the United States in matters that can often be of much importance to the airlines and the public. Yet it would prove unwieldy and fraught with long delays if matters such as these could not be finalized by the negotiators but had to be brought home and added to the pile of backlogged treaty actions awaiting the attention of the Senate. This would be particularly bad when a bilateral agreement is subject to a relatively minor amendment, as often occurs, such as adding a point to an established route.

Both bilateral agreements and any amendments to them are negotiated either in the United States or abroad and are signed by relatively high-ranking officials such as an ambassador, a foreign minister, or an assistant secretary of state.

What is most interesting, and to many people troublesome, about the negotiating of bilaterals is that they involve what the U.S. government calls "an equitable exchange of economic benefits," which is a polite way of saying "horse trading." The United States does not grant a route merely because the foreign government wants it for its airline, or even because service by an airline of that country might be beneficial to U.S. travelers. Instead, the grant of a route is viewed as a concession that the U.S. government is in no way obliged to make. Usually the United States wants rights for U.S. airlines in the foreign country, and there is a swapping of such rights. In legal Latin, the term *quid pro quo* is employed to describe what each government trades.

In the past, prior to the emergence of the regulatory reform philosophy, foreign governments often wanted to get their airlines into several U.S. cities but could not do so because they could not offer the United States any *quid pro quo* that the U.S. airlines wanted. Belgium, for example, had only Brussels to offer, and it had long ago traded Brussels (including "beyond" rights) for New York. Its government was handicapped in trying to obtain an additional route to San Francisco or Los Angeles for its airline. However, pursuant to the regulatory reform philosophy, the United States now rather freely trades U.S. points in return not so much for foreign points as for liberal arrangements concerning (1) frequency and capacity, (2) Fifth Freedom, (3) multiple designation, and (4) rates. (We shall discuss these shortly, except for the last, which will be covered in Chapter 6.) But it should be emphasized that the procedure is still one in which each government drives for the best bargain it can get. The pattern nowadays often is that a government grudgingly accepts the above-mentioned liberal arrangements as the only way to win entry into desired traffic-rich U.S. cities. Thus, the "open skies" agreement, just like the traditional agreement, is the result of bargaining.

To some of us this horse-trading procedure may seem a bit uncivilized between friendly nations in a world crying out for greater international cooperation. And there have been attempts at a multilateral agreement whereby every government would make a blanket grant to airlines of every other signatory government of the right to freely establish service to any point in its territory. These attempts, however, have had very little support, and there is little reason to think that each any such agreement is likely in the immediate future. Yet, looking into the more distant future, we should perhaps note that the "bilateral" system is neither sacred nor perfect as a device for allocating entry into international markets.

It is interesting that the ocean shipping of the world is not under such a bilateral bargaining procedure. The right of a shipping company to establish a route to and from a port in another country is considered to be a natural concomitant of friendly relations, and there is no need for any bilateral governmental bargaining procedure. This right is a historical outgrowth of international custom and general commercial treaties.

Another criticism of aviation's bilateral procedure is that the bargains struck are sometimes the result of factors that have nothing to do with aviation, such as a desire by the United States to incur the favor of the foreign government in a certain situation, for example, the establishment of a naval base in that country. In practice, the Foreign Office in a government (the State Department in the United States) may often pressure the aviation officials of the government to make a route grant or other concession that is generous by strict bargaining standards, simply to improve the general political relationship between the two governments.

Frequency and Capacity Restrictions

We said that we would examine any major limitation on the degree of entry, and in the international sphere there is such a major limitation. We refer to restrictions on frequency and capacity.

The word *frequency* means, of course, the number of scheduled flights, measured usually by the week. The word *capacity* means the total number of seats made available during a particular period, again usually a week. It will be obvious that the two terms overlap, but they are not identical.

If an airline has been offering one flight a day in a market, using a 180-seat aircraft, and increases the frequency to two flights a day, with the same size aircraft, then both frequency and capacity will have doubled. In practice, it often happens that the increase in frequency involves a directly proportional increase in capacity, and in such situations the two terms may be said to overlap completely. But capacity may be increased without increase in frequency, simply by introducing larger aircraft without increasing the number of flights. It can even happen (though seldom) that an airline may increase the one while decreasing the other—for example, decreasing the number of flights per week in a market while introducing a much larger aircraft so that the aggregate number of seats carried is greater than before.

Although the two words are generally thought of in terms of passenger service, they are also applicable to cargo service, whether speaking of all-cargo flights or of the cargo-carrying capacity of passenger flights. Here the measurement of capacity relates not to the number of seats but to the maximum cargo-carrying ability of the aircraft.

The philosophy of the United States has traditionally been that airline management should have maximum freedom to determine frequency and capacity once its airline has been granted entry into a market. This is reflected in our domestic law wherein DOT, under Section 41109(a) (2) (B) of the transportation statute, is specifically directed that it must not prescribe flight schedules or types of aircraft. This philosophy goes back to the old Civil Aeronautics Act of 1938 and, of course, is firmly reinforced by the regulatory reform movement. With the exception of a short time in the 1970s, the U.S. position has been to try to eliminate or at least minimize limitations on frequency or capacity in bilateral agreements.

Not all other countries, by any means, agree with the U.S. philosophy. In fact, many governments favor so-called predetermination of capacity— meaning that an airline must obtain governmental approval before it may increase the frequency or capacity it is offering in a market. The U.S. airlines often may find themselves in a situation on their international routes where their own government does not tell them how many flights to schedule or what size aircraft to use, but a foreign government may do just that, depending on the terms of the bilateral agreement. Where there is an "open skies" bilateral, of course, this problem does not arise since that type of bilateral does not allow predetermination of frequency or capacity.

In many intra-European markets, the traditional prevailing practice used to be that the governments would regulate tightly the amount of service between each pair of points, allocating it about equally between the carriers of the two countries. Competition was thus held to near zero. In recent years, however, there has been a gradual liberalization trend. In fact, with respect to the 15 nations that make up the European Union (EU), unrestricted service has been permitted since 1997, between any pair of points within the 15 countries for airlines of the member countries. (The members of the EU as of 1999 were Austria, Belgium, Denmark, Finland, France, Germany, Greece, Ireland, Italy, Luxembourg, the Netherlands, Portugal, Spain, Sweden, and the United Kingdom.)[26]

Although the United Kingdom has accepted this highly liberal arrangement for airlines of the EU within the EU area, it has been a strong holdout with respect to concluding an "open skies" agreement with the United States. Relationships between the United States and the United Kingdom with respect to airline service are of particular significance partly because of the sheer volume of traffic between the two countries, but also because for many years the bilateral agreement between the two governments served as a model, or at least a point of departure, for bilaterals with many other countries.

The first such agreement was drawn up at a conference in Bermuda in 1946. At that time, the British felt strongly that there should be some kind of control over the decisions of airline management concerning frequency and capacity that would protect the interests of British airlines in what was then foreseen as a severe competitive struggle with U.S. carriers. This might have been achieved by establishing an international agency with the power to decide what frequency and capacity were desirable for each airline. It might have been achieved by agreeing on some type of mathematical formula that would have divided the market at least approximately among the competitors. But all such arrangements were unacceptable to the United States.

What came out of the 1946 Bermuda meeting was a compromise whereby management was free to set frequency and capacity without prior approval of the foreign government, but that government had a right to protest to the airline's government if experience with a particular level of frequency or capacity showed that it was unreasonable in one or more respects. The language in the first Bermuda Agreement concerning frequency and capacity, which became known as the "Bermuda principles," was both complex and vague. It could be interpreted as requiring a complaining government to show that frequency or capacity of the other country's airline was unreasonably great and/or that an excessive proportion of Fifth Freedom traffic was being carried by it. (Fifth Freedom traffic means traffic that neither originates in, nor is destined for, the home country of an airline.) A complaining government could request a capacity consultation, and the other government was obliged to begin such a consultation within 60 days.

In a capacity consultation, aviation officials of both governments, advised by airline officials, would seek some form of compromise, perhaps a partial reduction of the earlier frequency or capacity increase. In some instances, the government of the offending airline would agree with the complainant government and require its carrier to cut back the entire increase. Usually the consultations would end in agreement, but if none could be arrived at, the problem could either be referred to arbitration or result in a notice of denunciation of the entire bilateral agreement in the manner we have already discussed.

For a few years after 1946 the United States succeeded in obtaining the Bermuda principles in many bilateral agreements, but by the 1970s there had been a falling away from this philosophy. Indeed, even the United States began showing a more lenient view of at least a degree of predetermination on some routes as overcapacity became a critical problem on them. The CAB even approved some temporary capacity limitation agreements between U.S. and foreign airlines, which were certainly a form of predetermination. Moreover, other governments, including the British, seeing their airlines in chronic financial problems due partly to overcapacity, took a steadily dimmer view of the Bermuda capacity principles. In 1976, the British gave the United States a one-year denunciation notice of the 1946 first Bermuda Agreement.

By 1976, when negotiations for the second Bermuda Agreement began, the United States was willing to go part way toward some form of predetermination but remained unwilling to see managements' hands so tightly tied that they could make no change without specific advance approval of the foreign government. The upshot was that the new agreement delineated a new, complicated mechanism for certain routes while leaving the old Bermuda principles and practices for the others. Under the new mechanism, where applicable, airlines were required to file proposed schedules in advance, the foreign government could object and call for a consultation, and a compromise would be worked out.

The old 1946 Bermuda language said, in effect, to airline management: "Go ahead and decide your frequencies and capacity, but remember not to overdo anything or you may be called to account afterward." The second agreement said: "Go ahead and decide what you'd like your frequencies and capacity to be, but remember that before you can operate them the foreign government has a right to challenge them, and you may end up being allowed only part of your desired increase." Thus, the second Bermuda Agreement put a heavier hand on managerial discretion. (This agreement, though negotiated in London, was formally signed in Bermuda for sentiment's sake, and thus is referred to as the second Bermuda Agreement.)

By the time this agreement was signed, however, in July 1977, political forces within the United States were already pushing toward enactment of the ADA and were soon to move U.S. policy on international airline service in a very different direction. Far from accepting any drift toward predetermination, the new policy was to strive for the complete removal from bilateral agreements of any governmental regulation of frequency or capacity, even of the ex post facto type of the first Bermuda Agreement. Many bilateral agreements have been renegotiated in this manner, with the United States trading entry to valuable U.S. points in return, leading in some instances to complete "open skies" arrangements. As for the British, however, long negotiations through the latter 1990s had not, as of 1999, brought about a liberalization, and remained tied to a proposed alliance between American Airlines and British Airways.

It remains to be seen how far some foreign governments will go in consenting to the relaxation of frequency and capacity restrictions. Despite the success of the United States in obtaining "open skies" agreements with many countries, some foreign airlines and their governments fear that the giant American carriers, with their domestic systems feeding massive quantities of traffic into their international routes, will drive their foreign competitors out of one market after another. Governments typically share an objective—more likely implied than stated—that the share of their airlines of traffic along their international routes will not be allowed to shrink too seriously. In short, there is an implicit understanding behind any bilateral agreement that to whatever extent the forces of the marketplace and passenger preference may be allowed to work, they will be curbed in some manner if the airlines of one country begin to dominate the routes granted in the agreement. Current U.S. policy reflects a willingness to let market forces determine relative shares of traffic, but foreign critics are quick to point out that American espousal of free international competition pre-supposes that U.S. enterprises will be reasonably successful. They point to our protected and subsidized merchant marine as evidence. So far, of course, U.S. airlines have more than held their own against foreign competitors, but if a time should come when their share of any major market began seriously shrinking, it is likely that Congress and American public opinion would demand protective measures such as the very frequency and capacity limitations that the United States is fighting against today.

Restrictions on Fifth Freedom

There are limitations on entry other than those relative to frequency and capacity. One of these is a restriction on carrying Fifth Freedom traffic. To understand this problem, it is first essential to master a classification of international traffic that originated back at the time of the Chicago Conference on International Civil Aviation in 1944 and remains in current usage today. Under this classification, traffic is broken down into five categories called freedoms, defined as follows:

First Freedom—the right to fly over another country without landing.

Second Freedom—the right to make a "technical stop" in another country, meaning a stop for fuel or repairs without taking on or leaving off passengers or cargo.

Third Freedom—the right to take on passengers or cargo in the home country of the airline and carry them to a foreign point.

Fourth Freedom—the right to take on passengers or cargo at a foreign point and bring them in to the home country of the airline as their destination.

Fifth Freedom—the right to pick up passengers or cargo at a point not in the home country of the airline and take them to a destination that is also not in the home country of the airline.

Most countries of the world (significant exceptions today being Brazil, China, and Russia) grant the first two freedoms through a multilateral agreement called the International Air Services Transit Agreement. (Usually it is referred to merely as the Transit Agreement or Two Freedoms Agreement.) It is the other three freedoms that involve the establishment of scheduled airline service; these must be granted through the bilateral process.

Governments generally agree that an airline has a greater right to carry traffic to and from its own home country (that is, Third and Fourth Freedoms) than to carry traffic that neither originates in, nor is destined for, its home country (Fifth Freedom). We have seen this reflected in the old Bermuda capacity principles where Fifth Freedom was tied in to capacity. But, entirely aside from capacity, governments often pursue a practice of flatly prohibiting a foreign airline from carrying Fifth Freedom traffic along certain routes or portions of certain routes. India, for instance may permit a U.S. airline to fly from Calcutta to Bangkok, Thailand, on a route extending through the Far East to California but prohibit the airline from taking on at Calcutta any traffic destined for Bangkok. Such traffic is Fifth Freedom when on a U.S. airline, since neither the origin nor the destination of the passenger is in the home country of the airline; but it is Third Freedom if carried by an airline of India, since the passenger's point of origin would be in the home country of the

Indian airline. Thus, it is argued that the Indian airline has a greater right to the traffic than the U.S. airline, and in this instance India elects to bar the U.S. carrier altogether from this particular piece of business.

Similarly, the United States could permit a European carrier to conduct its service to New York via Montreal but prohibit carriage of traffic traveling only between Montreal and New York. But U.S. policy over the years has been to oppose any prohibition on Fifth Freedom rights. Deviations from this policy have often had to be made in order to obtain a bilateral agreement, but current policy is to push strongly for the removal of all Fifth Freedom restrictions.

Let us insert here two hints to the student that may simplify the often confusing matter of Freedom classification: (1) In classifying a passenger in a Freedom, it is the nationality of the *airline* that counts, not the nationality of the passenger; (2) Third and Fourth Freedoms probably should have been lumped together originally as one Freedom, as they are the same thing only in opposite directions, and when one is granted, the other invariably is also.

The term *Sixth Freedom* is sometimes used to describe a peculiar type of traffic. Let us suppose that the Netherlands airline, KLM, carries some passengers from a city in the Middle East to Amsterdam in its home country, then carries them on to New York. The Netherlands government has contended that, so far as the United States is concerned, these passengers are Third Freedom because they entered New York from the home country of the airline. The U.S. position, however, is that the true origin of the journey should be governing and that the proper classification is Fifth Freedom. Occasionally one also hears the term *Seventh Freedom*, meaning what would ordinarily be classified as Fifth Freedom except that it is over a route that does not touch the home country of the airline. Such services are unusual, and bilateral agreements generally do not grant them. To the present writer, both Sixth and Seventh Freedoms are merely varieties of Fifth, and it would be preferable—and simpler—to consider them as such.

The right to carry Fifth Freedom traffic, and how much of it, remains a bone of contention as far as some governments are concerned—Japan, for example. Obtaining an "open skies" pact with them will obviously be difficult.

Multiple Designation

Multiple designation is a term used in international air transportation to mean that one country designates more than one of its airlines to fly a particular international route. U.S. policy, at least up until the second Bermuda Agreement, has been to insist that bilateral agreements permit multiple designation without any numerical ceiling on the number of airlines on any route. Bilateral agreements have used the expression "an airline or airlines designated by the Government of . . . ," although many foreign governments have granted this right reluctantly. Many countries have only one airline, sometimes government-owned, or only one large airline that they wish to operate on long international routes. They have no interest in multiple designations for themselves and are understandably reluctant to see their one chosen carrier competing with two or more U.S. carriers.

At the time of the second Bermuda Agreement in 1977, the United States accepted a ceiling of two U.S. airlines on each transatlantic route to Great Britain: New York–London, Los Angeles–London, and so forth. Since then, however, U.S. policy has been not only to push hard for unlimited designations, but to certificate numerous carriers over international routes. The easing of both policy and procedural requirements for issuance of international certificates, described earlier, combined with a willingness to trade multiple U.S. cities for, among other things, unlimited designations, has resulted in a great increase in the number of U.S. airlines serving international markets.

Expansion of Gateways for International Service

Airline service to Europe and Asia, whether by U.S. or foreign carriers, was operated for many years mostly out of the larger cities along the eastern and western seaboards and the Great Lakes. Passengers from inland points had to change planes at these gateways. But in recent years there has been a great expansion of service to inland points and also to somewhat smaller seaboard cities. Examples include Atlanta, Cincinnati, Dallas, Houston, Orlando, Raleigh/Durham, and St. Louis. It is not uncommon today for large European airlines, such as British Airways and Lufthansa, to serve a dozen U.S. cities. Nor is it uncommon to find U.S. cities with a dozen or more airlines, both U.S. and foreign, connecting them directly with points across the oceans.

CURRENT TRENDS IN INTERNATIONAL AIRLINE SERVICE

The trend to ever larger airlines has given rise to the term *megacarrier*, although there is no agreement as to how large an airline must be before the term applies. American, Delta, and United—by reason both of their total revenues and the great geographical extent of their route systems— might be put in that category today, as might British Airways.

The terms *global carrier* and *globalization* are also frequently heard, again without precise definition. Far-flung route systems, of course, are nothing new. By the late 1930s, Pan American had transatlantic and transpacific services as well as an extensive network in Latin America, while carriers such as the British and the Dutch were extending their services to what were then their distant colonies in Asia and the East Indies. Pan American by the 1950s had a round-the-world service. Today, however, market forces are pressuring the industry to where it may—as Professors Tretheway and Oum put it—"eventually 'globalize,' just as a number of other industries such as energy, automobile production, etc. have switched from national to global orientation and operations." They suggest that the term *global carrier* be limited to an airline with hubs in several countries "which can gather feed traffic from many widely separated points throughout the world, and channel that feed onto its long-haul routes." They conclude, "at present, no true global carriers exist in the world, although much talk has been heard recently about their potential emergence."[27]

Many foreign airlines, especially smaller ones, look fearfully at the competition of the large U.S. carriers and, in an effort to combat it, some have considered mergers that cut across nationality lines. There are, however, the problems with mergers that we have mentioned in discussing mergers among U.S. airlines, such as labor difficulties, different types of aircraft in the respective fleets, and differing corporate cultures. Moreover, public opinion in some countries may not be willing to accept the loss of their airlines' national identity in view of the long tradition of investing national pride in one's "flag" airline. As a result, the emphasis in the 1990s, instead of on transnational mergers, has been on operating alliances, marketing alliances, and code-sharing agreements, so that two or more carriers may operate almost as one entity, while retaining their separate national identities.

Alliances including both U.S. and foreign airlines have developed extensively through the 1990s. An early one was between Northwest Airlines and the Netherlands carrier, KLM, approved by DOT in 1993, under which the two airlines coordinate their scheduling and pricing. Since then, three additional alliances have been formed, so that, as of early 1999, there were the following four such large global groupings:

1. Atlantic Excellence—Delta Air Lines with Austrian, Sabena, and Swissair.

2. Oneworld—American Airlines with British Airways, Canadian Airlines, Cathay Pacific, Finnair, Iberia, and Qantas.

3. The Star Alliance—United Airlines with Air Canada, Lufthansa, SAS, Thai Airlines, and Varig, with membership pending for Air New Zealand, All Nippon Airways, and Ansett Australia Airlines.

4. Wings Alliance—Northwest Airlines with KLM, with negotiations seeking possible admission of Air France, Alitalia, and Continental Airlines.[28]

As to the precise nature of what is agreed to in these alliances, one authority has said: "Although the specific aspects of these alliances vary, basic provisions include code sharing, joint advertising and selling, joint frequent flyer programming, flight and schedule coordination, cooperation of computerized reservation systems, co-marking, joint product development, and joint cargo services."[29] To this we should add that an alliance may even involve purchase of equity in one member by another.

Note that membership in these groupings is not static—airlines enter and leave. Note also that the *extent* of cooperative activity within an alliance is limited by U.S. antitrust laws unless exemption from those laws has been granted by DOT. (DOT's authority to do so, and the policy it should apply, are found in Sections 41308 and 41309 of the transportation statute.) For example, the degree of cooperation within the Oneworld Alliance is limited because, as of the end of 1999, DOT had not approved the request for exemption. The great size of American Airlines and British Airways has raised the question of whether extensive cooperation between them would be highly anticompetitive. The proposal is also tied in with renegotiation of the U.S.–U.K. bilateral, as we have earlier noted.

A common feature of alliances is code sharing, whereby the airline identification code of one carrier will be used both on tickets and in computer reservations systems for a through service, although one or more airlines in the alliance are used in the service. We will look at computer reservations systems in detail in Chapter 5. Code sharing should be distinguished from the long-prevailing practice of interlining. Under interlining, while the carriers may establish joint fares and coordinate their schedules, "each carrier retains its own identity, and flight segments are clearly labeled as to which carrier is providing the service."[30]

Some critics, such as Professor Alan R. Bender, have charged that these alliances reduce intercarrier rivalry and thus reduce competition while offering no benefit to the public, and that they may result in crushing smaller airlines and new entrants.[31]

Foreign Airline Investment in U.S. Airlines

U.S. airlines ran tremendous deficits in the early 1990s, aggregating some $10 billion in the three years 1990–92. While their financial status improved greatly during the latter 1990s, it remains true that over the years they have not been a very profitable industry. Attracting capital in such a situation may sometimes be difficult, yet an infusion of capital is greatly needed. The Air Transport Association estimates that it will cost U.S. airlines about $144 billion for aircraft on order or on option at the end of 1998—this equipment being necessary both to replace older aircraft and to expand their fleets to meet expected traffic increases.[32] In this situation, investment by a foreign airline in the stock of a U.S. airline may be welcomed. The foreign carrier may see an otherwise possibly dubious investment as a good one if it can thereby obtain secure access to the large U.S. passenger market at the command of the U.S. carrier, supplementing and giving a degree of permanence to its operating alliance with the carrier.

Foreign equity investment in U.S. carriers, however, raises both legal and policy questions. Section 40102 of the transportation statute requires that a U.S. air carrier be a "citizen of the United States" and defines the term to require, in the case of a corporation, that "the president and at least two-thirds of the board of directors and other managing officers" are citizens of the United States and "at least 75 percent of the voting interest is owned or controlled by persons that are citizens of the United States." This provision originated in the Air Commerce Act of 1926 and was expressed substantially in this language in both the Civil Aeronautics Act and the Federal Aviation Act.

Note that the language specifies "voting" interest. DOT permits foreign ownership of up to 49 percent of the stock, so long as the *voting* stock share is limited to 25 percent. It announced this policy in January, 1991, when approving the Northwest-KLM alliance, which involved such a stock purchase. Of course, any investor buying nearly half the equity of a corporation will want an equivalent portion of the ultimate control of the corporation; if it is to accept less to meet the strictures of the transportation statute, it will need a special incentive. The need we have referred to of some foreign airlines to acquire secure access to a U.S. domestic system has in some instances provided just such an incentive. However, in the summer of 1991, DOT announced that it favored a change in the law to allow noncitizens to own up to 49 percent of *voting* stock in a U.S. air carrier in order to encourage more capital to flow into the U.S. airline industry. Bills to this effect have been introduced in Congress since then, but as of 1999 none had been enacted.

Some objections to foreign investment in U.S. airlines—and some responses to them—are as follows:

1. If the foreign airline is subsidized, part of the subsidy might flow to the benefit of the American carrier, enabling it to undercut the fares of its competitors. Perhaps DOT should not approve an arrangement with a subsidized airline.

2. Negotiating of bilateral agreements could be made more difficult since U.S. carriers participate in preparatory work for such negotiations and may participate as observers in some sessions. An American carrier with part foreign ownership would have divided loyalties. However, the U.S. government does

not give the airlines confidential negotiating information, and if necessary, a foreign-controlled U.S. carrier could have the degree of its participation limited.

3. The Defense Department is concerned about the impact on its Civil Reserve Air Fleet program (CRAF). As we noted in Chapter 2, about 500 aircraft of U.S. airlines, with flight crews, are on call in a military emergency and were of great value during the Persian Gulf War. Such flight crews would have to continue to be limited to American citizens with security clearances. As for the willingness of a foreign-controlled American carrier to participate in the program, it would have twin economic motives to do so—obtaining peacetime charter business from DOD (eligibility for which is a reward for CRAF participation) and serving as a balance against the drop in commercial traffic likely to follow any emergency that required activation of CRAF.

4. Airline labor is concerned that a U.S. airline controlled by a foreign airline might be used primarily to feed passengers to the foreign airline's connecting routes. Also, there is concern as to the attitude of a foreign owner toward the whole concept of bargaining with unions. However, the rights of employees under the Railway Labor Act (which, as we will see in Chapter 4, is applicable to airlines) would not be altered by the fact of foreign ownership. And, of course, bringing in foreign equity might save a weak U.S. carrier and save jobs for American labor.

Foreign ownership and/or control of U.S. airlines promises to be a subject of continuing controversy. The opinion has been expressed in DOT and elsewhere that close alliances, especially those with substantial foreign investment, should be limited to those cases where the foreign airline's country has a liberal bilateral agreement with the United States. This was the case with the Netherlands carrier, KLM, when it formed its alliance with Northwest, and continues to be DOT's position. In fact, the refusal of the British government to agree to an "open skies" bilateral agreement has resulted in a continuing refusal by the United States to approve the American Airlines–British Airways alliance.

Cabotage

There is growing sentiment to change U.S. cabotage laws to permit a foreign airline to carry U.S. domestic traffic on flights that originate in or are destined for foreign points. An example would be a British Airways flight from London to Miami via New York; today it is prohibited by law from carrying a passenger who merely wished New York–Miami service. Most countries have laws of this sort. They are traditional in both maritime and air law, but they result in the wasteful carrying of empty seats and the denial to the public of a service option.

At present, the only authority possessed by DOT to permit foreign airlines to carry cabotage traffic is limited to emergencies (such as when

U.S. carriers are on strike) and for 30-day periods, although authority for additional 30-day periods may be granted if the emergency continues. Section 40109(g) is the applicable law.

It is important to distinguish between *fill-up* (also called *consecutive*) cabotage, where the flight must have come in from or be destined to a foreign point, and *full* or unrestricted cabotage, where a foreign airline could operate between two points in the United States without any connection with an international flight. Most favorable sentiment today refers only to the fill-up variety. The Canadian and British governments, for example, have been seeking to exchange such rights with the United States.

There is sentiment within DOT to seek legislation that would permit it, in the course of bilateral bargainings, to include fill-up cabotage rights. Reciprocity would, of course, have to be granted, and here the philosophy of the equitable exchange of economic benefits intrudes. There are pairs of points within Canada, for example, between which U.S. carriers might wish to carry fill-up cabotage traffic, but there are far more pairs of points within the United States that Canadian carriers could profitably serve on a fill-up basis. The bargain would be very much in Canada's favor. Even more extreme is the imbalance with respect to small European countries such as Belgium and the Netherlands, where there is only one major airport in each country and no pair of points within the country between which cabotage rights could be exercised. Actually, all of the Western European countries, by reason of their small geographical areas, lack valuable cabotage segments to concede.

The broad geographical expanse of the United States and the presence of many traffic-rich major cities at great distances as, for example, on opposite coasts, is really not equaled anywhere in the world. Still, there could be an equitable exchange of economic benefits if a mutual grant of fill-up cabotage rights were supplemented by concessions by the foreign country on other matters such as Fifth Freedom, multiple designation, and rates.

As we have noted, the European Union in 1997 extended its rules to permit any airline of its member countries to take traffic between any pair of points within the European Union. What we may yet see—and what could cause controversy with the United States—is a future EU policy that would forbid a U.S. carrier from taking traffic between any points within the EU area even though the points are not within one country. For example, a U.S. airline might have a route from the United States going through Paris to Rome and have Fifth Freedom rights to take Paris-Rome traffic. The EU members might interpret the Paris-Rome segment as cabotage, looking upon the EU as if it were one large country. The United States would then be asked to allow fill-up cabotage traffic on the various routes coming into the United States from the EU countries in return for the reciprocal right to be able once again to serve segments within the EU on which it had previously had Fifth Freedom rights. Such a policy would tend to force the hand of Congress to amend the transportation statute to authorize inclusion of fill-up cabotage rights in foreign air carrier permits.

Generally speaking, U.S. airlines are dubious concerning any grant of cabotage rights, seeing competition on their valuable domestic routes balanced by less valuable rights for them abroad. Airline labor is deeply troubled by the idea, fearing that the diversion of traffic on domestic routes would lead to loss of jobs. It is by no means certain that the necessary legislation will be enacted by Congress.

Privatization of Government-Owned Airlines

There is a trend to privatization of government-owned airlines. We have noted that, except for the United States, the prevailing practice around the world has been for each government to own (or have a controlling interest in) a single major airline that conducts that country's long international routes. (In the past certain countries such as Canada, France, and Great Britain have also allowed a second carrier, privately owned, to operate some long international routes.)

In recent years, however, many of these airlines have been sold to private investors, with the government retaining either a minority interest or no equity holding at all. In the 1980s this occurred with two of the largest world airlines, British Airways and Japan Air Lines. Subsequently, some of the world's largest airlines, such as Air Canada, Lufthansa, and Qantas, have become fully privately owned, while others such as Air France and KLM are a mixture of government and private ownership. Even more remarkably, in Latin America, where government ownership of airlines was once dominant, most airlines have now gone to private (or predominantly private) ownership.[33]

According to the U.S. General Accounting Office, "Governments are considering privatizing their airlines for a variety of reasons: to raise revenue; reduce their deficits; free airlines' management from political interference; and enhance the airlines' commercial viability, efficiency, and, ultimately, profitability. After being privatized in 1987, British Airways dramatically improved its efficiency and profitability."[34]

Complaints of Unfair Treatment

U.S. carriers regularly complain of unfair treatment at foreign points in matters such as provision of airport facilities, currency exchange regulations, airport and airway charges, and taxation. For cargo, the list is longer and includes failure to furnish adequate cargo-processing facilities, prohibitions or limitations on air freight forwarder charters, and requirements that cargo at the foreign airport be handled by the competing national airline. (We will refer again to cargo problems in Chapter 7.) U.S. actions are not limited to negotiations with the governments concerned, but may include retaliatory measures at U.S. airports against the airline of the offending country, as authorized by the IATCA.

Proposed Multilateral and Regional Agreements

From time to time interest revives in the concept of a worldwide multilateral agreement to replace the whole bilateral system, or a regional multilateral agreement to cover, say, all airline service between North America and Europe.

In 1988, a State Department official suggested that a multilateral agreement between the United States and the countries of the EU (then called the EC) might some day replace the elaborate complex of bilaterals that governs transatlantic service. Such an agreement "would stress open entry, traffic rights to intermediate and beyond destinations, and unrestricted changes in aircraft size." The official suggested that the concept be tried first for all-cargo services.[35] In 1993, the secretary of transportation referred to "the outworn system of bilateral aviation agreements that so often triggers protectionist episodes." He described the bilateral system as "badly frayed by the pressures of a global—not a 'bilateral' economy" and urged "moving decisively beyond bilateralism to multilateral and regional accords."[36]

As of the end of the 1990s, nothing specific had resulted from such suggestions, and the emphasis had shifted to seeking "open skies" bilateral agreements. The enthusiasm shown from time to time by U.S. government officials for multilateral pacts may not be shared by some other governments, who will not fail to note that what the U.S. government seeks are broad rights to unlimited frequency, capacity, and Fifth Freedom, to multiple designation of carriers, and to unregulated rates— in short, what is contained in the "open skies" bilaterals.

As we have referred repeatedly to the "open skies" style of agreement, perhaps it would be well to quote a specific definition, prepared in 1992 when DOT sought approval of EU countries of the concept:

An open skies agreement allows access to all routes between the United States and the European country; provides for the greatest possible degree of freedom in pricing; prohibits restrictions on the capacity and frequency of flights on those routes; and allows unrestricted route and traffic rights, such as an airline's ability to serve intermediate destinations and points beyond the countries that are parties to the agreement, to change the size of aircraft used, to serve "coterminal" airports, and to exercise fifth freedom rights.[37]

It is sometimes also suggested that the World Trade Organization (WTO) might take on a role with respect to some aspects of international airline services now covered under the bilateral system. The WTO has had its jurisdiction extended beyond physical goods to include services, and thus could apply principles of free and fair trade to airline service. As of 1999, however, there seemed no immediate prospect of such a development. One authority who has researched this topic has concluded that for air transportation to fit into the WTO system "the first step the aviation community must take is to change its overall philosophy and consider all international air traffic as international property rather than national property."[38]

We turn now from the complicated topic of international entry—and, indeed, from the whole subject of entry and exit with which this chapter has been concerned—and in the next chapter will consider the cost or supply side of airline economics.

NOTES

1. Laurence E. Gesell and Martin T. Farris, "Airline Deregulation: An Evaluation of Goals and Objectives," *Transportation Law Journal* 21 (1992): 116.

2. Paul S. Dempsey, "Airline Deregulation and Laissez-Faire Mythology: Economic Theory in Turbulence," *Journal of Air Law and Commerce* 56 (Winter 1990): 316.

3. Robert L. Thornton, "Airlines and Agents: Conflict and the Public Welfare," *Journal of Air Law and Commerce* 52 (Winter 1986): 381.

4. John R. Meyer and Clinton V. Oster Jr., *Deregulation and the Future of Intercity Passenger Travel* (Cambridge, Mass.: The MIT Press, 1987), p. 56.

5. *Aviation Week and Space Technology*, March 14, 1988, p. 192.

6. Civil Aeronautics Board (CAB), Federal Aviation Act of 1958, revised March 1, 1977, Section 102(d).

7. Arthur D. Little, Inc., *Civil Aviation Development: A Policy and Operations Analysis* (New York: Praeger, 1972), p. 75.

8. CAB, "TWA, North-South California Service," *CAB Reports* 4 (1943): 373.

9. Civil Aeronautics Board, *Implementation of the Provisions of the Airline Deregulation Act of 1978*, Report to Congress, January 31, 1984, p. 125.

10. U.S. Department of Transportation News Release, November 1, 1993, p. 4.

11. U.S. General Accounting Office, *Airline Competition: Impact of Changing Foreign Investment and Control Limits on U.S. Airlines*, 1992, p. 16.

12. CAB, *Implementation of the Provisions of the Airline Deregulation Act of 1978*, App. E, pp. 1–2.

13. Scott Kilman, "Growing Giants," *Wall Street Journal*, July 20, 1987, p. 1.

14. Paul S. Dempsey and Laurence E. Gesell, *Airline Management: Strategies for the 21st Century* (Chandler, Ariz.: Coast Aire Publications, 1997), pp. 204–5.

15. Ibid., pp. 211–12.

16. Atef Ghobrial and Ken Fleming, "A Framework for Assessing the Role of

Aircraft Technology in Enhancing System Capacity," *Journal of Aviation/Aerospace Education and Research* 6 (Winter 1996): 27–32.

17. U.S. Department of Transportation, *U.S. Subsidized Essential Air Service*, July 1999.

18. Ibid., pp. 4 and 7.

19. Laurence E. Gesell, *Airline Re-Regulation* (Chandler, Ariz: Coast Aire Publications, 1990), p. 65.

20. "Southwest-Muse Acquisition Show Cause Order," Department of Transportation Order 85–5–28, May 10, 1985, pp. 6–7.

21. Lucile S. Keyes, "The Regulation of Airline Mergers by the Department of Transportation," *Journal of Air Law and Commerce* 53 (Spring 1988): 743.

22. Transportation Research Board, *Winds of Change: Domestic Air Transport Since Deregulation* (Washington, D.C.: National Research Council, 1991), p. 6.

23. U.S. Department of Transportation News Release, November 1, 1993, p. 5.

24. Raymond E. Neidl, "Current Financial and Operational Trends in the Airline Industry," in *Handbook of Airline Finance*, ed. Gail F. Butler and Martin R. Keller (Washington, D.C.: McGraw-Hill, 1999), p. 612.

25. Richard Smithies, "The Liberalization of Air Transport Services," in *Handbook of Airline Marketing*, ed. Gail F. Butler and Martin R. Keller (Washington, D.C.: McGraw-Hill, 1998) p. 31; *Air Cargo World*, November 1998, pp. 22–24; February 1999, pp. 18–20; and September 1999, p. 26.

26. *Miami Herald*, April 14, 1997, p. B-7; and *Daytona Beach News-Journal*, December 10, 1999, p. A-7.

27. Michael W. Tretheway and Tae H. Oum, *Airline Economics: Foundations for Strategy and Policy* (Vancouver, Canada: Centre for Transportation Studies, 1992), pp. 104–6.

28. G. Porter Elliott, "Learning to Fly: The European Commission Enters Unfamiliar Skies," *Journal of Air Law and Commerce* 64 (Winter 1998): 159; *Air Cargo World*, April 1999, p. 34; and Pablo M. J. Mendes de Leon, "Nationality and Privatization of Airlines in Light of Globalization," in *Handbook of Airline Finance*, ed. Gail F. Butler and Martin R. Keller (Washington, D.C.: McGraw-Hill, 1999), p. 51.

29. Elliott, "Learning to Fly," *Journal of Air Law and Commerce* 64 (Winter 1998): 182.

30. Tretheway and Oum, *Airline Economics*, p. 111.

31. Alan R. Bender, "Allied Airlines: The New Robber Barons?" *Aviation Week and Space Technology*, June 22, 1998, p. 70.

32. Air Transport Association, *Annual Report—1999*, p. 7.

33. Mendes de Leon, "Nationality and Privatization of Airlines," p. 52; and Uli Baur and David Kistner, "Airline Privatization: Principles and Lessons Learned," in *Handbook of Airline Finance*, ed. Gail F. Butler and Martin R. Keller (Washington, D.C.: McGraw-Hill, 1999), p. 72.

34. U.S. General Accounting Office, *International Aviation: Measures by European Community Could Limit U.S. Airlines' Ability to Compete Abroad*, 1993, p. 41.

35. *Aviation Week and Space Technology*, March 7, 1988, p. 15.

36. U.S. Department of Transportation News Release, November 1, 1993, pp. 9–10.

37. U.S. General Accounting Office, *International Aviation*, p. 53.

38. Ruwantissa I. R. Abeyratne, "Would Competition in Commercial Aviation Ever Fit Into the World Trade Organization?" *Journal of Air Law and Commerce* 61 (May-June 1996): 856.

SELECTED REFERENCES

How the major airlines have adjusted route strategies to compete in a deregulated environment both with new entrants and with one another is discussed in John R. Meyer and Clinton V. Oster Jr., *Deregulation and the Future of Intercity Passenger Travel* (Cambridge, Mass.: The MIT Press, 1987), pp. 55–72); the potential danger of concentration is discussed in the same book, pp. 207–14.

The development of hub-and-spoke networks is described in Steven Morrison and Clifford Winston, *The Economic Effects of Airline Deregulation* (Washington, D.C.: Brookings Institution, 1986), chap. 2, pp. 4–10.

The trend to dominant hubs, and its implications for airline profits and for merger policy, are analyzed in Atef Ghobrial, "Competition for Hub Dominance: Some Implications for Airline Profitability and Enplanement Share," *Journal of Aviation/Aerospace Education and Research* 2 (Fall 1991): 20–29.

Linear route systems are contrasted with hub-and-spoke route systems, with some criticisms of the latter, in Paul S. Dempsey and Laurence E. Gesell, *Airline Management: Strategies for the 21st Century* (Chandler, Ariz.: Coast Aire Publications, 1997), pp. 200–212 and 466–71.

The characteristics of successful hub-and-spoke networks are analyzed in Frank Berardino, "Integrating Airline Strategy and Marketing," pp. 106–8, and Peter Berdy, "Developing Effective Route Networks," in *Handbook of Airline Marketing*, ed. Gail F. Butler and Martin R. Keller (Washington, D.C.: McGraw-Hill, 1998), pp. 614–25.

The second Bermuda Agreement is analyzed in Ramon de Murias, *The Economic Regulation of International Air Transport* (Jefferson, N.C.: McFarland, 1989), pp. 141–46.

A critique of DOT's record in approving the wave of mergers in the mid-1980s can be found in Lucile S. Keyes, "The Regulation of Airline Mergers by the Department of Transportation," *Journal of Air Law and Commerce* 53 (Spring 1988): 737–64. Recommended for students with substantial background in economics.

For a labor-oriented approach to the emerging problem of airline concentration, see Frank A. Spencer and Frank H. Cassell, *Eight Years of U.S. Airline Deregulation: Management and Labor Adaptations; Re-Emergence of Oligopoly* (Evanston, Ill.: Northwestern University Transportation Center, 1987), pp. 1–6 and 29–49.

The trend to concentration since deregulation, barriers to entry, and desirable public policies are discussed in Robert M. Hardaway and Paul S. Dempsey, "Airlines, Airports, and Antitrust: A Proposed Strategy for Enhanced Competition," *Journal of Air Law and Commerce* 58 (Winter 1992): 455–86.

Foreign investment in U.S. airlines is analyzed in detail in David T. Arlington, "Liberalization of Restrictions on Foreign Ownership in U.S. Air Carriers," *Journal of Air Law and Commerce* 59 (September—October 1993): 133–92. The same topic is covered in U.S. General Accounting Office, *Airline Competition: Impact of Changing Foreign Investment and Control Limits on U.S. Airlines*, 1992, pp. 1–75; the Civil Reserve Air Fleet program is described in detail on pages 50–59.

For a worldwide view of airline service, analyzed region by region, see Nawal K. Taneja, *The International Airline Industry: Trends, Issues and Challenges* (Lexington, Mass.: D.C. Heath, 1988). It covers political and economic factors affecting the problems and policies of airlines and their governments. Though somewhat out-of-date, much is still pertinent.

A highly critical view of airline alliances can be found in Alan R. Bender, "Allied Airlines: The New Robber Barons?" *Aviation Week and Space Technology*, June 22, 1998, p. 70.

Alliances are discussed from a Canadian perspective in Ira Lewis, "United States–Canada Air Services: The Role of Alliances in a Future Bilateral Agreement," *Transportation Journal* 34 (Spring 1995): 5–12.

A detailed study of the pending American Airlines–British Airways alliance, and the complex problems that surround it, can be found in Jeff Mosteller, "The Current and Future Climate of Airline Consolidation: The Possible Impact of an Alliance of Two Large Airlines and an Examination of the Proposed American Airlines–British Airways Alliance," *Journal of Air Law and Commerce* 64 (Spring 1999): 575–603.

The legal and economic questions raised by foreign carrier investment in U.S. airlines are discussed in Joan M. Feldman, "Empty Gesture," *Air Transport World* (May 1999): 47–52; and John E. Gillick, "The Impact of Citizenship Considerations on Aviation Financing," in *Handbook of Airline Finance*, ed. Gail F. Butler and Martin R. Keller (Washington, D.C.: McGraw-Hill, 1999), pp. 41–50.

Privatization of foreign airlines is discussed in Pablo M. J. Mendes de Leon, "Nationality and Privatization of Airlines in Light of Globalization," pp. 51–70, and Uli Baur and David Kistner, "Airline Privatization: Principles and Lessons Learned," in *Handbook of Airline Finance*, ed. Gail F. Butler and Martin R. Keller (Washington, D.C.: McGraw-Hill, 1999), pp. 71–81.

Globalization and some problems it brings, together with possible solutions, are the topic of Eugene Sochor, *The Poltics of International Aviation* (Iowa City: University of Iowa Press, 1991), pp. 201–19.

The impact of U.S. "open skies" bilateral agreements on transatlantic airline service, and the possibilities of a multilateral agreement between the United States and the countries of the EU are analyzed in Benoit M. J. Swinnen, "An Opportunity for Transatlantic Civil Aviation: From Open Skies to Open Markets?" *Journal of Air Law and Commerce* 63 (August–September 1997): 249–85.

The complex problems of medium and short-haul air service, including the impact of the new regional jet aircraft, are analyzed in detail in Alan R. Bender, "Battle 2000: The New Jet Entrants Versus the Regional Partners?" *Journal of Aviation/Aerospace Education and Research* 6 (Fall 1995): pp. 7–16.

4

The Costs of Airline Service

This chapter focuses on the supply side of airline service. The supply side concerns the elements that are put together to make an airline service and what they cost.

ACCOUNTING CATEGORIES

Under the Federal Aviation Act, the CAB had authority to require the filing of data by airlines, including the power to prescribe the method of keeping airline accounts. Over the years, the board maintained a regulation containing a standard form for accounts, with interpretive rules that the airlines were required to follow. Although some information could be withheld as confidential company information, most of the accounts had to be filed with the board and were available to the public.

With the demise of the board, DOT took over this function. While there has been some relaxation of reporting requirements, consistent with the regulatory reform trend, much data are still filed and available to the public. These records show traffic and revenue, broken down in various ways such as by passengers and cargo, and aircraft statistics. Of course there are balance sheets and income statements. But the accounts also cover costs, the portion of them that we are concerned with in this chapter.

The cost data are reported in certain categories. We need not be concerned with the details here, but a look at a representative list of principal cost categories should give us a general appreciation of the subject of airline cost problems. Such a list is as follows:

Flying operations

Direct maintenance

Maintenance burden

Depreciation and amortization

Passenger service

Aircraft servicing

Traffic servicing

Reservations and sales

Advertising and publicity

General and administrative

Flying operations include crew wages and fuel. Direct maintenance covers the costs of labor and materials directly attributable to the maintenance and repairing of aircraft, including periodic overhauls, and other flight equipment. Maintenance burden means the overhead costs related to the upkeep and repair of flight equipment and other property, such as the administering of stockrooms, the keeping of maintenance records, and the scheduling and supervising of maintenance operations. This category could also be called "indirect maintenance costs."

Passenger service would take in the cost of food and providing cabin attendants. Aircraft servicing refers to routine servicing such as washing the aircraft and cleaning the passenger cabin, but not to mechanical servicing. It also includes landing fees. Traffic servicing includes ticketing and baggage handling.

Reservations and sales, as well as advertising and publicity, are self-explanatory, as are depreciation and amortization, but let us note that the latter item includes the cost of paying off the huge purchase price of modern aircraft. Lastly, general and administrative costs have been defined as: "Expenses of a general corporate nature and expenses incurred in performing activities which contribute to more than a single operating function such as general financial accounting activities, purchasing activities, representation at law, and other general operational administration not directly applicable to a particular function."[1]

Commissions paid to travel agents—a major expense for any airline—fall logically under "reservations and sales," but are often given a separate category.

There are other ways to categorize airline costs. One authority would use three categories: capacity costs, traffic-related costs, and overhead costs. The first would include wages of both flight crew and flight attendants, fuel, maintenance, landing fees, depreciation of aircraft, and charges for leasing aircraft. Traffic-related costs would include ticketing, baggage-handling, other terminal expenses, passenger food, and aircraft servicing. Overhead costs would include "the expenses of maintaining the organization, such as personnel functions, planning, and general management."[2] Another source would use a generally similar set of three categories, but would put aircraft depreciation and leasing costs under "overhead."[3]

ANALYSIS OF COSTS

Let us emphasize that the above sets of categories are merely accounting systems, are ways of *organizing* the costs. When the time comes to analyze airline costs, and make managerial and governmental decisions based upon them, we find ourselves in a much more difficult area. Not only is cost analysis inherently a complicated subject, but it is made even more difficult by problems of terminology. There are common costs, separable costs, constant costs, variable costs, fully allocated costs, out-of-pocket costs, direct operating costs, terminal costs, line-haul costs—just to mention a few. Airline management and transportation economists do not always use cost terminology consistently, and the classification of a cost as one type or another may also depend on the managerial decision being contemplated.

To simplify the discussion, we will limit ourselves to certain types of costs that commonly arise in airline decision making and will relate our discussion, so far as possible, to specific kinds of decisions.

Common versus Separable Costs

Separable costs are those that can be allocated clearly and on a logical basis to a particular service—food and cabin attendant wages and passenger ticketing may clearly and logically be allocated to passenger service, while the cost of handling freight at a terminal may clearly be allocated to cargo service. But the cost of the crew's wages, while obviously necessarily incurred to transport both passengers and cargo, cannot be allocated in a clear and logical manner between the two classes of traffic. Thus, we call this type of cost a common cost. The common versus separable duo can also be used for types of passenger traffic, such as allocating the costs of free champagne to the first-class passengers. Similarly, among different types of cargo, it is possible to have separable costs such as the special expenses resulting from carrying unusual cargo such as live animals.

Decisions as to the proper level of cargo rates when cargo is carried in the cargo compartments on passenger flights involve management deeply in the question of common costs.

Out-of-Pocket Costs, Constant Costs, and Fully Allocated Costs

These three terms are extremely important in rate decisions. Out-of-pocket cost is a familiar term in transportation economics; it refers to the added cost incurred when performing an additional service or accepting an added unit of traffic. It is the separable cost of an individual unit. Out-of-pocket costs are sometimes also called incremental costs and, generally speaking, are what economists would call marginal costs. (In this text we shall use out-of-pocket as synonymous with marginal cost, but the student should be aware that the term is sometimes used to mean marginal cost plus an allowance for a share of overhead or to mean average variable cost at the output level being considered.)

But one cannot simply scan an airline's accounts and designate some costs as out-of-pocket. The use of the term depends on the decision to be made. If an airline has a flight ready to take off and one more passenger comes running for the gate, the out-of-pocket costs of carrying this one additional person are almost nothing—merely the food eaten on board and the negligible amount of fuel consumption from the added payload. Crew wages will not change, nor will depreciation of the aircraft, nor will the salaries of management, just because one extra passenger is carried. A standby fare involves this cost concept.

But if an airline is operating, say, three flights a day in a market and decides to increase the frequency to four, such items as crew wages, fuel and landing fees are going to be out-of-pocket costs with respect to that decision. Moreover, if ticketing and baggage-handling facilities are already overloaded, the added flight may result in the airline's having to expand these facilities, and the resulting costs can be considered out-of-pocket with respect to that flight.

Constant costs are ordinarily defined as those costs that do not vary with changes in the amount of traffic. Very often the term *fixed cost* is used interchangeably with constant cost although, strictly speaking, fixed costs are those that will continue to be incurred so long as the airline goes on operating as a corporation, even if it suspends services. In practice, decision-making personnel in management and government will use either fixed or constant for all costs that are not out-of-pocket with respect to the decision being considered.

What, then, are fully allocated costs? The expression means the costs of carrying the particular unit of traffic, including both the out-of-pocket element and a fair share of the constant costs.

The out-of-pocket, constant, and fully allocated cost concepts find practical application in, among other things, decisions respecting the discount type of fare, such as an excursion fare aimed at the tourist market. Here some substantial saving is offered to a passenger who buys a round-trip ticket where the return coupon cannot be used until, say, two weeks after the departure flight. The airline may concede that such a fare does not cover costs on a fully allocated basis but will justify the fare as meeting out-of-pocket costs and making, in addition, a small contribution to constant costs. If the excursion fare attracts enough passengers who would not otherwise fly, and if they can be accommodated in seats that would otherwise be empty, the discount fare may indeed make very good sense, provided that not too many passengers will shift from regular fares to the discount fare.

Line-Haul versus Terminal Costs

Separating costs into line-haul and terminal is significant when explaining why the total cost per passenger-*mile* drops as the length of the trip grows. This phenomenon is called the cost taper and leads to a rate taper. Line-haul costs are those directly related to the mileage and time elapsing while the aircraft is actually in flight. Certainly this would include crew wages and fuel as well as direct maintenance costs and the wages of cabin attendants. Terminal costs—which are also called ground costs—would include the expense of activities at the terminal, such as aircraft and traffic servicing, and reservations and sales. These are costs related to the amount of traffic carried but independent of the mileage it travels.

An airline's costs at a terminal should be allocated equally among the passengers serviced since the costs of processing a passenger at an airport are about the same regardless of the length of the passenger's trip. The amount per passenger is then spread over the mileage traveled by the passenger to form part of the cost per passenger-mile for that trip. Spread over a journey of several thousand miles, this cost contributes a smaller amount per passenger-mile than if it were spread over a short trip. The effect is that the total cost per passenger-mile (line-haul plus terminal) tapers downward with the length of the trip. (Line-haul costs also taper downward somewhat since costs such as fuel are higher for takeoffs and landings and for slower speeds; line-haul costs per mile are lowest when the aircraft is cruising at high speed.)

In the case of cargo, the terminal costs include the entire process of receiving, weighing, sorting, guarding, and storing cargo, loading the aircraft, and unloading it at the destination. As we shall see in Chapter 7, terminal costs make up a big proportion of the total costs of cargo traffic, and they represent a major managerial problem area.

Often the cost taper, whether for passengers or cargo, leads to a tapering downward of the rate per mile on long hauls, although this is only one factor in rate determination, as we shall see in Chapter 6.

Direct Operating Costs and Indirect Operating Costs

Airline management frequently uses the term direct operating cost (often abbreviated DOCs) and typically will define them as those elements closely related to flying the aircraft, for example, crew wages and fuel. Indirect operating costs consist of the ground or terminal cost just mentioned as well as overhead expenses. The expression *ground and indirect* is sometimes used for these same costs, which is perhaps closer to literal accuracy, since many of the ground costs are, as we have seen, directly related to the amount of traffic though not to the actual flying of the aircraft.

Seat-Mile Costs and Other Ratios

The carrier's accounts, beyond merely listing cost figures, are the basis for some ratios that are of critical importance to management. One of these is the cost per available seat-mile. The word *available* is really unnecessary, and the simpler term *seat-mile* is commonly used. It means a seat carried for a mile, a measure of the physical output of the airline. The cost per seat-mile represents to management the total cost of a unit of output in passenger service.

The cost per revenue passenger-mile can also be computed. Usually the term *passenger-mile* is used, dropping the word *revenue*. The only significance of *revenue* is that passengers are occasionally carried free of charge or for a token sum, such as 10 percent of the normal fare (airline employees and their families, for example). These are not counted when computing passenger-miles, though a half-fare passenger such as a child is counted as one passenger.

A related ratio is the load factor, which relates the passenger-miles to the seat-miles. An aircraft with 100 seats flying 1,000 miles performs 100,000 seat-miles. If 55 percent of the seats are filled with paying passengers, the passenger-miles would be 55,000, and the load factor would be 55 percent. The term *breakeven load factor* is in common use in airline economics. It means the percentage of seats that must be occupied by paying passengers in order that the revenues from the operation will just cover the costs.

In the case of cargo, one may compute the cost per *available ton-mile* or per *revenue ton-mile*. A load factor may also be computed, although with cargo there are really two load factors (or two ways of computing a load factor). One is to calculate the relationship of the revenue ton-miles to the available ton-miles. This reflects the traditional manner of measuring cargo in all modes of transportation—by weight. But the critical figure for air cargo is usually the volume or "cube" of the cargo, as we shall see in Chapter 7. On many flights the cargo space is filled well before the weight limit of the aircraft is reached. A load factor based on weight alone might show a cargo flight with, say, a 70 percent load factor when the plane was completely filled. To reflect this situation, a volume-related load factor could be computed that relates occupied space to available space.

The Short-Haul Problem

Seat-mile costs are particularly significant in the short-haul problem, although the problem involves both cost and demand considerations. Not only is the cost per seat-mile higher for shorter stage lengths, but the demand is highly elastic (that is, highly price-sensitive), since alternative modes of transportation, notably the private automobile, are relatively attractive over shorter distances. To attract traffic in a short-haul market, an airline must keep its rates low, but to cover its seat-mile costs it must keep its rates high. Every mode of transportation has this short-haul dilemma, but in air transportation it is acute.

There are a number of reasons why seat-mile costs are higher for short hauls, some of which have already been mentioned in explaining cost taper. One reason is that the cost of processing passengers and cargo at terminals is about the same regardless of how long the flight is. It costs as much to ticket passengers and handle their baggage if they are going on a 100-mile trip as if they are going on a 3,000-mile trip and, for the shorter trip, there are far fewer miles over which to spread these terminal costs. Another factor is that fuel consumption is heavy during takeoff and landing, and this charge must be spread over fewer miles for the short hauls. Landing fees payable to the airport must be similarly spread.

The short haul also results in higher crew-wage costs per seat-mile because of the slower average speed of the aircraft. If a stage length is only 100 or 200 miles, the aircraft may not get up to maximum speed before it is time to slow down again. (Crew wages are usually determined by a formula that includes mileage flown and the weight of the aircraft, but the hours worked remain a major factor.)

It is little wonder that the local service carriers, flying stage lengths some of which were only 50 or 100 miles, had high seat-mile costs that, taken together with the demand problem mentioned above, kept most of them dependent on subsidy. As they moved into a longer-haul route pattern, the short-haul problem was handed down to the commuter air carriers—and with it the subsidy. However, the turboprop aircraft generally used by the commuters could operate at lower cost on short hauls than the larger jet aircraft of the local service carriers. Hence, as we have seen, the changeover from the locals to the commuters resulted in a drop in subsidy payments. As we have noted, in the late 1990s many regional carriers and some commuters were purchasing new jet aircraft in the 50 to 70 seat range, which may result in lower seat-mile costs on short hauls.

The short-haul cost problem results today in giving small points service only at fares that are quite high considering the length of the trip. Thus, although a service may offer the advantage of connecting a minor point with a larger city from whose airport there are numerous connections throughout the country and the world, a passenger at the small point is faced with an initial expensive short haul. Under deregulation theory, of course, this is appropriate as reflecting the true costs of the service.

It should be noted that the short-haul cost problem is not confined to regional and commuter carriers or to small points. Major airlines sometimes fly short stages as part of a longer route—for example, Philadelphia to New York as the last leg of a flight from California—and must consider the extent to which the cost taper runs against them when they schedule such stages. In fact, the shuttle services in the Washington— New York and Boston—New York markets to some extent reflect a short-haul cost problem.

The cost taper does not go on forever. At some point, as the haul gets very long, it becomes necessary to reduce the passenger load in order to squeeze the maximum mileage (within safety standards) from the maximum fuel-carrying capacity of the aircraft. The cost per passenger-mile begins to increase rather than decrease with the additional length of haul. In practice, airlines seldom fly such extended stage lengths.

A possible future development that could have a major bearing on short-haul air service is high-speed rail passenger transit. Proposals have been made for such service—for example, between Miami, Orlando, and Tampa; between Los Angeles and San Diego; and in the Texas triangle of Dallas, Houston, and San Antonio. Though some airlines oppose this development, others favor it, seeing a resulting relief of congestion of airports and airways.[4] Good rail service could compete with air service between cities such as these—of substantial size and within 100 to 300 miles of each other.

THE PRODUCTION FUNCTION AND FACTOR COSTS

In elementary economics we talk about factors of production and break them down into land, labor, capital, and managerial entrepreneurship. We also consider how these factors are brought together in certain proportions to create a particular output. An industrialized country may put a lot of capital and a little labor together to produce an article. A country with low-wage labor and not much capital will use a lot of labor and little machinery to produce the same article. Similarly, in the United States a few workers and a great deal of machinery produce on our farms a quantity of crops that in many other countries would be produced by many people and few machines. The proportion of one to the other—not the cost or wage levels as such, but the proportion of labor to machinery to land—is called the production function.

A good way to look at the term is to take the word *function* in the sense that it is used in mathematics. (What it does *not* refer to is a machine "functioning" to produce something.) Suppose we have an equation and a graph that shows the relationship of x to y; for this we use the word *function*.

The production function, then, may be defined as the relationship between the quantities of each input and the quantity of output. But what are the inputs for an airline service? Breaking it down beyond the usual general categories of "capital," "labor," and so on, we can readily name such factors as the aircraft, the flight crew, and the fuel. The cost of buying the aircraft, including financing charges, and the cost of maintenance might be considered as "capital." Crew wages, fuel, and landing fees are also major operational costs. There are all sorts of other costs, such as ticketing facilities, executive expenses, and so on, but we may simplify matters by saying that you produce air transportation of passengers, cargo, and mail by putting together an aircraft, a flight crew, fuel, and a landing strip at each end of the flight.

When you put this together as a production function, you find that there is little difference between one airline and another. One economist, Mahlon Straszheim, uses the word *homogeneous* to describe this similarity. He is, of course, looking at the international scene, where he finds that there is little difference in the production function even when comparing airlines of countries with widely differing levels of technological development.[5]

As an example, let us consider a New York–London service where American Airlines is competing with Air India. While the wage level in India is so low that typically their industries use much labor in proportion to capital, Air India uses machinery that is anything but primitive. The machinery is aircraft it has bought in the United States. It flies the same aircraft as American, the Boeing 747, on this route. It has the same required-size flight crew as American. For each flight between the two cities, each airline uses about the same amount of fuel and pays the same number of operational fees, one to each airport.

It is important to distinguish clearly between the amounts of each factor and the *price tag* on each factor. If each airline uses the same type of aircraft, the same number of flight personnel, and the same number of gallons of fuel, and pays the same number of landing fees, then the production function is the same, even though the *cost* of a factor to one carrier may be different from the *cost* to the other carrier flying between the two cities. The production function is homogeneous for airline service, and the underlying reason seems to be that to run an airline service at all, you simply cannot use primitive machinery but must use a machine that represents an extremely high level of technology and moreover is largely a standardized product of a handful of manufacturers.

Exceptions can be found to the above in areas of the world where low living standards may make feasible some local or regional services using old piston aircraft. Here the input of labor is greater and the input of capital lower. The aircraft are relatively cheap; but, due to both the small capacity and slow speed of the plane, many more man-hours are required to perform a given number of seat-miles than is the case with modern jet aircraft.

But how is it possible for high-wage countries to compete with low-wage countries in their airline services? In particular, how can it happen that an airline of a high-wage country may have a lower-cost operation than an airline of a low-wage country? This has happened. There have been years in which Pan American was the example of low-cost operations on the Atlantic. Straszheim's answer, derived from his own research, has to do with what he calls "scheduling of inputs." He finds that the skills of management in scheduling the utilization of aircraft, flight crews, and other inputs tend to be more effective in the airlines with the high-wage problems.[6]

More recent information indicates that Latin American carriers have costs averaging about 25 percent higher than their U.S. competitors, despite their lower wage rates, and that a major cause is their less efficient use of labor.[7] Another study said of the airlines of the EU countries that "the rates at which crews and aircraft are utilized are relatively low compared to the rates in the United States."[8] And a 1988 study by the International Labor Organization comparing North American (U.S. and Canadian) airlines with "European, Asian, African, and South American airlines," found that the North American carriers "had the lowest ratio of labor costs to operating revenues, showing that the North American airlines generate more revenue per unit of labor cost than airlines elsewhere in the world."[9]

How many hours are the crew actually flying the plane? How efficiently do you use your other personnel? And how many hours out of 24 is each aircraft actually flying? With today's expensive aircraft, the utilization rate is a figure over which management is well advised to brood constantly. Depreciation charges are severe, and they apply whether a plane is working or idle. (The presumed life of an aircraft is about 15 to 20 years.) Good management, then, is called on to do an expert job with the crazy-quilt pattern of allocating aircraft and crews over its entire system.

If you get your aircraft to the end of the line and it lays over, how long will the layover be? And how far can you crowd all this? Management must consider what passengers want in terms of the time of day of a departure and of an arrival. Experience shows that a utilization rate of 8 to 9 hours a day (that is, out of 24 hours) is good. This will vary, of course, with the airline, the type of route, and the type of aircraft. Time on the ground involves time spent loading and unloading, time spent fueling and for maintenance, but the major time on the ground results from the fact that an airline must please its passengers by using its fleet at the times of day when the passengers want the service.

It should be noted that aircraft utilization, as the term is ordinarily used in air transportation, refers to the time that the plane is engaged in revenue flights and does *not* have anything to do with how well the *capacity* of the plane is being utilized by filling it with revenue passengers. In short, aircraft utilization and load factor are two different ratios altogether. But there is a relationship between them that is important in running an airline: it can be a bad management decision to achieve high aircraft utilization by having numerous flights even though experiencing low load factors. The fleet is kept busy but at the expense of scheduling beyond what the traffic justifies. The impact on profits is clear.

While on the subject of aircraft utilization, we might mention that there are factors affecting it in addition to managerial skill, such as the seasonality or other peaking tendencies on an airline's system, the amount of competition from other airlines, and limitations on the discretion of management as to how many flights they wish to schedule. The latter is particularly evident in international operations.

Utilization of reservations, ticketing, and baggage-handling personnel can also be critical to cost control. Here, in addition to managerial skill, a major factor is the extent to which an airline serves large cities with a constant flow of traffic so that personnel and airport facilities can be kept rather steadily busy.

Flight scheduling obviously plays a central role in the optimal utilization of an airline's resources. Here is a good description, by Robert L. Crandall, then-president of American Airlines, of the complexity of the scheduler's job:

For each segment to be flown, the scheduler must consider how large a market is expected and how it will fluctuate by day of week and hour of day. At some airports, he must adapt to a shortage of slots for landings and departures. At others, curfews may shorten the flying day. The scheduler considers on-board loads by looking at local traffic, through traffic, and traffic that connects at some intermediate point with another flight, and must pay particular attention to building efficient complexes with multiple cross-feed. Aircraft must be scheduled to end their day's flying at the point of origin of the next day's flight pattern, and that pattern must bring the aircraft into maintenance shops on a predetermined schedule.[10]

THE TWO MAJOR AIRLINE COST AREAS

Labor and fuel are the two biggest costs of operating an airline. It is not unusual today for labor to represent over one-third and fuel, with its great price swings, somewhere between 10 and 25 percent of an airline's total operating costs. Each of these major cost areas will be examined separately.

Fuel Costs

In 1972 the average price paid by U.S. scheduled airlines for jet fuel was 11.5 cents a gallon; by the end of 1980 it was approaching $1.00 a gallon, nearly a ninefold increase. Peaking at $1.09 a gallon in 1981, a year when fuel represented 31 percent of operating costs, it dropped gradually over a five-year period to about 50 cents by late 1986, but rose again to 61 cents a year later. Since then the price has been reasonably stable except for a period in 1990–91 when, during the Persian Gulf War, it jumped as high as $1.14. From 1992 through 1997, jet fuel prices have been in the 55–65 cent range, dropping to 50 cents in 1998, but rising again in 1999.[11] The future course of fuel prices is hard to predict with any degree of exactness, but since the world's petroleum supply is limited and world consumption great, the ultimate course would appear inevitably to be up. Moreover, world political conditions, especially in the Middle East, could send prices up sharply again at any time. Thus, the emphasis in aircraft selection and obsolescence should continue to be heavily on fuel efficiency. Other managerial decisions such as choosing to enter or leave a market will continue to be influenced by the changing costs of fuel.

The price paid for fuel will differ from one carrier to another due to the bargaining strength of the big user in negotiating fuel contracts and also, to some extent, to the higher price often charged at small airports typically served by the smaller carriers.

Despite great improvements in fuel efficiency, the modern airline still consumes fuel liberally. In terms of passenger-miles per gallon, airline fuel efficiency improved from 17.5 in 1973 to about 31 in 1983, but this is still in the range of a private automobile with no one in it but the driver. In terms of our national policy to conserve fuel by encouraging people to use mass transit, the airlines do not come out too well. More recent data, however, suggest a continuing sharp improvement of fuel efficiency in the newest aircraft models.[12]

One step the airlines are taking is to purchase more fuel-efficient aircraft, to put more fuel-efficient engines on existing aircraft, and to drop from service older aircraft that are quite fuel-consuming. Another is to adjust routes to eliminate small points and reduce short hauls. Still another step is to seek higher load factors by such devices as curtailing the number of flights in leaner markets and especially by developing effective hub-and-spoke networks, as previously explained. Here their success was limited for many years, but in the latter 1990s, load factors have risen substantially. Passenger load factors averaged in a 59 to 63 percent range through the 1980s and early 1990s, but have climbed steadily from 1993 (63.5 percent) to 1998 (70.9 percent).

Looking ahead, there seems little likelihood of an amelioration of the fuel problem. The world's supply of petroleum, though still great, is ultimately finite, and a time will come when petroleum will become scarce, though the experts differ on when this will occur. Long range plans are now being developed whereby jet fuel might be made from the United States' abundant coal and shale reources. Research is also being done on alternative types of fuel, such as liquid hydrogen, which could be manufactured from coal. It remains to be seen, however, whether and when one or more of these plans can be brought to practical reality. Meanwhile, fuel costs remain a continuing challenge to the airlines.

Labor Costs

The scheduled airlines of the United States employed about 621,000 persons as of 1998, of whom about 64,000 were pilots or copilots. In the ten years between 1988 and 1998, while passenger-miles grew about 46 percent, total airline employment rose by only about 29 percent.[13] There has been a long-term trend in increased output, measured in passenger-miles, per employee, reflecting such efficiencies as larger and faster aircraft, computerization of reservation systems, engines requiring less maintenance, and changes in work rules deriving from the weaker position of labor since deregulation. The impact of hub-and-spoke networks on labor productivity, however, is a matter of controversy. A flight crew operating a well-filled (high load factor) aircraft may appear to be delivering well with respect to passenger miles, but the delays caused by hubbing, which we have earlier discussed, may cancel out any efficiency. The use of somewhat smaller aircraft under the hub-and-spoke system will also tend to reduce labor output per passenger-mile.

The relationship of an airline with its employees presents many difficulties. Compared with many other industries, airline labor is highly skilled and assumes a high degree of responsibility. Thus, strict standards in employee selection and training are essential. The nature of airline service requires 24-hour operations every day of the year and the physical scattering of employees around the country—and, indeed, around the world. Wage settlements must reflect the nature of the operations and thus can be quite complex.

The majority of employees of most airlines are union members, although new entrants into the airline business under regulatory reform are frequently nonunion. Airline labor unions are organized on a craft basis—that is, there is no single union that represents the whole labor force of an airline, but one union representing pilots, one mechanics, one flight attendants, and so on. A disadvantage to this arrangement is that a strike by one craft union may cause a shutdown of the airline. There may also be disputes as to what constitutes a craft and which jobs belong in which craft.

Airlines, like other transportation enterprises, are likely to be particularly hurt by strikes because, unlike manufacturing industries, they cannot store their product. An airline anticipating a strike cannot pile up an inventory of its product, as can a manufacturer, to tide it over the work stoppage, and the unions know this. The seasonality of the demand for airline service may also increase labor's bargaining power, in the sense that a union can select an approaching seasonal peak as the time to press its advantage.

Labor relations of the airlines are under a special federal law applicable only to them and to the railroads: the Railway Labor Act of 1926. Originally, as its name indicates, applied only to railroads, it was made applicable to airlines in 1936. Under this law, if a management-labor disagreement on a major matter occurs, such as an inability to agree on the renewal terms for a union contract, a governmental body called the National Mediation Board (NMB) attempts to mediate. The NMB consists of three members appointed by the president who serve for three-year terms and have a small staff of skilled mediators. If the NMB's efforts to bring the parties together prove unsuccessful, the NMB may try to get them to agree to submit the matter to arbitration. Once they submit the dispute to arbitration, both management and labor are considered obligated to accept the findings of the arbitration panel, but for this very reason it may be difficult to get them to accept arbitration in the first place.

If there is no agreement to arbitrate, and if mediation continues to be unsuccessful, a strike may occur and an airline may be shut down for weeks or even months. Usually a strike on a single airline is simply allowed to run its course. But if a strike is about to occur that would seriously inconvenience the public—such as a strike on several airlines simultaneously—the NMB may recommend that the president appoint an emergency board. Under the Railway Labor Act, such a board investigates a dispute and recommends a solution. The parties are enjoined by law from a work stoppage while the emergency board is investigating, for a 30-day period, and for an additional 30-day period after their decision. But even the decision of this presidential board is only a recommendation, and a strike may begin, or continue, despite all these efforts. Should a major shutdown of airline service present a grave emergency to the country, it is likely that the president would ask Congress for special legislation to deal with the emergency. Fortunately, this ultimate step has never proved necessary.

Minor disputes, under the Railway Labor Act, are treated in a very different manner. An example of a minor dispute would be an interpretation of a provision in a contract. If the matter cannot be worked out by direct negotiations between management and labor, it may be referred to a System Board of Adjustment containing an equal number of airline and union representatives. The decisions of this board are considered to be binding, but it may prove difficult to obtain a decision in view of the equally balanced number of airline and union representatives. (Note that these boards of adjustment, although set up pursuant to the Railway Labor Act, are not composed of government officials.) A deadlock may sometimes be resolved through having an additional member appointed by the NMB or by the private organization known as the American Arbitration Association.

In an effort to improve their bargaining power with the unions, a group of trunk lines in 1958 drew up the so-called Mutual Aid Pact whereby they agreed that if one of them were struck, the others would pay to the struck carrier the profits they realized from the strike. When one airline is shut down, passengers and cargo travel on its competitors, who realize windfall profits. Precise calculation of these profits is not possible, but formulas were agreed upon that attempted to measure the added revenues of each nonstruck carrier and to deduct the added costs of moving this traffic.

In the spring of 1959, the CAB approved this agreement, and it continued in effect, subject to various amendments, until it was given statutory disapproval by the ADA in 1978. The original participants were the then–Big Four domestic trunk lines—American, Eastern, TWA, and United—together with Pan American (which later withdrew) and the then-existing small trunk line Capital Airlines. Several small trunk lines later joined; two of them, National and Northwest, received substantial payments from pact members during prolonged strikes. In 1970 the pact was broadened, with CAB approval, to admit local service carriers, six of which subsequently joined.

Labor consistently and strongly opposed this pact, sought unsuccessfully to have the courts set it aside, and fought to have Congress outlaw it. Labor contended that the pact did not serve to prevent or shorten strikes, but had the opposite effect because a carrier might be able to withstand a prolonged shutdown if payments by the other members of the pact from their windfall profits covered much of the struck carrier's losses. Labor even contended that in some instances a carrier benefited financially from being on strike.

On the other hand, the airlines that were parties to the pact contended that it was necessary to redress a severe imbalance in bargaining strength. They noted especially that unions had used "whipsaw" tactics whereby a union sought a new contract from the airline in the weakest bargaining position and, having achieved the expected good bargain, used the new contract as a basis for demands on other airlines. One practical result of the Mutual Aid Pact, it was argued, was to diminish the effectiveness of this "weakest carrier" strategy.

While the ADA declared all existing mutual aid agreements void, it allowed for new agreements of this sort, but subjected them to such severely limiting conditions that no such pacts have been established. The ADA's provisions were thus a substantial victory for labor. (These provisions are now contained in Section 42111 of the transportation statute.)

It has been charged that, with respect to both wages and work rules, labor contracts were unduly favorable to labor over the many years of governmental regulation because both management and labor felt protected from new entrants—very likely to have nonunion labor—into the airline business. Advocates of regulatory reform sometimes used this point as a reason for anticipating greater labor efficiency and greater output per wage-dollar with open entry. And, with the entry of many nonunion enterprises into the airline business, far-reaching changes did indeed begin in the labor cost situation throughout the industry.

The difference between labor costs of a unionized airline and those of a nonunion airline may be more a matter of work rules than of wage rates. For example, an airline's mechanics may be fully competent, and licensed, to work on both engines and airframes, but the labor contract may require that those assigned to work on engines do nothing whatever involving the airframe, and vice versa. Since work on an engine may well require some work on the mounting of the engine on the airframe, one mechanic from the airframe group must stand by to perform these operations even though they might be readily and quickly done by the mechanic working on the engine. Other work rules may require that high-wage mechanics perform tasks that could as well be done by lower-wage customer service agents, such as directing aircraft into and out of gates. Other work rules may define the pay status of flight crews in periods before and after a flight. This problem exists in any mode of transportation, and of course it would not be permissible or equitable to pay flight crews only for the precise time the aircraft is in motion, although in a sense these are the hours of principal productivity.

As an example of the impact of work rules, data for 1995 show Southwest Airlines' pilots averaging 70 hours flying time a month, while United Airlines' pilots were averaging 53 hours a month.[14] The discrepancy, however, would very likely be partly due to the differing operational patterns of the carriers, not to work rules alone.

Back in the pre-deregulation era, Delta was unique among the trunk lines in that, except for its pilots, its employees were not unionized. To attract qualified personnel and to keep them contented so that they would not wish to unionize, Delta paid wages to its nonunion employees comparable with those of their union counterparts in other airlines. But Delta achieved high productivity due, at least in part, to the absence of the severely limiting work rules found in labor contracts of the other trunk lines. This high productivity was a factor in keeping Delta among the most profitable of the airlines of that era.

Changes in the Labor Cost Situation

Even in the brief heyday of the new nonunion airlines, before the wave of mergers described in Chapter 3 had greatly reduced their number, their traffic was only a small proportion of total airline traffic. Yet their influence on labor costs throughout the airline industry has been great. Typically their work rules have allowed for maximum worker flexibility. For example, one employee may work at a ticket counter, then as a flight attendant, then handling baggage, all in the same day. Flight crews may fly the maximum hours per month permitted by the FAA and may also be used for duties such as flight training and dispatching. Since the employees are new, their wages do not reflect seniority increments and generally average substantially lower than those of the old-line carriers, or at least lower than the pre-deregulation wage levels at those carriers. Often the new airlines have given each employee a direct financial stake in improving productivity through a profit-sharing or stock ownership plan.

The unionized airlines have responded to the challenge of the nonunion carriers (and perhaps also to the increased competitive pressures resulting from deregulation) by negotiating union contracts that differ remarkably from those of the past. There have been suspensions of scheduled cost-of-living and other pay increases and, in some cases, actual reductions in wages. Some airlines introduced a two-tier pay system under which newly hired employees are under a pay schedule at a lower level from that of the other employees. There are profit-sharing and stock ownership plans. But perhaps most significant are far-reaching changes in work rules affecting such matters as pilot workloads and the cross-utilization of employees.

These concessions did not come easily. They represented a remarkable shift in the bargaining power between management and labor, which may have been partly the result of the high level of unemployment in the nation in the early 1980s. As Professors Spencer and Cassell put it, "High unemployment, in effect, defanged union leaders whose members were more anxious to preserve their jobs than to strike for increases or to support the interests of other unions or future employees."[15] The drop in national unemployment of the late 1980s shifted the bargaining balance back somewhat toward labor, and there was a slowing of the process of making concessions. Many airlines abandoned the two-tier system or modified it so that newly hired employees would advance to the upper tier after a period of time with the company.

The two-tier system has been criticized as leading to animosity between workers at the two pay levels. Those on the lower tier are likely to resent being paid less than other workers who do the same work, solely on the basis that the latter were employed before a particular date. The upper tier employees may worry that management will have an incentive to refrain from promoting them or to push them into early retirement so that they can be replaced with lower-paid colleagues.

The early 1990s saw further labor concessions, but the driving force was the perilous financial condition of the major airlines. Faced with such examples as the demise of Eastern Air Lines, with its high labor costs even after many concessions, airline labor made what concessions appeared necessary to keep their carriers alive. In the late 1990s, however, with the greatly improved financial condition of the airlines, the mood of labor has swung from a willingness to make concessions to a desire to share better in the airlines' profits.

Still, the strike as a bargaining weapon has lost some effectiveness in recent years. As one study puts it, "An overall diminished support for unions has affected both the number of employees willing to honor a strike and a strike's ability to generate public support.... Greater numbers of union members are refusing to honor their colleagues' picket lines."[16] Also, the image of pilots as high salaried makes it difficult, if they strike, to win public sympathy.

These same authors note, however, that there are measures short of the strike that can bring pressure on an airline during contract negotiations. These include publicity campaigns directed at travel agents, frequent flyers, government agencies, and the general public, stating the union's case and sometimes going so far as to imply mismanagement or even safety compromises. More severe measures that can seriously disrupt an airline's operations, yet still be short of a strike, are work slowdowns and so-called sickouts, where many employees call in sick. These measures are forbidden under the Railway Labor Act while contract negotiations are in progress, but to enforce the prohibition it is necessary to prove that union leaders have directed the use of these measures, which is difficult to do. The employees can act without specific instructions by a tacit understanding or word-of-mouth grapevine, and operations can be severely hurt without action being possible under the RLA's prohibition. One example of an effective slowdown technique is for pilots to "work to rule." As the previously quoted study puts it, "Because of the enormous decision making power pilots have over whether an aircraft is fit to fly, their means of slowing down a departure or even canceling a flight are virtually endless."[17]

Mention should be made here of the use by an airline of bankruptcy proceedings as a device to void a union contract. This occurred with Continental in 1983. It halted operations, filed for reorganization under Chapter 11 of the bankruptcy laws, and then resumed operations in a few days on a smaller scale, rehiring many of its employees but at wages well below the union scale. The voiding of its union contracts was challenged in the courts, but Continental was upheld, and by July 1984 had increased operations to their prebankruptcy level. Subsequent legislation amending the bankruptcy laws has made it more difficult for a carrier to obtain changes in, or complete voiding of, a union contract simply by declaring bankruptcy under Chapter 11. Under this legislation, which was inspired in part by Continental's action in 1983, an airline now must demonstrate to the bankruptcy court that the steps are necessary to carry out the proposed reorganization intended to save the company. The court will balance the airline's needs against the employees' interests.[18]

One device available to a carrier is the creation of an "airline-within-an-airline," spinning off part of its service into a subsidiary or a separate division that would conduct no-frills, point-to-point services on short to medium hauls, and offer lower wages than on its regular routes. Patterned along lines of Southwest Airlines, the service would use the carrier's regular jet aircraft. The routes, while relatively short, would not compete with the shorter hauls serving low-traffic points of the regional and commuter carriers.

Two long-run developments may tend to shift the bargaining balance in labor's favor. One is that the employees of small new-entrant airlines may not be content for long to remain nonunion. The other is that if airline traffic continues its historical long-run increase, the demand for skilled airline labor will grow.

Were airline employees overpaid in the pre-deregulation era? Although the prevailing view seems to be that they were, this is an area where comparisons are often difficult and where conclusions involve value judgments. For example, should the size of the aircraft affect what the flight crew are paid? And how much is seniority worth, if anything? For that matter, does labor have an unlimited right to press for all it can get, and does an airline have an unlimited right to squeeze wages down as much as it can get away with? Perhaps the lesson to be learned is that the public interest is best served by moderation, and if airline labor becomes powerful again it ought to refrain from pressing its advantage too far, especially in the area of work rules.

Employee Ownership of Airlines

The concept of granting employees shares of stock in their airline in return for wage and work rule concessions is not new. In the early 1980s, for example, such arrangements were made by Eastern, Pan American, Republic, and Western. But in none of these did the employee share approach a majority interest.

By the mid-1990s, however, there was substantial employee ownership in three of the major passenger airlines—Northwest, 33 percent; TWA, 30 percent; and United, a majority holding of 55 percent. In each instance, the employees have paid for their shares by substantial concessions on wages, fringe benefits, and work rules, spread over a period of years. Also, in each instance, the employees appoint members to the board of directors.

One objective of these plans was to get the large labor concessions that appeared essential to rescue the carriers, given the extraordinary financial losses of the early 1990s. Another objective was to give the employees a stake in the carrier's profitability, thereby inducing each employee to work harder and contributing generally to worker morale. Of course, these plans raise the question of how bargaining for a union contract is to take place when the employees, in effect, sit on both sides of the table. This is especially true in the United arrangement where the employees hold a controlling interest.

The United Airlines Employee Stock Ownership Plan (or ESOP, as these arrangements are called) was put forward by the unions representing the pilots and the machinists (including baggage handlers and other ground crews), with participation by some salaried and management personnel. Flight attendants declined to join. Individual employees, not the unions, are the owners of the stock and are paying for it at a valuation of $4.9 billion over a six-year period through accepting lower wages and fringe benefits, together with changes in work rules. Despite holding a majority share of the airline, the employees do not manage the company. They have only three representatives on United's 12-member board of directors, while five represent the other shareholders and the four others are independent directors. An extremely complex voting system governs the workings of this board, designed along lines that check and balance the power of each interest.[19]

Included in the plan was employee consent to establishment of an "airline-within-an-airline," of the sort we have earlier mentioned. Certain aircraft from United's fleet were designated to offer a low-fare, no-frills service in markets not over 750 miles long. The service is largely point-to-point turnaround style, patterned after Southwest's style, rather than the hub-and-spoke style characteristic of United's other services. Originally nicknamed "U2," it was later called the United Shuttle. The work force continues to be represented by the current unions, but pay and work rules are less generous.

Under the United ESOP, according to Professor Jeffrey N. Gordon, "employees will receive stock in respect of foregone wages and benefits during a six-year investment period. New hires toward the end of the period will receive proportionately less stock; those hired after the period will receive no stock. As employee shareholders retire, their preferred stock converts into common, which they can sell."[20] Thus, as time goes on and retiring employees elect to sell their stock, the proportion of shares held by employees will gradually be reduced, so that majority interest will not last very long. When the level of employee owenership drops below 20 percent, the power of their representatives to elect directors will cease. Professor Gordon predicts that the United and other ESOPs will prove eventually to have been merely transitional measures to enable cost reductions at a time of financial pressure.

Perhaps the real test of ESOPs will come if an airline with such a plan gets once again into difficult financial troubles. The value of the stock for which workers have sacrificed wages and other benefits will drop, perhaps sharply, which may cause employees to view the whole plan in a dimmer light. More seriously, employee representatives on the board of directors may resist the wage cuts and furloughs or layoffs that may be the rational, though painful, steps for the airline to take. In short, a real test of ESOPs may come when the ever-cyclical airline industry goes into a slump.

AIRCRAFT SELECTION AS A DETERMINANT OF COSTS

Nowhere is airline management more severely tested than in making decisions on the types of aircraft it will have in its fleet and the number of each type. Often commitments must be made for delivery dates many years in the future, with all of the uncertainties that implies, and large sums of money must be obligated. For instance, in 1996 American ordered $6.5 billion worth of aircraft from Boeing, United ordered a combination of Boeing and Airbus aircraft for $4.4 billion, and US Airways ordered aircraft from Airbus costing $4.5 billion.[21] Of course, deliveries and payments are spread over a number of years, but the obligation that each airline undertakes is a massive one, made even more critical by the sensitivity of the airline industry to economic cycles. Commitments made by an airline in prosperous times, such as the late 1990s, can have the result that aircraft may be delivered (and payment expected) when traffic has dropped and they are least needed. To alleviate this problem, there are efforts by aircraft manufacturers to reduce manufacturing lead times, as well as efforts by the airlines to arrange long-term contracts that spread deliveries more uniformly and avoid sharp delivery peaks.[22]

Beyond the cost impact of carrying the huge investment that an airline fleet represents, there is the even greater cost consideration of the operating efficiency of the fleet. New aircraft offer savings on fuel and maintenance which, over time, may well justify their great initial cost.

The Aircraft Market

There are two major manufacturers of the medium-range and long-range jet aircraft used by the airlines of the world—Boeing and the European consortium called Airbus Industrie. Formerly there were three U.S. manufacturers, but Lockheed ceased making commercial airliners in 1981, while McDonnell Douglas was acquired by Boeing in 1997. The engines for these aircraft, however, are made by separate companies, notably General Electric, Pratt & Whitney, the British firm Rolls-Royce, and the French firm Snecma.

The aircraft of Boeing and Airbus now dominate the fleets of U.S. airlines and of the long-haul and much of the medium-haul services of airlines around the world. (By contrast, the small short-haul/aircraft used by regional and commuter carriers are often of foreign manufacture—for example, Brazilian, British, Canadian, and Swedish.) Airbus Industrie is a consortium of Western European countries which, in the late 1970s, began penetrating both the U.S. and the world markets with an aircraft called the A-300, nicknamed the Airbus. It has since become a major rival to Boeing and has expanded its output in a series of models denominated as A-300, 310, 320, 330, 340, etc. There are other foreign firms, such as British Aerospace and the Netherlands firm Fokker, that are trying to penetrate the market, but thus far with little success.

Because the research and development that go into a new aircraft, or even into a new jet engine, has become very expensive, joint ventures—where two or more firms share the work and the financial risk—are becoming common. Boeing had such an arrangement with a German and an Italian firm when developing the 767, and has one with a Japanese firm in the development of the 777. Joint arrangements with foreign firms to develop new engines have been entered into by both General Electric and Pratt & Whitney.

Even the actual assembly of what we think of as U.S. aircraft may take place abroad. An interesting glimpse of the growing multinationalizing trend was given by Robert Durbin, the manager of aircraft trading for the McDonnell Douglas Corp:

We have our airplanes built all over the world, including the People's Republic of China where the MD-80 is now being constructed. The air doors are being made in Shanghai, the wings in Canada, the tails in Japan, and the fuselage panels in Italy. Typical of many large aircraft, this one is a real international product.[23]

Jet airliners can be divided into narrow-bodied, with tunnel-like cabins; wide-bodied, with 10 or 12 seats abreast; and regional, with a 50 to 70 seat range.

Narrow-bodied aircraft

Two of the old original jet models introduced in the late 1950s and early 1960s—the Boeing 707 and the Douglas DC-8—can still be found in service, although, with the exception of some DC-8s that have been retrofitted with modern engines, they are obsolete with respect to noise standards and fuel efficiency. More modern narrow-bodied jets are of medium size (100 to 200 seats) and designed largely for medium-range flights; examples are the Boeing 727, 737, and 757, and the McDonnell Douglas DC-9, MD-80, and MD-90. (The earlier DC series of aircraft from Douglas Aircraft Co. continued under the MD initials after the corporate name became McDonnell Douglas. Boeing has acquired McDonnell Douglas, as we have noted, but as of 1999 was continuing to use the MD initials to identify these aircraft.)

During the 1970s, the 727 was by far the most popular aircraft in the fleet of the U.S. scheduled airline industry; by 1980, it made up about 40 percent of that fleet. It is, however, a three-engine aircraft and thus less fuel-efficient than its twin-engine cousin the 737. "Stretched" versions (that is, enlarged by lengthening the fuselage so as to increase passenger capacity) of the 737, with seating in the 135 to 155 range, have displaced the 727 in popularity. In 1983, Boeing shut down production of the 727 after a 22-year production run. In the previous year, Boeing had introduced a new medium-sized, medium-range, twin-engine, narrow-bodied aircraft, the 757, with high fuel efficiency, seating 170 to 210 passengers. Airbus sells narrow-bodied aircraft designated the A-319, A-320, and A-321.

It should be emphasized that there are several versions (or "series") of each aircraft model. Within the 737 category, for example, there are the 737–100, 737–200, 737–300, running up to a 737–800, with differing characteristics that include seating capacity, speed, range, fuel efficiency, and minimizing of noise and air pollution.

Wide-bodied aircraft

Wide-bodied jet airliners are designed for long hauls and have seating in the 200 to 500 range. From the U.S. manufacturers we have the Boeing 747, introduced in 1970, the Lockheed L-1011 and McDonnell Douglas DC-10, introduced shortly thereafter, and the Boeing 767, introduced in 1982. In 1990, McDonnell Douglas began delivery of a replacement for the DC-10, called the MD-11; however, Boeing, having acquired the company, reportedly intends to discontinue making this aircraft. In 1995, Boeing began delivery of a new wide-bodied model, the 777, seating in the 250 to 350 range, with two engines. Airbus also makes several wide-bodied models: the A-310, A-330, and A-340, the latter being designed for very long hauls.

Interestingly, the newer wide-bodied aircraft—the 767, 777, MD-11, and the latest Airbus models—are all smaller than the 747, which was designed over 30 years ago for a maximum of about 490 seats and remains the largest airliner in commercial service. Airbus, however, reportedly is planning a very large capacity airliner, to seat some 650 passengers, while Boeing may respond with an expanded 747 with seating approaching that number.

The 1980s saw a trend toward smaller aircraft. The causes appeared to spring from deregulation—intensified competition, whether among the major carriers or between them and new entrants, and the hub-and-spoke networks. The pressing need was for frequent departures and for minimizing empty seats on those departures, that is, to maintain high load factors. The 1980s saw the removal of many wide-bodied aircraft from domestic services, though they remained dominant on long international routes.

Earlier, in the 1960s and 1970s, the trend had been toward larger aircraft. This not only greatly increased the seat-miles per worker-hour, but also permitted a great increase in the number of passengers with negligible increase in the number of flights. Between 1969 and 1979, for example, the U.S. airlines in domestic service increased the number of flights only slightly, from 5,058,371 to 5,144,117, while the number of passengers nearly doubled, from 154,407,000 to 292,537,000. If the average aircraft size had remained the same during the period, with resultant nearly doubling of flights to carry the nearly doubled passenger load, the result would have been a severe overtaxing of the airways and of major airports. But the reverse trend of the 1980s, with smaller aircraft and increased flight frequencies, has made airport and airway overload a growing problem. In the 1990s, there are indications that the airlines may be reversing the trend once again, turning back to larger aircraft as a means for getting the most out of tight airway and airport facilities.

A modern airliner is extremely expensive. As of 1998, a new Boeing 737 cost in the $30 to $35 million range, while a new 747 cost over $150 million. The total U.S. airline fleet in 1998 came to about 4,800 aircraft, with about 1,200 more on firm order and options on another 1,680.[24]

With the dissolution of the Soviet Union and the opening of its society to the world, the Russian and Ukrainian aircraft manufacturing industries, with their three model lines—Antonov, Ilyushin, and Tupolev—could become significant factors in the world market, giving competition to Boeing and Airbus. It remains, however, for these manufacturers to demonstrate to the world the technology and cost efficiencies of their aircraft.

Regional aircraft

In Chapter 3 we noted that the regional and commuter air carriers have developed largely into adjuncts of the major passenger carriers, either owned or closely linked with those majors, and moving traffic between their hubs and relatively small traffic points, usually over short hauls. We have also noted that these services have been conducted largely with turboprop aircraft of foreign manufacture. In the mid-1990s, however, some foreign manufacturers began to bring on the market pure jet, rather than turboprop, aircraft, at a 50 to 70 seat level. These models have cruising speeds of about 500 miles per hour, whereas the turbo-props are limited to about 300 miles per hour. They have a range of 1300 to 1600 miles, compared to 500 to 800 miles for the turboprops.

As early as 1993, one regional carrier began using a Brazilian-made regional jet, and, in the latter half of the decade, British and Canadian manufacturers followed the Brazilians in bringing out similar aircraft. As of September 1998, U.S. regional airlines were operating 177 jet aircraft with 188 more on firm orders.[25] The purchase price of one of these air-craft is in the $16 to $25 million range, compared to $9 to $13 million for a turboprop, but their operating costs per seat-mile are lower and their larger seating capacity allows a lower passenger-mile cost, assuming reasonable load factors.

Regional jets are also being used in substitution for larger aircraft such as the 737, where traffic on a particular route does not justify the larger equipment. In such instances, the operator may be a major airline. When such a substitution is made, the diminished number of available seats will mean many fewer seats available for discount traffic, which can raise a public interest question.

Both U.S. and foreign aircraft manufacturers have plans to develop aircraft in a seating range that will blur the line between "regional" and larger jets. One authority describes the situation as follows:

In the second half of 1998 aircraft manufacturers announced plans to develop jet aircraft with 90 to 100 seats, including Bombardier Aerospace with its 90-seat jet aircraft; Airbus Industrie with its A-318 aircraft (100 seats), a derivative of the A-319 aircraft (124 seats); the Boeing Company with its B-717 aircraft (100 seats); British Aerospace with its Avro RJ100 regional jet (100 seats); and Fairchild Aerospace with its 90-seat aircraft. These larger jets—closer in size to aircraft such as the DC-9 and the B-737—are being marketed along with the 50- to 70-seat regional jets that are already in service. What is unclear at this time is what share of the regional jet markets that are currently under development will also support service using these larger aircraft.[26]

The Aging of the Fleet

There is concern from a safety standpoint about a tendency for airlines to keep old aircraft in use. In the early 1990s, about a quarter of the fleet of U.S. scheduled airlines was over 20 years old. Twenty years is a rule of thumb for what is called the "economic design life" of an airliner. More recent figures (1996) show the average aircraft age by carrier for the larger U.S. passenger carriers (in years) as: Southwest, 7.9; American, 9.0; United, 10.9; Delta, 11.5; US Airways, 12.0; Continental, 14.3; TWA, 19.0; and Northwest, 19.2.[27] Note that these are *averages*, including some new or nearly new equipment; thus, TWA and Northwest undoubtedly would have aircraft over 25 years old in daily usage.

Chronological age is only one factor in assessing the safety of an old aircraft. Another is the number of cycles it has gone through, a cycle being one takeoff and landing. The pressurization and depressurization in a cycle places stress on the "skin" of the aircraft. At 60,000 cycles an aircraft has met its economic design life even if it is not yet 20 years old. The aging process is also affected by environmental factors such as humidity and temperature.

An allied problem complicating the question of aging is the regulation of noise. Federal regulations divide aircraft into three groups based on the noise they make on takeoffs and landings. Stage 1 aircraft, the noisiest, have been eliminated from the fleets of U.S. scheduled airlines. The airlines were required to eliminate all Stage 2 aircraft by the end of 1999, and as that date approached it was expected that they would meet this deadline. Many Stage 2 aircraft were modified to meet Stage 3 noise standards either by replacing the engines with modern engines or by modifying existing engines through a process known as "hush-kitting." It costs about $10 million to put Stage 3 engines on a 727 aircraft or $2 million simply to hush-kit its three existing old engines. The cheaper procedure, of course, leaves the airline not only with an old aircraft but one with the same old engines.

The effect of the required phaseout of Stage 2 aircraft on the aging question has been to hasten the removal of some old aircraft from airline fleets, but also to postpone the retirement of the re-engined or hush-kitted aircraft well into the future. A very old airframe with new or noise-adjusted engines leaves us with the controversial question of whether there is some finite limit beyond which no airframe, no matter how well maintained and inspected, should be considered safe.

Aircraft Selection

The management of an airline approaching a decision on aircraft purchase must consider many factors. First, there is the price of the aircraft, which may be a matter for negotiation with the manufacturer, especially if there is to be a single commitment to purchase a substantial number of planes. Credit costs must be reckoned; aircraft financing usually involves extension of credit by a major bank, life insurance company, or other large financial institution, but sometimes by the aircraft manufacturer itself on terms designed to encourage the sale. Then there are break-in costs whenever a new model is introduced into an airline's fleet—notably initial crew training costs.

Performance characteristics must be matched against the carrier's existing and proposed routes, the stage lengths, and the flow of traffic now and in the future. What are the seating capacity and the cargo capacity of this aircraft? What is its range—that is, how many miles can it be flown without having to curtail payload? What is its effective speed for different lengths of haul? What maintenance costs may be anticipated over the years? What size flight crew will be required? How many seat-miles will it deliver for each gallon of fuel consumed?

From all this an attempt is made to calculate the cost per seat-mile (or per available cargo ton-mile) at foreseeable load factors. The aircraft must, of course, meet government standards with respect to noise and air pollution, and it should have passenger appeal.

Final decisions call forth all the skills of modern management. Fleet planning models, with an elaborate mathematical balancing of goals and constraints, are prepared by research personnel of the airlines through sophisticated use of computers, often with assistance from the manufacturers. But the final decision, fraught as it is with possibilities for profit or calamity, is made by top management in a manner that applies a delicate art to a great deal of science.

Financing and Leasing Aircraft

An airline will very rarely acquire an aircraft by simply buying it entirely with its own funds. Far more likely it will obtain financing in the form of a secured debt comparable to a mortgage on a person's home, only here the aircraft is the collateral and the legal instrument may be called an equipment trust or a conditional sales contract. Nowadays, however, it is also very common for an airline to lease the aircraft, perhaps by a simple rental or by a long-term lease with a right to purchase. The legal instruments under which these expensive aircraft are financed or leased are many and varied, and, as one lawyer puts it, "the range of secured debt and lease financing devices represents an almost continuous spectrum, and the line between one and the other is indistinct."[28] The complexities of this area of the law are best left to the lawyers.

Leasing has become an increasingly popular way for airlines to add to their fleets. Estimates as of 1995 were that about half the U.S. scheduled airlines' fleets were leased. Through leasing, an airline conserves its own capital but loses the residual value of the aircraft when it is turned back to the lessor, unless an option to purchase has been included in the lease. Leasing may also help an airline keep its capacity closely tailored to its traffic.

One disadvantage to leasing is its effect on the cash flow of the airline. When an airline owns an aircraft, it allocates a portion of its revenue to an account that covers the depreciation of that aircraft. Then as Professors Tretheway and Oum put it, "depreciation is an accounting charge and does not require an actual outlay of cash." They go on to say:

In recent years, this cash flow relationship has changed dramatically. Whereas in 1961 three percent of aircraft were leased, by 1988, 42 percent of aircraft were leased. With an aircraft lease, the airline does not lay out cash up-front when the aircraft is acquired. Instead, cash is laid out throughout the lifetime of the aircraft. With the adoption of leasing by airlines, carriers are now experiencing required annual cash outlays roughly equal to their cash inflows. Because of this, when difficult times are experienced—such as a recession or fuel crisis, carriers can experience negative cash flows. As a result, airlines are more likely to experience bankruptcy.[29]

With the great expansion of aircraft leasing by airlines throughout the world, several large companies have become major lessors with worldwide operations. Financial institutions from around the world participate in their ownership. Among the largest of these are AerFi (formerly GPA Group), General Electric Capital Aviation Services, and the International Lease Finance Corporation.[30]

Published Aircraft Cost Data

From time to time, data are published in tabular form in trade publications such as *Air Transport World* and *Aviation Week and Space Technology*, which show the cost experience of each airline with each type of aircraft that it flies. A table may show, for example, the expenses for a calendar quarter, broken down by carrier and type of aircraft, for flight crew, fuel, insurance, maintenance (including maintenance "burden" or overhead) and aircraft depreciation.

Using these figures, it is possible to make comparisons between types of aircraft or to observe how one airline may be making more effective use of a particular type of aircraft than another airline with the same type of aircraft. Data needed to make rational comparisons are also given, such as average length of haul, average seating capacity, and average passenger load. Use of data of this sort from current issues of trade publications is recommended in order to become more familiar with aircraft costing methods.

IMPACT OF TECHNOLOGICAL ADVANCES ON COSTS

As we have seen, advancing technology in aircraft has enabled the airlines to achieve lower seat-mile costs as a basic trend. The small piston aircraft of the 1930s, such as the DC-3, had very high seat-mile costs. The advent of larger piston aircraft caused seat-mile cost to drop, as did the arrival of turboprop planes. The introduction of turbojets caused a major further drop, and the coming of wide-bodied jets still another. The drop in seat-mile costs, however, has been counteracted by the inflation the whole economy has been experiencing.

Note that when a new type of aircraft is introduced, the savings on seat-mile costs (to whatever extent they may not be canceled out by inflation) may only slowly be reflected in reduced fares. There are various break-in costs, such as the training of personnel to fly and service the new model. And typically the new aircraft attracts passengers; thus, when an airline's fleet consists of some of the new type and some of the old, the airline will certainly not cut its fares for flights on the new ones when they are the ones to which the passengers are flocking. This was particularly noticeable when jet aircraft first began to replace piston aircraft; some airlines even imposed a jet surcharge based on superior passenger appeal, despite the fact that the seat-mile cost was lower than on the piston aircraft.

It appears that, at least in the immediate future, the impact of technological advances on costs will come not so much from larger or faster aircraft but from fuel efficiency and maintenance savings. Advances in airframe and engine technology can lengthen the periods between both routine maintenance operations and long-term overhauls. Other advances with a favorable impact on costs need not be confined to the aircraft itself—improved maintenance equipment, for example, or more efficient equipment for processing passengers, baggage, and air cargo. The elaborate computerization of reservations procedures is an example of a technological advance that, although requiring a large initial investment, provides a long-run saving in labor expense as well as improved service to the passenger.

Supersonic Transport Aircraft

If supersonic transport aircraft (SSTs) should some day come into general usage by the airlines, we would very likely see an exception to the trend relating lower seat-mile costs to new technology. While cost figures for some future aircraft are necessarily speculative, the one SST now in airline service, the Anglo-French Concorde, involves seat-mile costs higher than those of other airliners. According to information published by DOT, the Concorde "consumes 20,857 gallons of fuel to carry 110 passengers over 3,000 nautical miles. By comparison, the Boeing 747 uses 24,285 gallons of fuel to carry 375 passengers over the same distance."[31]

In 1976, Air France and British Airways began service to the United States with the Concorde on the basis of a premium fare above first class. Twenty-three years later, they were still the only two airlines operating SST flights to or from the United States, and the fare was still at a premium above first class.

The former Soviet Union had an SST, the TU-144, which was used on Aeroflot's internal routes. The airline withdrew it from service in the early 1980s citing high operating costs.

In 1970 Congress discontinued federal funding for the development of a U.S. supersonic transport aircraft. Opponents of the funding expressed doubts as to the economic feasibility of the project, and many were deeply concerned about environmental problems such as the sonic boom and possible effects on the earth's atmosphere. Some research continues, and U.S. aircraft manufacturers occasionally make predictions concerning an efficient, environmentally acceptable SST. There appears, however, to be little likelihood of any general introduction of SSTs in the near future. Some major technological breakthroughs with respect to the environmental problems and fuel efficiency, should they occur, would, of course, change this.

An even faster aircraft, described as "hypersonic," is the subject of some research and is reportedly of interest to the military. One version was nicknamed "The Orient Express" and was intended to cross the Pacific Ocean in two hours. Whether the hypersonic aircraft could become a practical, cost-effective aircraft for commercial airline service is at this time a matter of conjecture.

NOTES

1. CAB, *Handbook of Airline Statistics* (Washington, D.C.: 1974).

2. John R. Meyer and Clinton V. Oster Jr., *Deregulation and the New Airline Entrepreneurs* (Cambridge, Mass.: The MIT Press, 1984), p. 52.

3. Elizabeth E. Bailey, David R. Graham, and Daniel P. Kaplan, *Deregulating the Airlines* (Cambridge, Mass.: The MIT Press, 1985), p. 48.

4. Kathy Fox Powell, "Southwest Airlines v. High-Speed Rail," *Journal of Air Law and Commerce* 60 (May-June 1995): 1092–95 and 1137–38.

5. Mahlon R. Straszheim, *The International Airline Industry* (Washington, D.C.: Brookings Institution, 1969), p. 56.

6. Ibid., pp. 57–60.

7. Susan Carey, "Flying South," *Wall Street Journal*, December 8, 1993, p. A–6.

8. U.S. General Accounting Office, *International Aviation: Measures by European Community Could Limit U.S. Airlines' Ability to Compete Abroad*, 1993, p. 16.

9. U.S. General Accounting Office, *Airline Competition: Impact of Changing Foreign Investment and Control Limits on U.S. Airlines*, 1992, p. 62.

10. Robert L. Crandall, "Marketing Planning," in *Airline Economics*, ed. George W. James (Lexington, Mass.: D.C. Heath, 1982), p. 233.

11. Air Transport Association, *Annual Report—1999*, pp. 7–8.

12. Michael E. Irrgang, "Fuel Conservation," in *Handbook of Airline Economics*, ed. Darryl Jenkins (Washington, D.C.: McGraw-Hill, 1995), p. 367.

13. Author's calculations from Air Transport Association, *Annual Report—1999*, pp. 5 and 9.

14. Paul S. Dempsey and Laurence E. Gesell, *Airline Management: Strategies for the 21st Century* (Chandler, Ariz.: Coast Aire Publications, 1997), pp. 374–75.

15. Frank A. Spencer and Frank H. Cassell, *Eight Years of U.S. Airline Deregulation: Management and Labor Adaptations; Re-Emergence of Oligopoly* (Evanston, Ill.: Northwestern University Transportation Center, 1987), pp. 11–12.

16. William F. Herlehy and Tracy Ingalls-Ashbaugh, "Airline Employee Slowdowns and Sickouts as Unlawful Self-Help: A Statistical Analysis," *Journal of Aviation/Aerospace Education and Research* 3 (Winter 1993): 18.

17. Ibid., pp. 19–20.

18. Jonni Walls, "Airline Mergers, Acquisitions and Bankruptcies: Will the Collective Bargaining Agreement Survive?" *Journal of Air Law and Commerce* 56 (Spring 1991): 883–85 and 892.

19. Jeffrey N. Gordon, "Employee Stock Ownership as a Transitional Device: The Case of the Airline Industry," in *Handbook of Airline Economics*, ed. Darryl Jenkins (Washington, D.C.: McGraw-Hill, 1995), pp. 585–92.

20. Ibid., p. 589.

21. Dempsey and Gesell, *Airline Management*, p. 110.

22. Steve Skinner, Alex Dichter, Paul Langley, and Hendrik Sabert, "Managing Growth and Profitability across Peaks and Troughs of the Airline Industry Cycle," in *Handbook of Airline Finance*, ed. Gail F. Butler and Martin R. Keller (Washington, D.C.: McGraw-Hill, 1999), pp. 28–29.

23. Robert Durbin, quoted in *Air Cargo World*, February 1988, p. 16.

24. Air Transport Association, *Annual Report—1999*, p. 7.

25. Linda J. Perry, "The Financial Implications of Regional Jet Service at Selected Airports," in *Handbook of Airline Finance*, p. 544.

26. Ibid., p. 545.

27. Dempsey and Gesell, *Airline Management*, p. 223.

28. Michael D. Rice, "Current Issues in Aircraft Finance," *Journal of Air Law and Commerce* 56 (Summer 1991): 1032.

29. Michael W. Tretheway and Tae H. Oum, *Airline Economics: Foundations for Strategy and Policy* (Vancouver, Canada: Centre for Transportation Studies, 1992), p. 116.

30. Timothy M. R. Lintott, "Securitization of Aircraft Assets," in *Handbook of Airline Finance*, ed. Gail F. Butler and Martin R. Keller (Washington D.C.: McGraw-Hill, 1999), pp. 378 and 383.

31. Robert B. Donin, "British Airways v. Port Authority: Its Impact on Aircraft Noise Regulation," *Journal of Air Law and Commerce* 43 (1977): 698.

SELECTED REFERENCES

Airline cost analysis, using the accounting categories, may be found in Paul Biederman, *The U.S. Airline Industry: End of an Era* (New York: Praeger, 1982), pp. 35–48, and in David A. Swierenga and Mark W. Crandall, "Airline Revenues, Costs, and Productivity," in *Airline Economics*, ed. George W. James (Lexington, Mass.: D.C. Heath, 1982), pp. 4–15.

Some practical applications of cost analysis are discussed in William M. Frainey, "Network Profitability Analysis," in *Handbook of Airline Finance*, ed. Gail F. Butler and and Martin R. Keller (Washington D.C.: McGraw-Hill, 1999), pp. 165–67.

The flight scheduling problem is analyzed in Dempsey and Gesell, *Airline Management* (Chandler, Ariz.: Coast Aire Publications, 1997), pp. 249–52.

Methods of controlling airline fuel costs are covered in detail in Michael E. Irrgang, "Fuel Conservation," in *Handbook of Airline Economics*, ed. Darryl Jenkins (Washington, D.C.: McGraw-Hill, 1995), pp. 367–78.

Airline wages, including the complex formula for pilot pay, in the era prior to the 1982–84 wave of wage concessions, are discussed in Elizabeth E. Bailey, David R. Graham, and Daniel P. Kaplan, *Deregulating the Airlines* (Cambridge, Mass.: The MIT Press, 1985), pp. 97–102 and 229. The concessions made in the 1982–84 period are detailed, airline by airline, in John V. Jansonius and Kenneth E. Broughton, "Coping with Deregulation: Reduction of Labor Costs in the Airline Industry," *Journal of Air Law and Commerce* 49 (1984): 532–36 and 544–52. For an analysis of the concessions, updated to 1987, see Frank A. Spencer and Frank H. Cassell, *Eight Years of U.S. Airline Deregulation: Management and Labor Adaptations; Re-Emergence of Oligopoly* (Evanston, Ill.: Northwestern University Transportation Center, 1987), pp. 8–29.

The history of the Railway Labor Act and the way it works in practice are detailed in Athanassios Papaioannou, "The Employer's Duty to Bargain over Lay-Offs in the Airline Industry," *Journal of Air Law and Commerce* 55 (Summer 1990): 941–50.

The advantages and disadvantages of ESOPs are the subject of Paul Caver, "Employee-Owned Airlines: The Cure for an Ailing Industry?" *Journal of Air Law and Commerce* 61 (February–March 1996): 639–81. Details on the United Airlines ESOP can be found in Jeffrey N. Gordon, "Employee Stock Ownership as a Transitional Device," in *Handbook of Airline Economics*, ed. Darryl Jenkins (Washington, D.C.: McGraw-Hill, 1995), pp. 585–92.

An excellent review of the whole topic of airline labor relations can be found in Frank A. Spencer and Frank H. Cassell, "Emergence of Policy Bargaining," *Handbook of Airline Economics*, pp. 549–61. For a book-length treatment of the whole topic try Robert W. Kaps, *Air Transport Labor Relations* (Carbondale: Southern Illinois University Press, 1997).

Airline fleet selection is described in detail in Nawal K. Taneja, *Airlines in Transition* (Lexington, Mass.: D.C. Heath, 1981), pp. 191–212.

Types of aircraft leases are outlined in Rod D. Margo, "Aspects of Insurance in Aviation Finance," *Journal of Air Law and Commerce* 62 (November–December 1996): 425–26. An analysis of leasing as a method of financing can be found in Dempsey and Gesell, *Airline Management*, pp. 140–46.

Aircraft leasing companies and the economics of their operations are analyzed in John H. Taylor, "Fasten Seat Belts, Please," *Forbes*, April 2, 1990, pp. 84–88.

How airlines are to meet the government's timetable for quieter aircraft is the subject of Peter B. Coddington, "A Cost Analysis: Re-engining a Boeing 727–200 (Advanced) versus Buying a New Boeing 757–200," *Journal of Aviation/Aerospace Education and Research* 4 (Fall 1993): 25–32.

5

The Demand for
Airline Service

SOME DEMAND CHARACTERISTICS

There are certain characteristics of the demand for airline service that,
while not unique to airlines, are at least unusual.

Air transportation is what economists sometimes call an intermediate
good (and the demand for it a derived demand), in the sense that most
people use air transportation as a means to achieve some other purpose.
Very few passengers fly merely for the sake of flying. Consequently,
when trying to estimate passenger demand, it is necessary to go into all
the various reasons that make a destination city attractive. Tourists flying
to Hawaii have as their objective the happy vacation they expect to spend
there; the air trip is largely or entirely a means to this objective. Business
travelers have as their objective the business they are going to discuss
or transact at the destination; their air trip also is largely or entirely a
means to this end.

Passengers can be divided into categories by looking at the purpose
of their trip. Typically the simplest of the divisions is into tourist or
business travel, the latter including government travel. Another category
would be visiting friends or relatives, often classified as "VFR" traffic.
And there is always a "miscellaneous" or "other" category, which would
include someone traveling to a new job or to attend college, for example.

For each of these groups an airline will try to work out the elasticity
of demand. Actually there are two elasticities involved: the *price* elasticity
of demand and the *income* elasticity of demand. In economics the term

elasticity of demand is assumed to refer to price elasticity. That is, what is the sensitivity of the public to the price of a product? As the price is lowered, how much more will they buy? How much less as the price is raised?

But the other type of demand elasticity is particularly important to air transportation, especially with respect to the tourist market. We look at the level of income in a country (or in a city or in a segment of the public) and ask how much of any increase in real income is likely to go into air travel. Conversely, if real income drops, what will be the proportional drop in air travel? The basic concept here is that, as real income rises, people will spend proportionally less on necessities such as food and shelter and proportionally more on luxuries or semiluxuries. Economists call this behavior pattern Engel's Law.

Let's compare the average per capita income in the United States with the average per capita income in a very poor country. If the real income of U.S. citizens goes up, say, 10 percent in a year, very little of this increase will be spent on food, somewhat more on housing, and quite a bit more on luxuries such as travel. (Real income, of course, makes allowance for inflation; if your dollar income goes up 10 percent and prices go up 10 percent, your real income has not gone up at all.) The reason for this disproportionate effect on luxury purchases is that most U.S. families (not all, to be sure) are in a position where basic necessities are taken care of quite adequately, while an airline trip to a vacation spot is something that will be undertaken only as the budget will allow. This is fine for the airlines in prosperous times, but it also means that airlines are particularly vulnerable to economic recessions.

If we look, however, at people in very poor countries, an increase in their real incomes of 10 percent will flow largely into food and other necessities and very little into air travel. Changes in their income levels will have little or no impact on air transportation, and hence we say that the income elasticity of demand for airline service is low.

What about business travel? Income elasticity of demand is less important than with respect to tourist travel, but when a corporation's profits are down, it may take a closer look at its expenditures for the travel of its executives.

To the extent that deregulation-inspired low discount fares have increased the proportion of leisure to business passengers, the average income elasticity has risen and with it the degree of vulnerability of airlines to recessions.[1]

Returning now to the more familiar elasticity concept—*price* elasticity of demand—we find a similar distinction between business and tourist travel. Both have some price elasticity, but that of the tourist is greater. If air fares rise, some business firms will tighten up on their travel budget and may send employees by other modes or by rented automobiles. But the airlines have found that the tourist market is far more price-elastic, and this fact gives rise to the many discount fares weighted with conditions that make them suitable to vacationers but not to most business travel. For example, a discount may apply only when the ticket is bought a month in advance of the flight. Or the discount may be offered only for a round trip where the person must be gone for at least a specified minimum time including a full weekend. Business travel generally requires available space on short notice, often with same or next-day return. In our next chapter we will look at how airlines tailor fares to each segment of the market.

The price elasticity of demand for the "visiting friends and relatives" category (as well as the "miscellaneous" or "other" category) is as varied as the reasons for each trip, and consequently it is hard to generalize about it.

Secular Increase in Demand

Another characteristic of the demand for airline service is the secular (or long-term) increase, reflected in the astonishing growth rate over the years, as noted in Chapter 1. As can be seen from Table 1, passenger-miles on U.S. scheduled airlines more than tripled in the 1950s and more than tripled again in the 1960s. Although growth slowed in the 1970s, the decade nevertheless showed nearly a doubling of passenger-miles. Cargo (including mail) on U.S. scheduled airlines, which had grown even faster than passenger traffic in the 1950–70 period, grew much more slowly in the 1970s, but revenue ton-miles still increased by about 41 percent in the decade.

The 1980s showed an 80 percent increase in passenger-miles, less than the previous decades but still impressive. The figure for the first eight years of the 1990s is a more modest 35 percent. Cargo revenue ton-miles grew 78 percent in the 1980s and 72 percent between 1990 and 1998.

We should not, of course, assume that a growth in the number of passenger-miles (or cargo ton-miles) necessarily means an increase in demand. To the extent that the increase is due to a reduction in airline rates, economists would describe the change as an increase in the "quantity demanded" rather than in the demand itself. Students not clear about this distinction should review it in any basic economics textbook.

Relative Advantage with Trip Distance

Another important characteristic of the demand for airline service is that the advantage of airlines over other means of travel grows with the length of the trip. Consider a person trying to decide whether to use the family car or go by bus, train, or plane. The longer the trip, the stronger the inclination to choose air. Clearly this is a factor of significance in estimating passenger demand between any two cities.

Variability Factor

Passenger demand for any mode of transportation varies greatly by the hour of the day, the day of the week, and in most markets by the season of the year. *Variability* is the general term that describes this built-in headache of the transportation industry.

Surveys of U.S. airline traffic show a definite *seasonality*. Professors Dempsey and Gesell show the peak month (August) with 20–25 percent more traffic than the slackest month, which is January in domestic service, February in international service.[2] Deregulation has alleviated the seasonality problem for some airlines by permitting them free entry into markets with winter peaks, such as from northern cities to Florida. Under free entry a carrier could even elect to enter a tourist market for the vacation season only. On the other hand, to the extent that deregulation has given rise to deeply discounted fares, it has had the effect of increasing the amount of vacation travel, the chief component of seasonality.

The aging of the U.S. population, and consequent higher proportion of retirees who are free to travel at any time of year, is a factor tending to alleviate seasonality that may be of considerable long-run significance.

Variability by day of the week will often reflect whether a market is dominated by business or by tourist travel. A market oriented to business travel will have slack days on weekends, whereas one oriented to tourist travel may show quite the opposite pattern. However, Dempsey and Gesell show Sunday to be the peak day (26 percent above the lightest day, Tuesday) because business travelers may be leaving that evening while leisure travelers are returning, and many of the latter may be returning on Sunday because of Saturday overnight restrictions on their discount tickets.[3]

The most severe variability in any market is likely to occur by hour of the day, even if we disregard the hours in the middle of the night when traffic drops to nearly zero. There is an effect somewhat comparable to commuter rush hours, with the hours of 5 and 6 P.M. and around 9 A.M. being the daily peaks. In considering hourly variability we must, of course, be aware of at least some degree of circular causation: maybe some passengers departing at the 9 A.M. peak are doing so only because the airline has scheduled its only morning flight to their destination at that hour. Airlines naturally schedule heavily at peak hours and, by so doing, may attract passengers who would just as soon leave at a late-morning trough. (This would not happen, of course, in a very busy market where flights are available at every hour through the day anyway.)

Along a similar line of reasoning, an airline that offers a night coach special low fare will show figures that seem to indicate a jump in passenger demand at 11 P.M. and midnight over lower apparent demand at 8 or 9 P.M. But what is really being measured by those figures is an increase in the quantity demanded because of the lower price; the demand, in the economist's sense of the word, can be said to increase only when the increase in traffic is not related to price.

Variability is a constant major problem of airline management in planing the best utilization of aircraft, flight crews, ground personnel, and so on. They must plan around it, and on occasions they will try to cope with it by pricing policies, such as the night coach mentioned above and off-season fares in vacation markets. The term *off-peak pricing* is used for such fare policies. In Chapter 6 we will see how the modern practice known as yield management relieves the variability problem.

Electronic Substitutes for Travel

In Chapter 2 we mentioned the use of computer links, conference telephone calls, and videotelephones as alternatives to airline trips. Many businesses are relying on these and other electronic substitutes for air travel. Of the several techniques, the one that comes closest to a personal visit is the videoconference: if two or more or a group of persons can both see and converse with one another, there may often be no reason left for the bother and expense of air travel. A business can equip itself with the necessary videoconference equipment for about $20,000 at each end of the communication, and conduct conferences for about $20 an hour.[4]

The opinion has been expressed, however, that teleconferencing is largely "a substitute for interoffice travel within the same company, where those communicating know each other and know the company business and policies." By contrast, for business travelers "who, for example, are traveling to negotiate a contract, there is still the need to 'look their business partners in the eye' and assess their body language."[5]

On a much smaller scale and intended for household use is the small-screen videotelephone. Here the impact on air travel would be from trips to visit friends and relatives as well as from the business segment. As of 1993, AT&T was advertising videophones under lease-purchase plans whereby the equipment could be bought for about $1,200. Of course, the person at the other end would also have to have a videophone.[6] As of the end of the 1990s, however, the personal videophone had not as yet caught on with the public.

Tourist travel is likely to be least affected by these electronic techniques, since they may substitute for a visit or a conference, but hardly for a vacation. But the demand for business and some personal air travel will be diminished in future years, to a degree that is hard to predict, as these technologies are improved and become less expensive.

Limited Managerial Control over Demand Factors

Airline management has only a limited control over some of the factors affecting passenger demand, and it has no control at all over others. It has no control at all over people's income levels or over the general state of the economy, or over services and prices of competing modes. It has only very limited control over technological advances that result in improved speed and comfort. Looking back to the time when the airlines changed their fleets from piston to jet aircraft, with a great improvement in both speed and comfort, we can say that each airline made the actual decision to purchase the new aircraft and that the airline industry encouraged the manufacturers to produce jet transports. But the technological development itself was the product of factors such as defense-oriented government financing, and an individual airline had no practical choice but to adopt the new type of aircraft once its competitors were doing so.

An airline has only a limited say as to the prices it will charge. No matter to what degree its rates have been freed from governmental controls, it usually finds that as a practical business matter it must meet the competition. This problem will be examined in Chapter 6. (To keep our economics terminology correct, let us note that this particular demand factor involves the quality demanded rather than demand as such.)

Two areas where airline management has broad control are flight scheduling and the services aboard the flight. Flight scheduling includes the number of flights in each market, the time of day that each departs, the number of nonstop services, and the number of seats that are generally available. (An airline that is stingy on the capacity it schedules in a market is obviously the one that may not have a seat for a prospective passenger.) For domestic U.S. services, the airlines control scheduling decisions subject only to the pressures of competition and sometimes to limitations on airport space. For schedule changes in international services, however, management (1) may have to obtain prior consent of the foreign government, (2) may be free to initiate changes subject to ex post facto challenge by the foreign government (one of the original Bermuda principles), or (3) may have complete discretion (the goal of U.S. policy in many current bilateral negotiations).

As for services aboard its flight—meals, drinks, movies, and so on— management generally has broad discretion, limited only by competitive pressures. Even here, however, there can be some limitations where rate regulation still exists (as on a few international routes) and where a tariff distinguishes between first class and coach fares in terms of such amenities.

Total Demand versus Market Shares

Some of the factors we have been discussing tend to attract people to air travel, others merely to attract to a particular airline some people who were going to fly anyway. The total demand for airline service was certainly affected by the quantum jump in speed and comfort when the airlines went from piston to jet fleets. And the general level of personal income also affects total demand for air service. But service amenities are another matter: very few people will decide to fly to a point merely because they can obtain food or drink or movies en route. When an airline emphasizes the service aspects in its advertising, it is trying to increase its share of the traffic by winning people away from its competitor airlines. Flight scheduling may have either result: the existence of a flight at a particular hour may cause people to fly rather than to drive their own cars, but in many other instances flight scheduling will merely win a passenger who was going to fly anyway.

Much airline advertising does little to promote air travel as such but concentrates on winning or holding a share of the market. Advertising a new lowered fare very likely does more to promote air travel than the extensive advertising of service amenities. And much advertising—reflecting the intermediate-good nature of the product—promotes air travel by presenting mouth-watering pictures and descriptions of tourist meccas. The latter may present the problem that the expensive advertising by one airline may cause people to travel to the attractive point by competing airlines or by train, bus, or private automobile. (Airline figures show advertising expenses averaging in the 1.5–2.0 percent range.)

METHODS OF ESTIMATING DEMAND

Having considered some of the peculiarities of the demand for airline service, let us turn our attention to some of the methods by which economists and airline managers seek to estimate the demand in the different markets.

Can we take a market (that is, a pair of cities) and study it by one or more methods that will reveal at least a good approximation of the demand elasticities? Efforts have been made to develop mathematical formulas in which the different elements affecting demand for airline service are quantified in some manner and relationships among them are worked out. While such formulas may well be useful to management, they must be used with the understanding that despite their apparent mathematical precision they are only giving estimates. Four methods that underlie the formula approach will be considered below.

Polling the Passengers and Prospective Passengers

This method consists simply of quizzing passengers or prospective passengers, either by personal interview or by printed questionnaires. Often an airline will simply leave a copy of a questionnaire on each passenger seat on certain flights and compile data from those that are turned in. The disadvantages of this procedure are obvious: There is no way to compel passengers to fill out the questionnaire, nor to know whether those who turn in completed forms are a typical sample of all passengers, nor even to know whether some passengers may give an answer intended to support a desired result. (If you were traveling on a discount fare and were asked whether you would be taking this flight even if there were no such fare, how would you reply?)

Typical questions asked are purpose of trip (business, tourism, visiting relatives, and so on), duration of trip, age bracket of the passenger, family income, and the fare (first class, coach, or discount by type). From such surveys come data on both price and income elasticity of demand, which can be broken down by the purpose of the trip, or in other ways such as age groups.

The polling technique is not confined to airline surveys of actual passengers. Professional poll takers will contract to survey a sample of the population of a city, a region, or the country as a whole. The range of questions may include a person's past flying experience (number of flights in the past year, purpose, whether at regular or discount fares, and so on) and future plans to travel. Breakdowns by age and income levels are often used, and people may be asked what fare level would induce them to take trips, say, to Europe or Hawaii. Or they may be asked what fare level in a particular market would induce them to fly instead of using their own automobiles.

Figures collected in this way are analyzed in an effort to determine what fare policy ought to be. As in any business, airline management is operating against an unknown: it can never be certain how the public will react to a new fare. Use of polling methods is one way to reduce the uncertainty.

Polling on a national scale reveals that many U.S. citizens have never flown at all. It also brings out the importance to airlines of the income elasticity concept. As personal income rises, people are more likely not only to travel, but to travel by more expensive means (air over bus) and to travel longer distances (where air has the strong advantage).

Price elasticity also has a feature that surveys can bring out: the number of passengers in a market may not increase at all in response to a very small fare reduction but may increase greatly when the fare cut is large enough to attract the public's attention and have a significant effect on the passenger's pocketbook. If the fare in a long-haul vacation market is $380, a reduction to $370 may not induce even one person to decide to take the trip. But a discount fare of $280 may bring passengers by the thousands. Surveys may help to reveal the true shape of the demand curve in a particular market.

Cross-Section Analysis

Another method for seeking to estimate demand may be called a cross-section analysis of a market wherein we look at all factors that may have a bearing on air travel between the two points.

In this method, population and income figures for each of the two cities are used, as is the geographical distance between them. These and other factors are employed to try to determine what the traffic between them by all modes ought to be and what fraction of it ought to go by air. Then management looks at what the airline traffic between them really is and compares that figure with the "ought to be" figure. An airline not serving a market may use the cross-section method to judge whether the airlines already serving are doing a good job of developing the market. If not, perhaps it should consider entering.

Another factor to be considered is the type of city, whether predominantly a manufacturing, commercial, tourist, or institutional city. These terms are rather general, and not all cities are easy to classify under just one of them. Simpler ones to classify are Pittsburgh (manufacturing), New York (commercial), Las Vegas (tourist), and Washington (institutional). (The term *commercial* includes finance, insurance, port and transport activities.) It has been found that commercial cities tend to generate more traffic than manufacturing cities. The tourist point will obviously be a good traffic point, while the institutional city will usually also be a good traffic point, since the adjective *institutional* typically means a state or national government capital or a college town. Too much emphasis should not be placed on this typing of cities, since the categories are inexact, but at least we may plausibly infer that the predominantly manufacturing city will be likely to generate less traffic than a city in the other classifications of comparable size and income levels.

A more basic factor is the distance between the two points. A principle of surface transportation is that traffic tends to be inversely proportional to the distance between two points. Thinking of one's own automobile, or bus or train, the farther away the point, the greater the investment in time and money and sheer travel weariness it takes to get there. We tend more readily to decide to go somewhere if it is closer at hand. The planning of surface common carrier transportation takes this human tendency very much into account. But with airlines the matter becomes more complicated: for longer distances the principle applies, but for shorter distances the tendency runs in reverse.

Let us take an "other things being equal" situation—that is, where all the cities concerned are of about equal population and income level and there are no special facts, such as one of them being a particular tourist attraction. If we are in city A and are contemplating a trip to city B, 20 miles away, it is exceedingly unlikely that we will decide to go by airline, if indeed any airline even serves so short a haul. If instead we wish to travel to city C, 50 miles away, the chances are somewhat greater that we will fly, and greater yet if we are heading for city D, 100 miles away. For these short distances, then, the amount of traffic is *directly* (not inversely) proportional to the distance. As the trip length increases, it becomes more and more worthwhile to put up with the delays, expenses, frustrations, and uncertainties of the whole process of getting to and from the airports, standing in check-in lines, waiting out operational delays, and so on.

But if we are contemplating trips of 500, 1,000, and 3,000 miles, we shall very likely make an immediate decision that the airline is the best way to get there, but our decision to travel will be limited by the cost of the trip. (Another factor may be the time we have off from work as a proportion of the cost; to travel 500 miles for a weekend away is a more likely action than to travel to Europe for only a weekend.) For these longer distances the basic transportation principle starts to apply: The amount of traffic will be inversely proportional to the distance, other things being equal.

Note that the phrase "other things being equal" has to be tacked on repeatedly, and herein lies one severe shortcoming of cross-section analysis. "Other things" are never really "equal" when we are comparing one city to another. The total air traffic between New York and San Francisco is much greater than the total air traffic between New York and, say, Salt Lake City, although San Francisco is the more distant point. What has happened to our inversely proportional concept? Simply that other factors, such as the greater population, tourist attractiveness, commercial importance, and so on of San Francisco, enter the picture and greatly outbalance the distance factor.

Still, partly just because the airplane lends itself so dramatically (and profitably) to the very long haul, it is quite important for airline management to keep in mind that for longer distances the tendency of the public to travel tends to diminish as the distance grows, however much this tendency may be covered over by other factors.

Note that we have not even tried to say what the distance is where the traffic ceases to be directly proportional and becomes inversely proportional. To isolate it would be a difficult task. The extremely heavy air travel between Washington and New York would tend to indicate that it is well under 200 miles.

The cross-section method, then, uses distance along with population, income levels, and the type of city in an effort to approximate passenger demand. Also used will be any index of the community of interest between the two points, such as the volume of long-distance telephone calls. It is theorized, doubtless with some justification, that the tendency to phone someone in the other city indicates a degree of personal or business interest that may result another time in a trip to the other city. (A possible flaw in this idea is that a telephone call may be a *substitute* for a trip.)

Cause-and-Effect Analysis

The third method of estimating demand involves a study of past situations where a specific action, such as the introduction of a discount fare or a general fare change, produced a particular result. We look at past experiences in specific instances and then try to predict future passenger behavior.

When a lower fare is introduced, management must ask itself two questions: how many new passengers will the fare change attract, and how much revenue will be lost because some passengers at the new fare would have traveled anyway at the higher fare? Past experiences in a particular market is a good, though not infallible, guide. Similarly, past experience can guide management with respect to fare increases—did the last round of increases, for example, scare away so much traffic as to offset the gain in revenue from each remaining passenger?

There are hazards, of course, in relying too heavily on past experience. A change in the mood of the public from the optimism of a year of prosperity to the caution of a year of recession may shift the demand curve. Also, predicting passenger behavior in one market from past experience in another market must be engaged in with judgment. Unless the markets are quite similar, the elasticities may be different.

Time-Series Method

The fourth method of estimating demand involves the familiar time series where trends are plotted against the passage of time. Changes in business or tourist or total travel in a market or region or nationwide may be shown from year to year, and a trend or trends deduced. Changes in airline fares, in the fare levels or traffic levels of other modes, and in income levels also lend themselves to time-series analysis. Out of such analyses of the various demand elements, it may be possible to work the demand elasticities.

PASSENGER OPTIONS

The S-Curve Controversy

Many airline officials will contend that passengers in a market are attracted to an airline in a proportion *greater* than that airline's capacity bears to the total capacity of all the airlines in that market. For example, if there are two airlines in the market and one has 60 percent of the capacity, prospective passengers will tend to think first of this dominant carrier when they decide to reserve space on a flight. Also they will be most likely to find the most desirable departure time and available space on that carrier. Thus, the airline with 60 percent of the total capacity will win *more* than 60 percent of the traffic. Or so the believers in this theory will contend.

The phenomenon is shown graphically by a curve with a flattened S shape (hence the term *S-curve*, a familiar one in airline economics), where the share of passengers flown on a route is plotted against the share of seats flown on that route.

The argument that passengers tend to behave in this fashion, and the consequent conclusion that there is an inherent tendency in the airline industry to overschedule, gained much prominence at the beginning of the 1970s. It was offered as part of the explanation for the severe over-capacity problem then existing. With the gathering of strength among the proponents of deregulation in the middle 1970s, the S-curve concept, which they generally decry, gained even more attention.

In 1975 the CAB described the "so-called S-curve theory" as "the claim that increases (or reductions) of marginal flights (those generating revenues covering out-of-pocket but not fully allocated costs) result in a greater-than-proportional gain (or loss) of market share, with the result that carriers have a short-term economic incentive to schedule excess capacity in highly competitive markets" (Order 75–7-98, July 21, 1975, p. 9). The board went on to express doubts whether such a phenomenon really existed "to any material degree."

Obviously there were other reasons for the extreme level of capacity in those years, such as the need to order aircraft several years in advance of delivery against a hoped-for traffic growth that did not fully develop. Yet, to the extent that the S-curve theory may be valid, it would seem to be an argument against removal of entry controls, since new entrants would overschedule in an effort to win an adequate share of the market, while the established carriers would retaliate by expanding their schedules further. But opponents of the theory will argue that it has a built-in absurdity: a carrier finding that it is losing money because it is flying too many empty seats will seek to correct the problem by further expanding the number of seats it is offering.

Perhaps there is a middle ground in the S-curve controversy. After all, there is a difference between saying that some passengers may behave in this fashion some of the time and saying that this is a major problem and that airline management is helpless to counteract it. Let us consider two examples:

There are three airlines in a market, one offering 40 percent of the capacity, the other two 30 percent each. Since each has a substantial schedule and thus should have clear identification in the market, it seems unlikely that a passenger would have any special tendency to contact the largest participant.

There are four carriers in a market, three with 30 percent of the capacity each, one offering only 10 percent. Perhaps some passengers would think of the three when making a reservation, but not of the minor participant. But the latter airline could counteract this tendency by vigorous advertising of the services it offers.

Moreover, the fact that the great majority of airline tickets are written by travel agents should surely have a tendency to limit any S-curve behavior. An agent would in all likelihood know all the carriers in a market. In any case, most agents, as we will later see, use a computer reservation system that shows for each pair of points a list of all flights by departure time. (There are bias problems with computer reservation systems, as we will shortly see, but they do not appear to have a bearing on S-curve behavior.)

The trend to hub-and-spoke networks, discussed in Chapter 3, might also be expected to reduce any S-curve tendencies by shifting emphasis from straight-out capacity rivalry to the size and strength of the feed from an airline's network of connecting flights. However, two earlier studies (1991 and 1992) concluded that an S-curve phenomenon might aid a carrier in strengthening its position at a hub. By adding flights on the spokes radiating out of a hub city, it wins *more* than a proportional share of traffic, and the process may go on until the carrier dominates these markets.[7] Two more recent studies find that once a carrier has achieved dominance at a hub, it may use its S-curve advantage to drive out other competitors, and that carriers use the S-curve (including the variations in it from market to market) in their decisions to add or reduce capacity.[8] It appears that the prevailing view today is that, contrary to the opinions of deregulation proponents in the past, there is indeed an S-curve in passenger behavior.

Whether one accepts the S-curve theory in whole or in part, the discussion revolving around it is part of a focusing on a basic dilemma of air transportation: how to adjust capacity, keeping in mind the variability factor, so that the public will have an acceptable service without the surplus of empty seats that is a major cause of high airline fares.

An airline not subscribing to the S-curve theory may nonetheless engage in frequency rivalry. It may add flights in a market not hoping for a more-than-proportional share of traffic but desiring merely to dilute the competitor's traffic. It may carry this practice all the way to the point where its load factors drop to a break-even level. Of course, it could instead engage in fare cutting, but it may fear a destructive rate war with a carrier whose costs may be lower than its own. Thus, even in a deregulated environment, and assuming an airline's disbelief in the S-curve theory, we may still have frequency rivalry, with resultant wasteful surplus of empty seats.

Price/Quality Options

An approach to the subject of passenger demand that gained great currency in the course of the regulatory reform debate of the 1970s was that passengers were not being offered enough price/quality options. It was contended that the airlines had largely geared themselves to the business traveler who wishes frequent departures and last-minute availability of seats and is willing to pay for these privileges. But, it was argued, other segments of the public would prefer lower fares even though this meant a reduction in the quality of service. The word *quality*, as used in this context, refers very little to the amenities such as food and drinks, and very much to flight scheduling and load factors. Let it be harder to get a last-minute reservation, and compensate for this by having lower fares, a balance between price and quality different from that desired by most business travelers. Thus, the word "quality" is employed to include (1) the length of time between the precise hour when a person would *like* to depart and the time when the flight is scheduled, and (2) the chances that that person will get space on that flight.

Attempts have been made to balance the fares that passengers pay against the value of their *time*. There is certainly some truth in the idea that the total "cost" to passengers of their journeys is not merely what they pay the airline, plus ground connection costs, but includes the value they place on their time, from the moment when they desire to depart to the moment when they actually get to their destinations. If a person wishes to leave at 9 A.M. but the first flight to the desired destination is not scheduled until 10 A.M., there is a presumed cost, which some economists would set at the hourly wage rate in whatever line of work the passenger is engaged. This last assumption, applied whether the trip is for business or pleasure, is certainly a debatable point. Then, if the 10

A.M. flight is sold out and the passenger must wait until an 11 A.M. flight, there is another presumed hour of cost equal to this person's wage rate. But perhaps many people would accept such costs in return for a sizable reduction in airline fares.

As part of the regulatory reform debate, figures were presented seeking to show a welfare loss in the sense that many passengers had had to travel at fares reflecting a higher-quality service than they really required, assuming they were prepared to trade delay for price.

As evidence of a large potential demand for lower-fare air service, advocates of regulatory reform called attention to the popularity and growth of charters and of low-priced scheduled services within California and Texas that were being offered by the then-intrastate carriers. They contended that deregulating both entry and rates would result in a variety of types of service, testing consumer preferences in different markets.

The period following deregulation saw just such a testing. The new services, however, while usually offering lower fares, did not generally do so at a sacrifice of seating availability. Several involved the use of lesser-used airports such as the Midway Airport in Chicago and the Long Beach Airport in the Los Angeles area. Some offered reduced amenities; People Express, for example, encouraged carry-on baggage and charged for each checked bag, served only cold food, and charged for meals. It later got into financial difficulties, moved toward full service, but was finally acquired by Texas Air.

More recently, Southwest Airlines, a pre-deregulation intrastate carrier, has become an outstanding example of a price/quality option. Based in Texas, it serves Dallas and Houston at lesser-used airports close to downtown. But it has expanded to a nationwide network and prospered at a time when the major airlines were running large deficits. In general, it has tended to serve smaller cities with stage lengths short enough so that meal service is not necessary. It holds down maintenance costs by having only one aircraft model in its fleet, the 737. It does no interlining. Its costs being low, it can charge low fares, but it avoids serving markets where it would be competing with the largest airlines. It serves a special niche, a special option in the industry.

It should be noted that Southwest ought not to be viewed as an example for other airlines to follow, despite its prospering when the majors ran heavy losses. As Professor Laurence E. Gesell puts it: "One must ask what would happen if all carriers behaved like Southwest. Travel would be difficult indeed, and the passenger would be faced with making complex and frustrating flight arrangements should he or she need to travel outside the short-haul parameters of a carrier like Southwest."[9]

There are quality limitations, employed by both new and old-line carriers, whose history goes well back into pre-deregulation days. Among these are closely packed seating and ticketing limitations such as an advance purchase requirement with a partial or total forfeit if the ticket is not used. Moreover, there is a drop in quality whenever intermediate stops are added to a formerly nonstop service and when a change of planes is imposed on a formerly one-plane service. The change from linear to hub-and-spoke networks, discussed in Chapter 3, may thus result in some quality changes, presumably compensated for by lower fares resulting from more cost-efficient operations. In a sense, these are price/quality options.

TRAVEL AGENCIES AND COMPUTER RESERVATIONS SYSTEMS

Travel agents have always been an important element in airline ticket sales, but the proportion of tickets written by them increased considerably following deregulation, apparently due both to the larger number of flights being offered and to the extremely complex and confusing fare situation. In the mid-1990s, it was estimated that about 80–85 percent of all airline tickets were being sold by agents, and there were at the time about 33,000 agents in the United States.[10] Starting in 1995, however, the major airlines began reducing commission rates and placing caps on the maximum commission on any one sale. In addition, the major airlines began a policy of encouraging passengers to book directly with the airline, thus saving the airline all commission.

Agencies run all the way from giant nationwide corporations with scattered local outlets, such as American Express, to small individually owned proprietorships, although the trend in recent years has been away from the latter into the larger units. While there were travel agents before there were airlines, and while they handle many other types of travel business such as cruise ship reservations, hotel reservations, car rentals, and package tours, airline ticketing has become a major element in their business. The standard practice is for an agent to sell an airline ticket at the same fare as if it had been bought at the airline ticket counter, with the agent's compensation coming from the commission paid by the airline, though there are variants permitted today, where an airline may sell a block of tickets to an agency, which then resells them at its own price. Another variant is a growing practice among some agents of charging a fee to the customer, this being an outgrowth of the above-mentioned limitations on commissions imposed by the airlines.

The commission received by agents traditionally was 10 percent, sometimes higher for international flights. To this there frequently was (and often still is) added an *override* commission where an airline rewards an agent for booking traffic on its flights above a specified amount. The override commission is usually not over 5 percent but can run as high as 10 percent.[11] This practice has been criticized as influencing an agent to book a passenger on the airline offering the highest override even where a different carrier's flight would be in the best interest of the passenger.

The reduction in commissions that began in 1995 was from a 10 percent rate to 8 percent, with a cap on any individual commission of $25 for a one-way ticket, $50 for a round trip. Further reductions followed, and, by late 1999, the 8 percent rate had been cut to 5 percent, with a maximum payment of $25 for a one-way domestic ticket, $50 for a round trip, and double these amounts for an international ticket.[12]

The travel agencies have obviously been injured financially by the limiting of their commissions. Where the airlines in the past eagerly sought business from the agents, their attitude toward them today can best be described as ambivalent—seeking to influence as many passengers as possible to bypass the agents, yet at the same time, for traffic that remains with the agencies, to lure as many passengers away from competing airlines. Thus, the airlines, on the one hand, have sharply curbed regular commissions, but at the same time may continue to use overrides.[13]

The agents have fought the commission restrictions on antitrust grounds, noting that each move by one airline to cut commissions has been swiftly matched by the others, but they have not been successful. They have also pointed out that there are personnel and other costs to an airline when it receives its reservation and ticketing requests directly from the public. The airlines, of course, can try to minimize such costs by encouraging so-called "ticketless" traffic, where the customer makes a reservation, purchases a ticket by credit card, and receives a confirmation number—all by telephone, with no paper ticket issued. Even so, it can be questioned whether the personnel and other costs to the airlines may exceed what they save by eliminating agent commissions. Yet the airlines strongly defend their commission-cutting actions as the legitimate cost-cutting acts of any business.

From a public interest standpoint, it can be argued that the reduced role of the travel agent tends to reduce competition among the airlines. An agent today searches computer screens to find the best deal for the customer out of the confusing and ever-changing mass of airline fares. While a large corporation with extensive employee travel can tie directly into that same computer system and have personnel trained to manage its complexities, the average individual customer can hardly be expected to do so. Also, an agent is far more likely than an individual customer to know of small new airlines struggling to compete with the majors.

One authority ties this concept into the oligopoly power of the major airlines, which we have discussed in Chapter 3. "Without the travel agents' ability to funnel customers and provide expert advice, and thereby foster competition via helping upstarts and supporting those with the best deals, airlines can more easily collude . . . By analogy, travelers who buy directly from the airlines will be more at the mercy of the airlines than travel agents, who are more aggressive in curbing airline oligopoly power."[14]

Intermediary Organizations

In 1945, the U.S. airlines, through their trade organization the Air Transport Association, established the Air Traffic Conference (ATC) which, among other things, was to serve as a regime through which the airlines dealt with the travel agencies. Since the agent actually writes an airline's tickets, and since the agent receives the money from the passenger, the airline naturally has great concern with each agency's competence, honesty, and creditworthiness. The ATC undertook the job of screening and accrediting agents, while the airlines for their part agreed not to allow their tickets to be sold by any agents other than those so accredited. A clearing-house was established within the ATC called the Area Settlement Plan, whose task it was to distribute among the airlines the ticketing revenues collected by the agents. Commission rates were set on a uniform scale. The CAB had to approve all details of the arrangements between the ATC and the airlines, including the commission rates, as otherwise they would have been in violation of the antitrust laws.

Shortly after the establishment of the ATC, IATA set up (and maintains today) a similar arrangement for international services, including the elements of accreditation, commission rates, and a clearinghouse for financial settlements.

In 1978, pursuant to the deregulation philosophy, the CAB began reviewing the ATC arrangements. The first change made was to open up all restrictions on commissions, so that the amount of a commission became a matter between the agent and the individual airline. Then the requirement limiting the sale of airline tickets only to those agencies accredited by the ATC was phased out, expiring in 1984. However, the Area Settlement Plan was permitted to continue indefinitely.[15] With the demise of the board, government policy on such matters became the responsibility of DOT. In 1985 the ATC was reconstituted as the Airlines Reporting Corporation, which now performs the clearinghouse function of the Area Settlement Plan and also issues accreditation to travel agents.

Computer Reservations Systems

Beginning in the mid-1970s, certain airlines began expanding their computerized reservations systems so that travel agents could tie in to them. Immediate information as to flight schedules, available seats, and fares between any two points could be shown on a computer screen in the travel agent's office, with the facility for the agent to make reservations through the system. United Airlines was first, calling its system "Apollo," and American Airlines followed with a system called "Sabre." These remain the two leading systems in the industry. Since most agents can afford only one computer reservations system (CRS), and since an agency would hardly be serving its customers well if it limited its offerings to the flights of one carrier, it was necessary for the airline owning each system (called the "host carrier," "host airline," or "vendor") to list the flights of its competitors as well as its own on the computer screens. By 1990, every major U.S. passenger airline except Southwest was listed in every CRS.

Agents rather quickly joined these programs, since by so doing they could offer faster service to customers, with large savings in their employee productivity. (One study found a 42 percent productivity gain through ticketing via a CRS.)[16] The earlier system involved looking up each pair of points in a large printed volume, issued monthly, called *The Official Airline Guide* (OAG), followed by a telephone call to the airline to check seat availability and make reservations. Over 90 percent of bookings today are made through CRSs. (The OAG is still published, however, and is useful, for example, in booking with carriers that are not in a CRS, for seeing what services exist between a seldom-traveled pair of points, or simply as a backup if the CRS is malfunctioning.)

As of the late 1990s, there were four principal CRSs available to U.S. scheduled airlines: Sabre, Apollo/Galileo, Worldspan, and Amadeus/System One. Sabre was still majority-owned by one carrier, American (actually by a subsidiary of AMR Corporation, the parent of American Airlines). Apollo/Galileo has 65 percent of its ownership among eleven airlines, including British Airways, United Airlines, and US Airways, but the other 35 percent is publicly traded. Worldspan is owned by a consortium of airlines (including Delta, Northwest, and TWA) and an Asian CRS called Abacus. Amadeus is owned by Continental, Air France, Iberia, and Lufthansa.[17] Each of these CRSs has grown into a worldwide system; the term *Global Distribution System* (GDS) has come into use as synonymous with a worldwide CRS.

An airline that owns a CRS has an obvious motive to favor its own flights over those of its competitors in the day-to-day operation of that CRS. This has been a chronic complaint of other airlines and of some agents and consumers. Moreover, it is likely that bias in the treatment of new airlines by CRSs was a factor in the demise of so many of them in the late 1980s, as discussed in Chapter 3.

An early complaint was of discrimination in favor of the host carrier's flights on the display screen, through practices such as listing those flights ahead of the competitors' flights or giving a higher display position to a flight with a change of planes but no change of carrier than to one involving two carriers. Another type of bias is delaying updating their systems with changes in a competitor's schedules or fares, especially when the changes offer more severe competition with the host carrier. The terms of the leases for CRS equipment are another possible source of bias; for example, the agency may be required to book a certain proportion of its business with the host carrier. In short, back in 1985 one writer could say, "CRSs have an infinite potential for abuse and vendors have infinite incentives for abusing CRSs."[18]

Before the demise of the CAB, that agency conducted an investigation of CRSs. In August 1984, it issued an order requiring host carriers to list flights on a nondiscriminatory basis. It also required that the fees charged by the host carrier to other airlines for carrying their flight information and processing their reservations on its system must be the same for all airlines unless there is cost justification for a difference. The board also put limits on certain provisions in CRSs contracts and leases. For example, a vendor is not supposed to prevent an agent from using an additional CRS, nor can contracts run for over five years.

The CAB order remains in effect today, with DOT responsible for its enforcement. Complaints of bias have been reduced but not wholly eliminated. DOT has worked with the industry in efforts to alleviate remaining biases. For example, every vendor now offers an option whereby the travel agent may directly access the internal reservations system of all of the airlines participating in the CRS, not just that of the vendor airline. Use of this technological option increases the accuracy of the information received by the agent and the confidence that the reservation, sale, and seat assignment will be properly recorded by the airline selected. DOT also now requires vendors to offer agents a three-year contract albeit at a higher monthly rate than the five-year contract.

In 1989, a bill was considered in Congress, but never enacted, that would have required the airlines to divest their ownership of CRSs. There can certainly be a reasonable argument for having CRSs owned and operated by companies that have no motives for favoring one airline over another, just as the OAG is published by a firm that has no airline ownership. But the vendor airlines that had pioneered the systems at great expense argued that they were entitled to profit from them, and that as airlines they understood the problems of operation better than could an outside firm. Moreover, as an International Civil Aviation Organization (ICAO) official put it, "The probable economies of scope available from operating both an airline and a CRS would be lost, . . . resulting in the prospect of higher user fees. In addition, vendors would lose some of the incentive to upgrade their systems as technology develops."[19] Pressure for divestiture has diminished greatly in the 1990s as the degree of bias has been reduced and as the trend has developed to have a CRS owned by several airlines rather than just one. Also, advances in technology may have made CRSs so much cheaper to develop that any abuse of economic power by the large systems is limited by the potential development of competing systems.

In 1989, the European Community (now called the European Union) adopted regulations governing the conduct of CRSs in its member countries, generally similar to the CAB/DOT rules. Meanwhile, the ICAO conducts studies, on a continuing basis, of possible abuses by CRSs and measures to minimize them. In light of the critical importance of CRSs in airline service and the ever-present possibility of their use as competitive weapons, they have become an element in negotiations for bilateral agreements. In its definition of "open skies" as a goal to be sought in such negotiations, DOT includes "explicit commitment for nondiscriminatory operation of and access for computer reservations systems."[20]

Looking to the future, there may be such a development of personal computers that a person at home may be able to access a CRS and, with all the information that would be available to a travel agent, make a reservation and buy a ticket charged to a credit card. This would reduce the significance of the whole travel agent industry.

NOTES

1. Michael W. Tretheway and Tae K. Oum, *Airline Economics: Foundations for Strategy and Policy* (Vancouver, Canada: Centre for Transportation Studies, 1992), p. 15.

2. Paul S. Dempsey and Laurence E. Gesell, *Airline Management: Strategies for the 21st Century* (Chandler, Ariz.: Coast Aire Publications, 1997), p. 45.

3. Ibid., p. 45.

4. *Wall Street Journal*, July 30, 1991, p. A-3.

5. Philip Shearman, "Airline Marketing: A Great Future but Different," in *Handbook of Airline Marketing*, ed. Gail F. Butler and Martin R. Keller (Washington, D.C.: McGraw-Hill, 1998), p. 137.

6. Advertisement in *Modern Maturity*, January 1994, p. 19; and telephone conversation with AT&T representative, March 7, 1994.

7. Tretheway and Oum, *Airline Economics*, p. 27; and Atef Ghobrial, "Competition for Hub Dominance," *Journal of Aviation/Aerospace Education and Research* 2 (Fall 1991): 20–29.

8. Peter Berdy, "Developing Effective Route Networks," in *Handbook of Airline Marketing*, pp. 623–25; and Steve Skinner, Alex Dichter, Paul Langley, and Hendrik Sabert, "Managing Growth and Profitability across Peaks and Troughs of the Airline Industry Cycle," in *Handbook of Airline Finance*, ed. Gail F. Butler and Martin R. Keller (Washington, D.C.: McGraw-Hill, 1999), pp. 32–33.

9. Laurence E. Gesell, *Airline Re-Regulation* (Chandler Ariz.: Coast Aire Publications, 1990), p. 75.

10. Dempsey and Gesell, *Airline Management*, p. 331.

11. U.S. Department of Transportation, *Secretary's Task Force on Competition in the U.S. Domestic Airline Industry*, 1990, pp. 14 and 26.

12. *Air Transport World*, November 1999, pp. 10 and 13.

13. Dempsey and Gesell, *Airline Management*, p. 339.

14. Ian E. Pate, "In Re Travel Agency Commission Antitrust Litigation," *Journal of Air Law and Commerce* 64 (Summer 1999): 974.

15. John R. Meyer and Clinton V. Oster Jr., *Deregulation and the Future of Intercity Passenger Travel* (Cambridge, Mass.: The MIT Press, 1987), pp. 126–28.

16. Derek Saunders, "The Antitrust Implications of Computer Reservations Systems (CRSs)," *Journal of Air Law and Commerce* 51 (1985): 163.

17. Dempsey and Gesell, *Airline Management*, pp. 323–24; *Air Transport World*, April 1998, p. 7; and Michael J. Durham, "The Future of Sabre," in *Handbook of Airline Economics*, ed. Darryl Jenkins (Washington, D.C.: McGraw-Hill, 1995), p. 487.

18. Saunders, "The Antitrust Implications," p. 195.

19. Chris Lyle, "Computer-Age Vulnerability in the International Airline Industry," *Journal of Air Law and Commerce* 54 (Fall 1988): 175.

20. Department of Transportation Order 92–8-13, August 5, 1992.

SELECTED REFERENCES

Detailed discussions of the demand for airline service, including techniques for forecasting it, may be found in Paul Biederman, *The U.S. Airline Industry: End of an Era* (New York: Praeger, 1982), chap 2; and in Nawal K. Taneja, *The Commercial Airline Industry* (Lexington, Mass.: D.C. Heath, 1976), pp. 131–45, and his *Airlines in Transition* (Lexington, Mass.: D.C. Heath, 1981), pp. 149–61. The first two of these are advanced treatments and require some background in economics.

The S-curve concept is explained in William E. Fruhan Jr., *The Fight for Competitive Advantage* (Boston: Harvard Graduate School of Business Administration, 1972), pp. 124–39.

More recent treatments of the S-curve concept, showing its relationship to hub dominance, can be found in Atef Ghobrial, "Competition for Hub Dominance," *Journal of Aviation/Aerospace Education and Research* 2 (Fall 1991): 20–29; and Michael W. Tretheway and Tae H. Oum, *Airline Economics: Foundations for Strategy and Policy* (Vancouver, Canada: Centre for Transportation Studies, 1992), pp. 27–28.

Demand factors, especially income and price elasticities for business and leisure travel, are analyzed in Tretheway and Oum, *Airline Economics*, pp. 14–17.

A clear explanation of demand curves and elasticities—including the distinction between a change in demand and a change in the quantity demanded—can be found in Alexander T. Wells, *Air Transportation: A Management Perspective*, 4th ed. (Belmont, Calif.: Wadsworth Publishing Company, 1999), pp. 329–39.

A detailed study of the travel agency business and of CRSs—as matters stood in 1989—can be found in U.S. Department of Transportation, *Secretary's Task Force on Competition in the U.S. Domestic Airline Industry*, 1990, pp. 1–30 and 43–99. More recent works on the history, structure, and functioning of CRSs—as well as predictions for their future—are Michael J. Durham, "The Future of Sabre," pp. 485–91; Lewis E. Elsworthy, "The CRS: A Global Electronic Marketplace," pp. 493–97; and Richard J. Fahy Jr., "The Cutting Edge of Technology and Regulation," pp. 499–506, in *Handbook of Airline Economics*, ed. Darryl Jenkins (Washington, D.C.: McGraw-Hill, 1995).

The case against the airlines in favor of the American Society of Travel Agents concerning commissions is argued in Ian E. Pate, "In Re Travel Agency Commission Antitrust Litigation," *Journal of Air Law and Commerce* 64 (Summer 1999): 941–76.

6

Airline Rates

This chapter is concerned with what the airlines charge for their product. First, we will look at the economics of ratemaking and see how the topics of the two previous chapters—costs and demand—interact in the pricing of airline services. Then we will examine changes in the airline passenger fare structure over the years and, in particular, the impact of deregulation on that structure. Then we will look at the role played by the CAB in the past in regulating airline rates, how this role changed by stages under the terms of the regulatory reform laws, and how much of it is now exercised by DOT. Last, we will examine the role of foreign governments in regulating rates of both U.S. and foreign airlines for services to and from the United States. In particular we will describe the controversial ratemaking function of the International Air Transport Association (IATA) and current U.S. attempts to negotiate alternative ratemaking systems in bilateral agreements.

BASIC RATEMAKING FACTORS

The factors that enter into determining a rate, whether domestic or international, may be divided into two broad concepts: the cost of service and the value of service. The first of these is easy to define but may be hard to arrive at in a specific case; the second is hard to define as well as hard to quantify in a specific case. The term *value of service* is, in a way, a polite way of saying that a carrier should charge what the traffic will bear. It is a term under which transportation economists group various demand factors.

What is the value of the service to each passenger (or to each shipper of cargo)? Is it a service that cannot be done without and for which no reasonable substitute can be found? If so, the value-of-service principle would cause the carrier to price the service high, perhaps very far above the cost of performing it. The concept can perhaps be clarified by some examples:

1. The "value" of the service on a long trip, as we have noted, is greater than on a short one. Air service saves us the several days' time and tedium of a transcontinental trip by rail or highway, and the time spent going to and from the airports, waiting for baggage, and so on is of relatively minor consequence.

2. The value of air service to a business traveler is often greater than to a tourist, as is evident from the fact that business travel is far less sensitive to fare changes than is vacation travel.

3. There is a tendency in pricing air cargo to let the value of the goods be a factor in determining the rate. Very expensive goods can bear a heavier transportation charge with only a minor relative impact on the retail selling price of the goods.

Rates are determined by a complex interaction of both cost-of-service and value-of-service factors. As an example, let us look at the familiar type of excursion fare, wherein a substantial discount, often on the order of 30 or 50 percent, is granted on regular coach travel if a person buys a round trip ticket on which the return coupon may not be used for, say, at least two weeks. Often there is an added condition that the ticket must be purchased at a specified minimum time, say 30 days, prior to departure. Vacation travelers often can meet these conditions, while business travelers usually cannot. The airline is seeking to attract additional tourist travel while minimizing the tendency for its business travelers to take advantage of the discount fare. However, the airline must allow for the revenue loss from those tourists who will use the discount fare even though they would have flown anyway, at the regular coach fare, had no discount fare been available.

The term *profit-impact test* is sometimes used. It means that the new fare must generate enough additional traffic to pay the out-of-pocket cost of carrying that traffic, with enough revenue left over to offset the revenue lost from those using the discount fare who would otherwise have traveled at full coach fare. The airline is looking at the elasticity of demand for pleasure travel (a value-of-service consideration) as well as the out-of-pocket cost of handling the additional traffic.

As we have seen, the out-of-pocket costs for fill-up passengers on a flight that would otherwise have departed with those seats empty are extremely low, being limited to the cost of food consumed and a tiny increase in fuel consumption. But if a discount fare proves very popular, the airline may have to run additional flights to accommodate the additional passengers; now costs such as crew wages and fuel become out-of-pocket costs deriving from the discounted traffic. Under these circumstances the airline may find that the impact of the discount fare on its profit is distinctly negative. Many airlines have tried to cope with this latter problem by limiting the number of discount-fare tickets they will sell on each flight; the term *capacity-controlled* has come into use to describe this practice. As we will shortly see, an elaborate, computer-facilitated practice called *yield management* has become the prevailing method of the airlines in applying the concept of capacity-controlled fares.

An airline must move cautiously when establishing a discount fare, and its task is made more difficult by the likelihood that its competitors will respond to its initiative by establishing similar or identical discount fares of their own. Now the new traffic—people who would not have flown had it not been for the discount fare—is scattered among the competitors, and each airline may get too small a share of it to compensate for regular traffic diverted from regular fares to the discount fare.

Determining how deep the discount should be on any discount fare requires a particularly close look at the shape of the demand curve. As noted in Chapter 5, a small reduction in fare may induce very few passengers to travel. Discounts, therefore, may be futile if they are in the 5 or 10 percent range; thus, such fares usually involve dramatic cuts in the 30–50 percent range.

Another example of interaction of cost-of-service and value-of-service factors in ratemaking is the tapering of rates with the length of a trip. In Chapter 4 we noted that the cost per seat-mile drops with the length of a trip, a phenomenon known as the cost taper. Rates also tend to taper with the length of a trip but, because of the intrusion of a value-of-service element, they often do not taper as rapidly as costs. The intruding element is that the desirability of air travel, in contrast with bus, train, or private automobile travel, is greater for longer trips. The airlines, knowing this, may not taper their rates as rapidly as the tapering cost would justify. Thus, it can be argued that long-haul passengers under these circumstances are paying more than their fair share and are indirectly subsidizing the short-haul passengers, a phenomenon described as cross-subsidization. The degree to which such cross-subsidization has existed in airline service was one matter in dispute during the regulatory reform debate, with proponents of reform being generally skeptical that very much such indirect subsidy really existed.

Still another example of the interaction of cost-of-service and value-of-service factors is peak-load pricing. Load factors of the airlines could be improved without serious inconvenience to passengers if the peaks and valleys of passenger demand could be partly smoothed out by a system of fares that would be lower on flights that operate at times of leaner demand—whether by hour of the day, day of the week, or season of the year.

A certain amount of such pricing has for many years been a standard practice of the airlines—examples being night coach fares and off-season fares, as well as the gearing of some discount fares to variability by making them unavailable for certain days of the week or busy seasons.

But the airlines have developed a far more sophisticated form of off-peak pricing, which we have already mentioned under the term *capacity-controlled fares*. As one writer remarks: "One difficulty with off-peak pricing until recently, however, has been the fact that the timing of the peak has varied from route to route, and even from one direction to the other on the same route. . . . The wide daily variation in demand on a given route made it difficult to find a definition of off-peak suitable for an entire airline system." This writer, transportation consultant Melvin A. Brenner, goes on to say:

The capacity-controlled fare retained the old idea of off-peak pricing, but gave the airlines the flexibility to make discounts available in specific relation to the demand fluctuations demonstrated by individual schedules on individual routes. This enabled the carriers to take advantage of new computer technology in handling reservations. With this technology, it is possible to predict the demand patterns of individual schedules, and thus predict the amount of space on future individual departures that could be used for promotional discount traffic.[1]

The precision with which the technology works has been described as follows: "If a particular flight is not filling up with full-fare passengers as rapidly as expected, more seats can be opened up for discounts, and vice versa. Thus the balance of discount and full-fare tickets can be continually revised and carefully targeted to respond to new competition."[2] The goal sought, of course, is to have every flight carry as many full-fare passengers as can be garnered, with all other seats occupied by discount passengers.

Ultimately, of course, an airline must recover its costs, however it may manipulate its fares in the process. As one source puts the problem:

Thus it becomes clear that pricing occurs in both the world of cost and the world of demand. As a result, skilled pricers will consider cost factors as constraints and demand factors as a primary driver . . . Many airline pricers make the mistake of being overly cost focused—cost recovery becomes an objective rather than a constraint (and costs may be ill-defined). Even more frequently pricers make the opposite mistake of ignoring costs. They and their associates in the sales department are often too eager to say yes.[3]

THE CHANGING STRUCTURE OF AIRLINE PASSENGER FARES

In the early days of the airlines, there was only one class of passenger service, and the air mode was an expensive way to travel. The competing passenger trains had first-class and considerably cheaper coach service, but the airlines set their rates, in the late 1930s, at the level of rail first-class. It was not until 1948 that the scheduled airlines introduced a second-class service in a separate section of the aircraft, which they called "air coach" and which offered a fare about one-third less than the regular fare (which now became "first-class").

Initially the coach fares had their own off-peak characteristic, being designed for overnight flights, and they were also characterized by crowded seating and little if any food service. By 1950, however, the night departure time requirement was removed by the CAB and as time went on such matters as food service were upgraded, although the closely packed seating has generally remained a feature of the coach section of an aircraft. Seating "configuration" (to use airline terminology) includes width of seats, "pitch" (the distance between each row of seats), width of aisles, and two-abreast or three-abreast seating on each side of the aisle.

During the 1950s, the airlines developed a family fare offering a discount as high as 50 percent to family members traveling with the head of the family who was paying full first-class fare. The 1960s saw the family fare extended to coach service and the establishment of other special fares for coach passengers. Among these were youth fares (for persons 12 to 21 years of age), standby fares, and a variety of excursion fares premised on purchase of a round-trip ticket with a minimum and maximum period in which the return coupon could be used. By the late 1960s it was commonplace to find passengers sitting side by side in the coach section receiving the same service, all at different fares.

In 1974, the CAB issued a decision in the Domestic Passenger Fare Investigation (DPFI) which held that rates should be based closely on costs, and that discount fares had to meet clearly the profit-impact test. Reversing its earlier stand, it prohibited further use of family or youth fares—an action that gave political impetus to the rising deregulation movement. The excursion type of discount fare remained in effect but the amount of the discount was limited.

By 1975, the regulatory reform philosophy was beginning to prevail at the CAB and elsewhere through the government. On the subject of rates, the position was that there was insufficient price competition among the airlines, and that rates should be freed from CAB regulation not only to promote lower fares via more competition, but to encourage innovative fares and services (the price/quality options previously mentioned). The late 1970s saw the introduction of the concept of *zones of reasonableness* (to be described shortly), giving carriers considerable pricing latitude, and, by the end of 1982, pursuant to the ADA, controls were removed altogether from domestic rates.

Domestic Rates after Deregulation

The deregulation of domestic rates has resulted in an expanding use of discount fares. This was especially marked in the 1980s. The proportion of discount traffic to total passenger miles in the domestic services of the major airlines rose from 57 percent in 1980 to 91 percent by 1987, and has remained close to 90 percent thereafter, with the average discount in the 60 to 65 percent range off the full fares.[4] These figures seem especially remarkable in light of the fact that the discount fare is capacity controlled—that is, built around the concept of carefully limiting the number of passengers on each flight who travel at such fares. Clearly the explanation must be that regular fares have been pushed to high levels in order that a great proportion of discount traffic can be carried without having revenue fall below breakeven levels. An analogy may be found in the merchandising of many products, where the list price is set artificially high and discounting is used as a marketing ploy with the tacit understanding that "nobody pays the list price any more."

It should be noted that the 90 percent figure is measured using passenger-*miles*. Since discounting is more likely on longer trips, the percentage would be lower if calculated in terms of numbers of *passengers*, leaving out the mileage factor.

A hazard of the dominance of discount fares is that their very success in filling empty seats may induce airline management to acquire more aircraft (as well as to expand personnel and reservations and ticketing facilities) to accommodate the growing traffic even though the fares being paid by the discount traffic do not cover the fully allocated costs of the added capacity.

We focus now on a familiar term in airline economics—the *yield*—which is the amount of revenue received by the airline per passenger-mile (or per cargo ton-mile). Let us assume that a regular coach fare results in a yield of 12 cents, but a discount fare puts a passenger in a coach seat for a yield of only 10 cents. If more and more people travel at the discount fare and fewer and fewer pay the regular fare, the yield for the coach section as a whole will drop without there having been any reduction in either of the two fares. Under pressure to improve load factors, management may pay insufficient attention to the impact on yield of filling more and more seats with discount traffic. As William H. Waltrip, then-president of Pan American World Airways, has phrased it, "With slight exaggeration one could say that some airline executives slash fares, match lower-priced competitors, liberalize or violate restrictions or conditions for 365 days a year, then on January first they ask: what happened to the yield?"[5]

The term *yield management* has become popular with airline management to describe the careful, computer-assisted control of the number of discount fares available on each flight, keeping them truly capacity-controlled fares, as we have previously discussed, while protecting the yield. In fact, the techniques of yield management are now being introduced into air cargo service, drawing on the passenger experience.

In using yield figures it must be kept in mind that the development of hub-and-spoke networks can distort their significance. Consider two passengers traveling between the same two points and paying the same fare, but with one on a nonstop flight, the other with a plane change at a hub. The yield will be lower for the latter passenger because the fare has been divided by the higher mileage traveled. Yet the lower yield does not mean that that passenger has received a better bargain; on the contrary, the nonstop passenger has received a better service for the same price.

The term *revenue management* has come into use as a development from the term *yield management,* and is really a more descriptive term for the whole procedure, since the goal is to maximize revenue, not merely yield. One source describes the relationship as follows:

Good revenue maximizers seek to obtain the best possible yields and load factors given the circumstances. Yet it is easy to get high yields by excessively raising fares and limiting the availability of discounts—and in the process ensuring nearly empty flights. Similarly, it is easy to maximize load factors by giving the product away. Neither strategy will lead to profitability. . . . The art is to obtain both high load factors and high yields at the same time.[6]

One feature of modern airline pricing is the almost instantaneous speed with which a change in a fare by one airline can be matched by its competitors. The mechanism involves the Airline Tariff Publishing Company (ATPCO), owned by 24 airlines, including the seven largest U.S. majors. The *Wall Street Journal* describes the procedure as follows: "Every carrier sends its fare changes to ATPCO, whose centralized computer system sends a download seven times a day to computer reservation systems used by travel agents—and to the airlines themselves . . . ATPCO says its two mainframe computers create a perfect marketplace, akin to a gas station owner being able to watch prices his competitor posts across the street."[7] To appreciate the remarkable complexity of this procedure, one should note that there are about 50,000 fare changes a *day* in the U.S. domestic market alone.[8]

Deregulation has also given rise to many new types of price/quality options, as its proponents had predicted. We have already given examples of these in Chapter 5—use of a secondary airport, reduced meal and baggage services, closely packed seating, fewer nonstop and one-plane services, advance-purchase and other ticketing limitations—all in return for actual or presumed fare savings. There are also price/quality options for those prepared to pay a *higher* price: a separate section for full-fare coach passengers, or a luxury service at a premium price. Many airlines have a "business class" at a fare above coach but below first class; these passengers have a separate section with more spacious seating and higher-quality meals than in the coach section.

What might also be considered a price/quality option, or at least a price option, is the negotiating of special agreements between airlines and corporations to obtain discounts for the corporation's employees when traveling on company business. Such agreements were forbidden in the days before deregulation. Although the airlines do not like to advertise the fact, it appears that the corporate discount practice has become extensive, although the favored rates may apply only on specified city pairs, not throughout an airline's system. Of course, it is the large corporation (and also the U.S. government) with a high volume of employee travel that has the bargaining power to win discounts. It is the smaller business entity that pays the high full fare for much of its employee travel. This situation may be questioned as a matter of fairness and of public policy, especially when it is realized that small firms are innovators and job creators.[9]

Airlines often offer special reduced rates for travel to business conventions. And, of course, the large discounts offered to lure the leisure traffic may be used for business travel if the advance purchase and other conditions can be met. Thus, much business travel is also discount travel, even where there is no negotiated corporate rate.

Frequent Flyer Programs

In 1981 the airlines began instituting frequent flyer programs, under which a passenger is awarded points (in the form of coupons or certificates) for every flight taken on one airline, the number of points being based on the flight distance and sometimes on the type of ticket purchased. For example, in 1988 American Airlines was awarding a mileage-based number of points for coach tickets, whether or not at discount fares, 120 percent of that number for a business-class ticket, 150 percent for a first-class ticket. After accumulating a sufficient number of points, the passenger may obtain free flights (subject to availability under a capacity-control system), discounts on flights, or free upgrades from one class to another. Many airlines have arrangements with suppliers of other services, such as hotels and car rental companies, so that hotel stays and car rentals may win points or may be part of what is earned through the accumulation of points.

Some airlines have tie-ins with foreign airlines so that they can offer trips to many foreign vacation sites as free trips earned by an accumulation of points. Many major airlines will award points for travel on the regional or commuter carriers with which they maintain code-sharing operating alliances, discussed in Chapter 3.

Through the 1990s, all the major passenger airlines had frequent flyer programs. According to a DOT estimate in 1990, there were about 33.9 million frequent flyer memberships, but because many persons held memberships with several airlines, the number of *persons* involved was "indeterminate."[10] A later estimate (1996) shows 38 million memberships.[11] While a person may hold membership in as many programs as desired, points won by traveling on one airline cannot be cashed in on another, except where "alliances" and similar tie-in arrangements include mutual acceptance of one carrier's points by another. In fact, the motive of an airline for establishing a frequent flyer program is to develop repeat customers. Since what the airlines offer is in many ways an undifferentiated product, as was pointed out in Chapter 1, it is an important marketing goal for an airline to capture passengers for repeated trips by getting them interested—the term "hooked" has been used by some critics—in the process of accumulating points toward a free vacation trip.

Though the programs are not by any means confined to business travelers, one widespread use has involved a person traveling at company expense on company business, earning points in the form of coupons that can be accumulated and later cashed in for free personal vacation travel. Some employers, of course, require that coupons so earned be turned in to the company to be cashed in for future company travel, but such policies apparently are the exception rather than the rule.

Businesses have had problems arising from frequent flyer programs, which burden them with wasteful costs. An employee has an incentive to take unnecessary trips at company expense, or to take circuitous routings on necessary trips, in order to earn frequent flyer mileage for later personal use. Or an employee who has been building up frequent flyer points on a particular airline may select that airline for business travel even though travel by a different carrier would be less expensive. A company may, of course, control such expenses by careful auditing of travel expenses.

Frequent flyer programs raise a variety of other problems. From the airlines' standpoint, it may well be that the process of winning repeat customers tends to cancel itself out, since every large passenger airline has such a program. Meanwhile, the airlines have built up a potential liability in the form of mileage credits earned but not yet cashed in. According to one estimate, in 1991 this was about $2.6 billion for the U.S. scheduled airline industry; a later estimate (1994) shows a liability of $380 million for American Airlines alone.[12] Such estimates, however, are not particularly meaningful for several reasons. Much mileage is never redeemed. Other mileage is used to upgrade from one class to another rather than for free travel. And the airlines apply capacity controls to frequent flyer redemptions along the same lines as they use to limit the availability of discount tickets; thus, to the extent that these controls are effective, the "free" passenger is filling an otherwise empty seat and the expense to the airline is only the small added or out-of-pocket cost. Consequently, an airline has a contingent liability, but it is far less than the face value of the outstanding mileage credits and hard to measure.

In addition to capacity controls on airline seats, seasonal blackout periods are being used, and capacity controls are being placed on free, mileage-earned hotel space at some points. Yet the airlines may face customer resentment, rather than the desired customer loyalty, from all these restrictions. Also, the obvious penchant of passengers to cash in their mileage for trips to the most popular vacation spots can result in pressure on an airline to relax capacity controls on these routes so as to avoid having to deny space to the frequent flyers whose goodwill it has sought to cultivate. Such relaxation, of course, means revenue lost from a paying passenger displaced by a free one.

From the standpoint of the public interest there are several criticisms of frequent flyer programs. Ultimately their costs must be covered by a generally higher fare level. These costs include the expense of administering the programs, the added cost of carrying the free passenger, and the total revenue lost if, despite capacity controls, an otherwise paying passenger is displaced. Then there is a lessening of the competitive pressure that deregulation was supposed to bring; passengers intent on building up points for future free flights will not select the lowest fare if that is not on the airline whose frequent flyer program they have selected. New and small airlines are placed at a severe disadvantage in competing with the majors; they do not serve enough cities so that a passenger can build up a great number of points, nor do they serve a large number of attractive distant vacation destinations that a passenger may look forward to as a reward. As a general rule, the larger a carrier's network, the more plausible it will be for a passenger to sign up for its frequent flyer program. Thus these programs become a factor in the trend back to oligopoly described in Chapter 3.

There is also a problem of government tax policy in those instances where an employee travels at company expense, then uses the accumulated points to obtain free personal travel. Free travel thus obtained could reasonably be construed as income. Despite this fact, as of the late 1990s the Internal Revenue Service was reportedly not insisting that the value of such free mileage be declared as income. Should it change its position, the attractiveness of the frequent flyer programs would be reduced, though not eliminated.

The Impact of Deregulation on Rates

What has been the overall impact of deregulation on the general level of passenger fares? Various studies in the 1980s generally show that basic fares rose, especially at smaller points and for shorter hauls, but discounting became so prevalent that the average passenger was paying less, sometimes much less, than in the era of regulation.[13]

All data as to the impact of deregulation on the level of passenger fares must be used with caution. We have already noted that hub-and-spoke networks typically involve greater mileage than would nonstop services and thus show a lower yield figure although there has been no reduction in the fare. It should also be noted that had there been no deregulation, overall reductions in real (inflation-adjusted) fares would likely have occurred due to cost savings from improved technology of aircraft and engines as well as labor through, for example, automated baggage handling and CRSs. This has been the long-run trend of airline history. Data from the Air Transport Association for the period between 1965 and 1995—approximately half before deregulation and half after—show a steady, nearly parallel drop in both passenger yield and total operating expenses for U.S. scheduled airlines, with figures adjusted for inflation.[14] Perhaps the best that can be said as to the impact of deregulation on airline fares is that it must remain a matter of conjecture in light of all the elements involved.

Certain aspects of the current fare situation, notably those that impose hardships, raise public interest questions. No-refund provisions, or high penalties for refunds, are an obvious example, especially when the loss to a passenger runs to hundreds or even thousands of dollars. Also, the high price of coach travel when the need to fly is a last-minute emergency bears heavily on the poorest among us whose only use of air travel may be at just such times. They would be better off if less discounting allowed for lower regular coach fares. Others among us may feel that fares have simply become too complicated and confusing to the point of being a hardship on the public. Perhaps there is a public interest in simplicity and stability.

RATE REGULATION

In 1938 the CAB was given the power to regulate rates for airline services both within the United States and between the United States and foreign countries. This authority was altered by the three major regulatory reform laws that were mentioned in Chapter 1: the act of November 9, 1977, which reformed the regulation of domestic air cargo; the Airline Deregulation Act of 1978; and the International Air Transportation Competition Act, enacted February 15, 1980. Under this legislation CAB authority over domestic airline rates terminated at the end of 1982 (except, perhaps, over fares for essential air service, as will be seen shortly). Regulation of international rates, however, continued under the CAB until that agency was abolished, and continues indefinitely under DOT.

It is unlikely that regulation of international rates can ever be entirely done away with while some foreign governments favor—indeed, insist upon—such regulation at their end of the international trip. However, regulatory reform legislation made changes in the goals and legal machinery in the Federal Aviation Act (now in the transportation statute) affecting international rate regulation, with the aim of enlarging managerial pricing discretion and increasing price competition. The general guidelines can be found today in Section 41509(a)(3) of the transportation statute. They include "whether the price will be predatory or tend to monopolize competition," and "reasonably estimated or foreseeable future costs and revenues for the air carrier or foreign air carrier for a reasonably limited future period during which the price would be in effect."

Governmental policy concerning airline rates often must balance the interests of the airlines against those of the consumer. This was a CAB problem in the days before deregulation, and is a problem today for DOT in monitoring international rates and for Congress in considering new legislation. Airline management, like the management of any business, will seek a profit for its stockholders, and in an expanding industry such as air transportation it is particularly necessary that the profit be adequate to attract new capital to invest in new plant—primarily in new and increasingly expensive aircraft. Governmental policy should assist the airlines to make just such a profit but at the same time protect consumers from rates that are unreasonable or unjustly discriminatory. Yet the interest of the consumer is by no means always in opposition to that of the airlines. Indeed, it certainly can be argued that the public has a great stake in having profitable airlines that can offer safe, efficient service and have the capital to invest in new and better aircraft.

At this point let us first have an understanding of a basic document that continues to be of at least some pertinence to international rates: the airline tariff.

What Is a Tariff?

Tariffs existed in the world of transportation long before there were airlines, and were considered complicated and even downright tricky documents, understood fully only by experts who spent their lives dealing with them. Fortunately, airline tariffs are simpler than those of other modes of transportation.

Basically, an airline tariff is a list showing the carrier's rates and rules. Where rates are regulated, a tariff consists, strictly speaking, only of those lists filed with and accepted by the regulatory agency (formerly CAB, now DOT), but the term is commonly used to mean any published list of airline rates and rules. Very likely an airline will have separate tariffs for passengers and cargo, and perhaps separate tariffs for charters or ones that contain no rates at all but merely list rules such as requirements for protective packaging for certain types of cargo. Nowadays the list will often be in computerized form. Today, since there is no domestic rate regulation, tariffs are required to be filed only (1) by foreign air carriers and (2) by U.S. airlines with respect to their international services.

The rate shown in a tariff filed with the regulatory agency is called the *legal rate*, meaning that it is the rate that the carrier is obliged by law to charge. However, the international rate tariffs filed with DOT have lost much of their significance in recent years, due to several factors:

1. Since there is no longer domestic rate regulation, the airlines do not have to file tariffs with DOT for these rates.
2. Nowadays, tariffs are no longer filed in document form, but electronically under rules established by DOT.
3. Many rate changes are allowed to become effective immediately upon filing, without the statutory 30-day delay.
4. DOT intervention to suspend or cancel a rate in a tariff is limited by the deregulation philosophy which seeks to give carriers maximum pricing freedom.
5. Where the United States has an "open skies" bilateral agreement (as explained in Chapter 3) a "double disapproval" rate clause is included for the express purpose of giving the carriers maximum freedom to set their own rates.

There also seems to be considerable discrepancy between theory and practice in the observance of international tariffs. Both U.S. and foreign airlines, for example, have been known to sell blocks of tickets to some travel agencies at wholesale prices, which the agencies then resell to the public at below-tariff rates. The practice offers consumers lower-fare travel and is arguably a pressure that promotes competition, thus having an appeal to the deregulation philosophy. There seems little desire in DOT to apply penalties to enforce tariffs.

It should be remembered, however, that DOT holds in reserve the power to suspend or cancel an international rate, either when a tariff change is filed or on its own initiative. Then, if the problem cannot be worked out informally with the airline, there can be a hearing procedure at the conclusion of which DOT may reject the proposed rate change or cancel an existing rate.

Grounds for Suspension, Rejection, or Cancellation

The Federal Aviation Act contained complex language defining the grounds on which DOT could suspend a proposed tariff change and, after hearings, reject or cancel an international rate. When that act was incorporated into the transportation statute in 1994, the language was simplified. The grounds can now be broken down into two categories— "unreasonably discriminatory" and, simply, "unreasonable" (Section 41509 [a][1]).

Unreasonably Discriminatory Rates

An example of a rate that is unreasonably discriminatory might be one where a bargain fare is introduced at one city that is not offered at a neighboring city. In justification, the airline would present data on costs and demand; in today's permissive regulatory climate it is likely that DOT would give the benefit of any doubt to airline management. Clearly, the word "unreasonably" placed before "discriminatory" in the statute gives DOT very broad latitude.

Although we have emphasized that DOT control over rates is limited to international operations, it is conceivable that DOT might, if it chose, assert authority over unreasonable discrimination with respect to a *domestic* rate under a different provision of the transportation statute, Section 41712, that bars "an unfair or deceptive practice" or "an unfair method of competition." The policy of DOT, however, has been to assume that the free market will correct discriminations. Intervention by DOT, whether the rate is domestic or international, is not likely except in an extreme circumstance where market forces not only did not justify the discrimination but seemed unlikely to correct it.

Notably, DOT does not intervene when the "yield management" process, which we have described earlier, results in passengers on the same flight receiving identical service but paying a multiplicity of different fares. Under the broad language of the statute, "unreasonably discriminatory" could be interpreted to apply, but in fact it is not.

One type of rate discrimination that might be challenged as unjust is where the fare to the end of the line is lower than the fare to an intermediate point. This is traditionally known in the transportation world as "long-short discrimination," requiring cost justification to be permitted. Fare discriminations of this sort occur often today, but DOT would hear the airline's cost and demand analysis and would likely give the benefit of any doubt to the airline.

Unreasonable Rates

A rate may be unreasonable when it is either too high or too low, and it is easy to find grounds for the former. If an airline is making extremely high profits for a substantial period of time, it can very plausibly be argued that its general level of rates is unreasonably high and that the airline is taking inequitable advantage of the public. Similarly, it may be found that rates being charged by an airline in a particular market or region are unreasonably high in terms of the cost of the service—that the profit margin in the market or region is unconscionable—or that a particular type of fare, such as a first-class fare, may be earning an unjustifiably high profit for the airline. How great a profit is unreasonable? This is an area of opinion, but it is possible to calculate the cost of the service against the revenue and compare the profitability of the fare with the general experience of the industry.

Regulatory reform theory, however, emphasizes competition, rather than governmental action, to hold rates to reasonable levels. Where profit margins in a market are high, other airlines will be attracted and will enter the market, with a resulting downward pressure on rates. Still, where competitive forces do not produce this desired result—as, for example, in an international market where entry control is insisted upon by the foreign government—we may in the future see action by DOT against unreasonably high rates.

We may also see such DOT action in a situation where an alliance among U.S. and foreign carriers includes coordinated fare-setting and where the alliance so dominates an international market that its members can charge high fares with little fear of effective competition.

Parenthetically, we should note that there is one domestic area where DOT has authority over the reasonableness of rates—the small-community essential air service program. It is permitted, when administering this program, to require that fares not be "excessive when compared to the generally prevailing fares of other air carriers for like service between similar pairs of points" (Section 41732 [b] [2]).

It may be more difficult to envisage when a rate is unreasonably *low*.

One instance is when the low-cost carrier in a particular market proposes a fare cut that its competitors cannot meet without severe losses. In the past the CAB often permitted such a fare cut on grounds that the more efficient airline should be allowed to set the pace and that the public was entitled to the benefit. On the other hand, there were situations where the board sought to protect the higher-cost carriers, even though it meant denying the public the lower fare, if it felt that it was more important to keep the other competitors in the market than to pass on to the public the advantages of the lower fare.

Regulatory reform theory now enters the picture. Airlines, it is argued, should not be protected from more efficient competitors; if they are forced to drop markets or go out of business altogether, the low-cost competitor who has done this to them will not for long enjoy a monopolistic situation because other efficient operators will come into the markets under a free entry policy.

Nevertheless, there is a type of unreasonably low fare, described as "predatory," that seems likely to continue to be the subject of governmental regulation. This is a fare set so low that it threatens to drive a competitor out of a market and that, moreover, is not justifiable by the airline's cost and demand situation. The term is a relative newcomer to the vocabulary of airline rate regulation, appearing for the first time in the mid-1970s, in an amendment to the Federal Aviation Act that added it to the "Rule of Ratemaking" applicable to foreign air transportation. It is now found in Section 41509(a) (3) (F) of the transportation statute and defined in Section 40102(a) (34) as "a practice that violates the antitrust laws." With the expiration of CAB jurisdiction over domestic passenger rates at the end of 1982, a predatory domestic passenger fare became the concern of DOJ, which applies to the airlines the regular antitrust laws that apply to all industries. DOT also could become involved with a predatory domestic fare if it elected to act under Section 41712 which, as earlier described, gives it the power to act against "an unfair or deceptive practice or unfair method of competition."

But it is with respect to international rates that the adjective *predatory* is likely to have its greatest application. If a foreign airline were to introduce a fare so low that the U.S. airline or airlines in the market could not match it except by accepting severe losses, the charge would very likely be made that this fare was predatory. The DOT would then employ the legal machinery with respect to suspension, rejection, or cancellation described earlier. A finding that a fare was predatory would be more likely if it could be shown that the foreign airline received a subsidy from its government that enabled it to institute loss operations to gain an advantage over its unsubsidized U.S. competitors. The "predatory" concept could also come into play if a powerful alliance of U.S. and foreign carriers (or of foreign carriers alone) were to introduce coordinated fares that threatened to wipe out their competition.

Zones of Reasonableness

The concept of a zone of reasonableness gathered favor during the 1970s as a device to give management greater latitude in pricing. The idea was that the CAB would not find a proposed rate change to be unreasonably low or high if it did not exceed a specified percentage.

Consumer groups and many other proponents of regulatory reform seemed to look upon the zone of reasonableness concept as a way to get *lower* fares by enabling the airlines to compete readily for the consumer dollar. The airlines, however, seemed to look upon the concept as a device to enable them to *raise* fares swiftly to keep up with inflationary costs.

The upshot was that the ADA placed zone-type limits on the CAB's authority to find domestic passenger fares unreasonable. The term *standard industry fare level* (SIFL) was introduced, meaning the fare level in effect on July 1, 1977, for each domestic pair of points for each class of service, with adjustments to be made by the board not less than every six months on the basis of the actual operating costs per seat-mile. A zone was then established around the SIFLs of 5 percent upward and 50 percent downward. The great difference in the two percentages reflects the airline practice of letting fares rise slowly with inflation of costs, while cutting fares by means of dramatic and attention-getting discounts.

The system of SIFLs was effective only for the transition period between the enactment of the ADA in 1978 and the termination of domestic rate controls at the end of 1982.

Of greater significance today is a similar provision for international passenger rates, put in the Federal Aviation Act by the IATCA in 1980, because, unlike the domestic provisions, it remains effective indefinitely, and administering it is an important duty of DOT. A *standard foreign fare level* (SFFL) has been provided for, based initially on fares as of October 1, 1979, for each international pair of points for each class of service, subject to adjustments at least every six months based on "the actual operating costs per available seat mile." A separate additional adjustment process was established, to be applied at least every 60 days, based solely on fuel costs. The zone is the same as the one established earlier for domestic passenger fares—5 percent upward, 50 percent downward. The downward percentage may be increased by DOT, but not the upward. A fare increase cannot be suspended if it is within the 5 percent zone unless it is found "unreasonably discriminatory." A fare decrease cannot be suspended if it is within the 50 percent zone unless it is "predatory or discriminatory." These provisions of the Federal Aviation Act were placed in the transportation statute in 1994, with no change in substance, as Section 41509(e).

With respect to international cargo rates, there was no similar provision put into the Federal Aviation Act by IATCA. However, the CAB in 1983 created for these rates a "zone of flexibility within which rates may be set without a requirement for economic justification." The term *standard foreign rate level* (SFRL) was used, and there was provision for periodic adjustment on a cost basis. CAB policy was that international cargo rates would not be suspended "except in extraordinary circumstances."[15] DOT administers international cargo rates in a similar fashion, maintaining the SFRL but leaving broad latitude to airline management.

The foregoing discussion of international rates (passenger and cargo) applies to the services of both U.S. and foreign airlines. However, two features of the transportation statute not yet mentioned apply only to the foreign airlines ("foreign air carriers" in the legal parlance of the statute). DOT may construe a fare of a foreign airline to or from the United States to be unreasonably high or low even if it is within the zone of reasonableness if there have been "unreasonable regulatory actions" by the airline's government with respect to fare proposals by a U.S. airline. There is also a provision of the statute, entirely aside from the question of zones of reasonableness, that grants to DOT the power to cancel or reject a tariff of a foreign airline if the agency concludes "with or without a hearing" that such action "is in the public interest" (Section 41509[a][2]). These rather sweeping powers are not, of course, intended for everyday use, but are bargaining ploys to be used in disputes with foreign governments.

The practical result of the use of zones of reasonableness today is that most changes in international passenger or cargo rates that airline management wishes to make can be made with little fear of U.S. government disapproval. However, when DOT does intervene, its actions in evaluating a rate reflect the type of rate provision in the bilateral agreement with the foreign country involved—a matter we will take up shortly.

The Role of the President in International Rate Regulation

Orders concerning international rates issued by DOT must be cleared through the White House before being issued if they suspend, reject, or cancel a rate. The president is empowered by Section 41509(f) of the statute to "disapprove the order on finding disapproval is necessary for United States foreign policy or national defense reasons." In practice, this means that the Departments of State and Defense are consulted and may urge presidential disapproval. The president has ten days to act; if there is no disapproval action within that time, the order is issued. Note that the president does not act affirmatively on international rate orders but merely acts to *disapprove* when unusual circumstances justify. Presidential action is thus very infrequent and reserved for a few controversial cases.

Reregulation of Domestic Rates

There have been many proposals to reestablish some degree of governmental control over the reasonableness of domestic rates. Some would simply restore the powers formerly held by the CAB, though now to be exercised by DOT. Others would leave domestic rates largely in the hands of the airlines, but would allow DOT to intervene under certain conditions—for example, a ceiling could be placed on rates in a market dominated by one airline. Interestingly, an early draft of the ADA in the 1970s would have retained such a power over unreasonably high rates in such markets, and the CAB (though by then dominated by pro-deregulation opinion) supported the proposed provision. The board would have defined a market where one airline carried 70 percent or more of the traffic as a market dominated by one carrier. Congress did not agree, and the provision did not survive into the final version of the ADA.

Other proposals would give DOT power to intervene selectively to set a floor under unreasonably low rates as well as a ceiling over those it found unreasonably high. This approach would seek to protect the public from excessive rates, to protect the airlines from destructive price wars, and to make it somewhat less difficult for small and/or new-entrant carriers to maintain themselves against the giants.

In April 1998, DOT proposed guidelines for determining when a carrier is engaging in unfair practices. In general, the guidelines would look at whether a major carrier, in competing with a new entrant, had met the new entrant's low fares or lowered its fares "substantially below" what they had been, and whether the number of passengers carried by the major at the new lower fares exceeded the number of low-fare passengers carried by the new entrant. The guidelines would also look at whether the major had added capacity in response to the new entrant and, especially, whether it had filled such capacity at a very low fare.[16]

DOT's proposal met with strong opposition from the airlines and in Congress. No final guidelines were issued and, as of late 1999, it did not appear that they would be.

INTERNATIONAL RATES—DEALINGS WITH FOREIGN GOVERNMENTS

The setting and governing of the rates that both U.S. and foreign air-lines charge for services between the United States and foreign points involve a basic principle: that, as with international entry, the airlines must have the approval in some form of the governments *at both ends* of the passenger's trip for the rate being charged (and likewise for cargo). This governmental approval may be tacit or blanket, although nearly always it involves some manner of rate control spelled out in the same bilateral agreement that grants entry rights, as discussed in Chapter 3.

Until the late 1970s most bilateral agreements provided that the basic job of ratemaking would be done by the association of world airlines called the International Air Transport Association (IATA), subject to the approval of the respective governments for each package of rates. (The abbreviation IATA is in extremely common use and is usually pro-nounced with the accent on the first syllable, "Eye-ata.") Since that time, the role of IATA in ratemaking has diminished so greatly, especially with respect to services to or from the United States, that we need look only briefly at its workings before examining the trend away from it in recent years.

The International Air Transport Association

Unlike bodies such as the United Nations or the International Civil Aviation Organization (ICAO), which are made up of governments, IATA consists of airlines, not governments, though some of these airlines are government corporations. Any airline that has international service may become a member, and most of the airlines of the world with sub-stantial international services belong.

IATA holds conferences at which airline officials seek to work out the rates that all of them will charge. Over the years, the CAB (and later DOT) reviewed what the airlines did at a conference and approved or disapproved a rate package, or disapproved particular rates in a package by placing reservations on an approval action. Approval includes ex-emption from the antitrust laws which the U.S. airlines would otherwise be violating. Today, IATA rate agreements are still being submitted to DOT, which approves them with the antitrust exemption, even though it views IATA rate actions as advisory, rather than binding, on the air-lines.

IATA is accused of being a cartel, and it certainly bears one aspect of a cartel: it sets prices, and its members are supposed to charge the agreed-upon prices. Other aspects of a cartel, however, are lacking. IATA does not allocate markets or determine the extent of participation in them by its members. That is to say, it has no jurisdiction over the decisions as to entry or frequency or capacity; as we have seen in Chapter 3, these are matters handled bilaterally between governments. Also, IATA is non-exclusive—that is, it must admit any airline that has an international service. And, as already noted, its rate decisions have no effect unless approved by the governments.

IATA has functions other than ratemaking, although the latter is its best-known and most controversial work. One important task is to act as a clearinghouse for ticket coupons. Thus, a passenger may buy a ticket from a domestic airline at an inland U.S. city to travel around the world with a series of stopovers involving the use of a dozen airlines of as many nationalities. The airline selling the ticket collects the money while each of the other airlines merely takes a ticket coupon from the passenger upon boarding each flight. The task of obtaining payments for these coupons resembles the behind-the-scenes work of our banking system with respect to checking accounts. IATA has a staff that performs the elaborate paperwork, made all the more elaborate by language barriers and the different currencies involved.

IATA also assists with other problems, such as fuel shortages, hijacking, navigation, and safety, and provides a useful forum for airing such topics, although its role is largely advisory.

The Changing U.S. Position on IATA

Over the years there has been much criticism in the United States of the IATA ratemaking function, and it was a favorite target of deregulation proponents.

In 1978, the CAB issued a show-cause order proposing that it terminate its approval of the whole IATA ratemaking system. This order caused such a furor among foreign airlines and their governments that final action was repeatedly postponed and the proposal finally was withdrawn. While the show-cause order was pending, IATA made two amendments to its procedures in an effort to placate the United States. One of these permitted an airline to belong to IATA and participate in its various functions—such as its clearinghouse for airline tickets and its safety and economic studies—without having to participate in the ratemaking function. The other change was to allow a loophole whereby two governments could permit experimental, innovative rates outside the provisions of the IATA package, as long as these rates applied only to traffic between their two countries.

Although the ADA, as amended by the Sunset Act, terminated some of DOT's functions with respect to exemptions from antitrust laws, the power was left intact to grant immunity for airline agreements concerning international services. As of 1999, DOT was continuing to approve

IATA rate agreements that it found acceptable, but the Department of Justice was on record as wanting DOT to cease such approvals.

Non-IATA International Rate Regulation

Even prior to the show-cause order on IATA, the U.S. government was attempting to negotiate changes in its bilateral agreements that would permit pricing outside the IATA system and that would increase managerial pricing discretion. In March 1978 it signed an agreement with the Netherlands amending the basic bilateral air transport agreement so as to introduce language concerning rates that was a novel departure from previous practice. The new language stated that the two governments "shall encourage individual airlines to develop and implement competitive fares, rates, and prices." Furthermore, the two governments agreed

that such fares, rates, and prices should be set by each designated airline based primarily on commercial considerations in the marketplace and that governmental intervention should be limited to prevention of predatory or discriminatory practices, protection of consumers from the abuse of monopoly power, and protection of airlines from prices that are artificially low because of direct or indirect governmental subsidy or support.[17]

A few months later, in August 1978, the United States and Israel signed an agreement amending their basic bilateral agreement so as to include an even further departure from earlier practice in the form of a "double disapproval" rate article. Under this article no airline rate between the two countries will be suspended by either government unless the other government concurs in the action.

There has also been recourse to "country-of-origin" rate articles. Under these the United States may regulate the rates of airline traffic outbound from the United States, while the foreign government regulates rates for traffic in the opposite direction. (A round-trip ticket is priced according to the country of origin.)

When the rate arrangements are either "country-of-origin" or "double-disapproval," the bilateral agreement typically will include the language quoted above from the Netherlands agreement of 1978, or very similar language. The idea is to state the *grounds* on which a rate might be disapproved, while the "country-of-origin" and "double-disapproval" provisions specify who does the disapproving. Of course, either of these provisions takes rates between the two countries out of the IATA system for all practical purposes, although IATA may still have a bearing on rates for third-country traffic along the routes in question.

Experimentation with rate articles of these types has occurred in a series of amendments to bilateral agreements. In order to obtain these rate provisions (as well as the liberal or nonexistent frequency/capacity limitations that have usually accompanied them), the United States has had to give the airlines of many of these countries routes to numerous U.S. cities, including inland points such as Atlanta and Dallas. Critics have charged that the United States has given more than it has received in the trade-off.

U.S. policy clearly favors the double disapproval rate provision in bilateral agreements. In fact, DOT included it in its definition of an open skies agreement (referred to in Chapter 3) in an order issued in 1992.[18]

Summary of the International Rate Picture

Earlier in this chapter we noted that most changes that airline management wishes to make in international passenger or cargo rates can be made today with little chance of DOT disapproval, but that in those instances where DOT chooses to intervene, its actions in evaluating a rate reflect the type of rate provision in the pertinent bilateral agreement. A look at this evaluation process with respect to international passenger fares may help to clarify the rather complex legal and administrative mechanisms we have been discussing.

There are three types of rate articles in bilateral agreements:

1. The double-disapproval type. Here an airline's rate initiatives can be interfered with only by both governments acting jointly. Thus, it is the article that gives the broadest latitude to management, the article under which international rates come closest to being totally deregulated. Not only is IATA irrelevant, but DOT ordinarily does not interfere with managerial discretion at all, and does not even use the SFFL.

2. The country-of-origin type, where each government regulates only the outbound rates. Here IATA is also irrelevant, and DOT usually elects not to interfere with managerial discretion, usually elects not to use the SFFL at all.

3. The Bermuda type, citing IATA as the source for rate determination and requiring approval of rates by both governments, sometimes called a "double-approval" article. DOT, wishing to give management maximum leeway, looks upon IATA rates as advisory rather than binding. It will usually apply SFFL standards, but will allow deviations from them in its discretion. The foreign government, of course, may require that IATA rates be charged, but the trend among many of them is to allow flexibility.

Where does all this leave IATA? One writer, Professor Paul S. Dempsey, has said: "In a practical sense, the IATA has been transformed from an international quasi-regulatory agency to an influential trade association."[19] But this comment may somewhat overstate the situation. IATA still makes rate packages, which DOT approves (although it is not much guided by them), and some governments in important airline markets still follow IATA actions.

A look at the international rate picture would not be complete without noting once again the prevalence of tariff violations in international airline services—the gap between theory and practice. We have seen that both U.S. and foreign airlines sell blocks of tickets at wholesale prices to agencies, and the agencies then retail them at below-tariff rates. There are other evasions, such as an airline's charging the appropriate fare but offering a bonus such as a free hotel stay or car rental. IATA used to have its own enforcement program, but it was felt to be ineffective and was abolished in 1978. And we have noted that DOT shows little enthusiasm for the difficult and unpopular task of ferreting out and punishing tariff violations, due likely, at least in part, to the fact that evasions of tariffs that offer the consumer lower fares appeal to the deregulation philosophy.

Thus far in this book we have been emphasizing airline passenger service, consistent with its role as generator of about 90 percent of airline revenues. Yet, for the future, air cargo is of great significance, both to the airlines and to the national and world economies. There are even predictions that someday cargo, instead of being a minor part of airline revenues, will become a major or even dominant proportion. Our next chapter will be devoted to the problems of air cargo.

NOTES

1. Melvin A. Brenner, "The Significance of Airline Passenger Load Factors," in *Airline Economics*, ed. George W. James (Lexington, Mass.: D.C. Heath, 1982), pp. 51–52.

2. John R. Meyer and Clinton V. Oster, Jr., *Deregulation and the Future of Intercity Passenger Travel* (Cambridge, Mass.: The MIT Press, 1987), p. 79.

3. Donald Garvett and Laurence Michaels, "Price Parrying: A Direction for Quick, Decisive, and Profit-Maximizing Pricing," in *Handbook of Airline Marketing*, ed. Gail F. Butler and Martin R. Keller (Washington, D.C.: McGraw-Hill, 1998), p. 335.

4. Paul S. Dempsey and Laurence E. Gesell, *Airline Management: Strategies for the 21st Century* (Chandler, Ariz.: Coast Aire Publications, 1997), p. 289.

5. William H. Waltrip, "International Planning," in *Airline Economics*, ed. George W. James (Lexington, Mass.: D.C. Heath, 1982), p. 291.

6. Donald S. Garvett and Kyle J. Hilton, "What Drives Airline Profits?," in *Handbook of Airline Finance*, ed. Gail F. Butler and Martin R. Keller (Washington, D.C.: McGraw-Hill, 1999), p. 181.

7. *Wall Street Journal*, November 3, 1997, p. A-6.

8. Robert G. Cross, "An Introduction to Revenue Management," in *Handbook of Airline Economics*, ed. Darryl Jenkins (Washington, D.C.: McGraw-Hill, 1995), p. 453.

9. Dempsey and Gesell, *Airline Management*, pp. 307–8.

10. U.S. Department of Transportation, *Secretary's Task Force on Competition in the U.S. Domestic Airline Industry*, 1990, p. 40.

11. Dempsey and Gesell, *Airline Management*, p. 229.

12. *Wall Street Journal*, April 30, 1991, p. B-4; Dempsey and Gesell, *Airline Management*, p. 229.

13. Civil Aeronautics Board, *Implementation of the Provisions of the Airline Deregulation Act of 1978*, Report to Congress, January 31, 1984, p. 79; Meyer and Oster, *Deregulation and the Future of Intercity Passenger Travel*, pp. 111–13 and 124; and Transportation Research Board, *Winds of Change: Domestic Air Transport Since Deregulation* (Washington, D.C.: National Research Council, 1991), pp. 98 and 129.

14. Anthony C. Homan, "Changes in Airline Operating Expenses: Effects on Demand and Airline Profits," in *Handbook of Airline Finance*, ed. Gail F. Butler and Martin R. Keller (Washington, D.C.: Mc-Graw Hill, 1999), p. 505.

15. Civil Aeronautics Board, *Implementation of the Provisions*, pp. 64 and 90.

16. Raymond E. Neidl, "Current Financial and Operational Trends in the Airline Industry," in *Handbook of Airline Finance*, ed. Gail F. Butler and Martin R. Keller (Washington, D.C.: McGraw-Hill, 1999), p. 620.

17. U.S. Department of State, *Protocol Relating to U.S.-Netherlands Air Transport Agreement of 1957*, T.I.A.S. no. 8998, art. 6(a), 1978.

18. U.S. Department of Transportation Order No. 92–8-13, August 5, 1992.

19. Paul S. Dempsey, "Aerial Dogfights over Europe: The Liberalization of EEC Air Transport," *Journal of Air Law and Commerce* 53 (1988): 625.

SELECTED REFERENCES

Pricing theory, airline price competition from the late 1940s to 1981, and the early effects of deregulation on rates are covered in Paul Biederman, *The U.S. Airline Industry: End of an Era* (New York: Praeger, 1982), chap. 7, pp. 103–22.

The impact of deregulation on domestic passenger fares is discussed in John R. Meyer and Clinton V. Oster Jr., *Deregulation and the Future of Intercity Passenger Travel* (Cambridge, Mass.: The MIT Press, 1987), chap. 7, pp. 109–24; and in Transportation Research Board, *Winds of Change: Domestic Air Transport Since Deregulation* (Washington, D.C.: National Research Council, 1991), chap. 3 and pp. 276–78.

The intricate details of yield management are delineated in Michael W. Tretheway and Tae H. Oum, *Airline Economics: Foundations for Strategy and Policy* (Vancouver, Canada: Centre for Transportation Studies, 1992), pp. 32–46.

Two more recent analyses of yield management, which the authors would prefer to call "revenue management," are to be found in Paul S. Dempsey and Laurence E. Gesell, *Airline Management: Strategies for the 21st Century* (Chandler, Ariz.: Coast Aire Publications, 1997), pp. 291–301; and Robert G. Cross, "Trends in Airline Revenue Management," in *Handbook of Airline Marketing*, ed. Gail F. Butler and Martin R. Keller (Washington, D.C.: McGraw-Hill, 1998), pp. 303–18.

Frequent flyer programs are described and analyzed in U.S. Department of Transportation, *Secretary's Task Force on Competition in the U.S. Domestic Airline*

Industry, 1990, pp. 31–42; an analysis of these programs, taking a dim view of them, can be found in Tretheway and Oum, *Airline Economics*, pp. 53–59.

A more recent analysis of frequent flyer programs can be found in Donald S. Garvett and Alex Avery, "Frequent Traveler Programs: Moving Targets," in *Handbook of Airline Marketing*, ed. Gail F. Butler and Martin R. Keller (Washington, D.C.: McGraw-Hill, 1998), pp. 567–76.

Corporation discounts, negotiated fares and rebates, and the relationships between business corporations and travel agents are analyzed in U.S. Department of Transportation, *Secretary's Task Force*, pp. 17–21.

7

Air Cargo

The historians Will and Ariel Durant, in their book *The Lessons of History*, say:

The development of the airplane will again alter the map of civilization. Trade routes will follow less and less the rivers and seas; men and goods will be flown more and more directly to their goal. . . . Coastal cities will derive less of their wealth from the clumsy business of transferring goods from ship to train or from train to ship. When sea power finally gives place to air power in transport and war, we shall have seen one of the basic revolutions in history.[1]

This quotation is really looking very far ahead. Air cargo has not even begun to make the merchant ship or freight train obsolete. Nor do we know whether it ever will. Yet air has drawn away from surface modes enough important and valuable cargo that it has become a significant factor in the U.S. and world economies.

The term *air cargo* is generally used in the broad sense, to include air freight (with which we shall be primarily concerned in this chapter), mail, and the several types of expedited small package services to which the term *air express* is now rather loosely applied. In short, almost everything that goes in the cargo compartment on a passenger flight is considered air cargo, except passenger baggage, which is treated as if it were part of the passenger.

The airlines got their start carrying the mails, then progressed into the passenger business, and moved last of all to substantial participation in the freight business. Yet, although it was the latecomer, air freight was once the fastest-growing segment of the airline industry. From 1961 through 1971, the ton-miles of freight carried by U.S. scheduled airlines had nearly a fivefold increase, while passenger-miles increased a little over threefold.[2] The 1970s showed slower but steady growth, about a 67 percent increase over the decade for ton-miles of air freight.

In the 1980s, small-package express services grew rapidly, and data for that decade reflect freight and express combined; they show an 85 percent increase in ton-miles in the ten years. Most recent figures show an increase of 71.8 percent from 1990 to 1998.[3]

Yet the whole category of services defined as air cargo accounted in 1998 for only about 12.7 percent of the total passenger-plus-cargo revenue of the U.S. scheduled airlines, even though two all-cargo majors (Federal Express and United Parcel Service) were included.[4] If we look at only the major passenger carriers, their cargo revenues were running at only 4.4 percent of the total passenger-plus-cargo revenue for the first half of 1999.[5] It is a basic complaint of airline cargo managers that important decisions of an airline, such as aircraft selection and flight scheduling, are made to suit the passenger market rather than the cargo market.

But it would be a mistake to downgrade the importance of air cargo simply because it is a small business compared with the passenger business. Because of its speed, and because of the many savings deriving from speed, air cargo service has become valuable to manufacturers, to retailers, and to consumers. A manufacturer of appliances may rely on the airlines for delivery of components, while retailers may use air for moving much of their merchandise to their scattered outlets. The consumer may benefit in many ways, such as quick receipt of urgently needed goods and being able to enjoy perishable foods brought in from a distance. The consumer also benefits indirectly to the extent that use of air may involve an overall cost saving in the manufacture and distribution of goods.

This chapter considers how the concept of physical distribution in our industrial system ties in closely with the future development of air cargo. We shall see that although transportation costs by air are nearly always higher than by surface carriers—often very much higher—there are often compensatory savings in such items as warehousing costs, inventory costs, losses from pilferage and damage, and the minimizing of stock on store shelves that the public just does not take to. Part of the daily task of the promoter of air cargo for an airline is to persuade manufacturers and retailers that these many savings more than cover the differential in the transportation charges for air over surface. The applicable term is *total cost concept*.

Many airlines specialize in carrying cargo. But much cargo is carried by the regular passenger airlines; most of it today travels in the cargo holds on passenger flights, rather than on all-cargo (freighter) aircraft. (The passenger airlines will be referred to in this chapter as *combination airlines* or *combination carriers*, signifying that they carry both passengers and cargo; the term is applicable whether the airline elects to operate some all-cargo flights or to put all its cargo on passenger flights.)

In 1949 the CAB established a class of airline called the *certificated cargo carriers*. The one member of that class that survived into the 1980s was The Flying Tiger Line, which developed a large worldwide network and, for a time, was the world's largest carrier of air freight. In 1989 it was acquired by the small-package carrier Federal Express.

The 1970s, 1980s, and 1990s saw a remarkable growth in small-package traffic, a phenomenon that we will consider in detail shortly. The term *integrated carrier* was initially used for small-package specialists that used their own trucks for pickup and delivery—"integrated" in the sense of one-company door-to-door service. In the 1990s, however, there has been a trend among some small-package carriers to expand into the carrying of heavy freight, the acquisition of Flying Tiger by Federal Express, mentioned above, being consistent with this trend. But not only have these carriers been expanding into air freight, some former air freight forwarders (traditionally handlers of heavy cargo, as we will later see) now operate their own aircraft and provide one-company door-to-door—"integrated"—service. An example of the latter would be Emery Worldwide.

A variety of cargo airlines—distinguished from integrated carriers in that they provide only airport-to-airport, not door-to-door, service—have developed in recent years. Some are quite small, others—such as Arrow, Atlas, and Evergreen—large enough to place them in DOT's "national" category. These all-cargo airlines typically specialize in providing service for forwarders or in operating on a contract basis for other airlines.

Regional airlines and air taxis (including DOT-designated "commuter air carriers" operating under the Section 40109 exemption) may carry cargo on either passenger or all-cargo flights. Many operators of small aircraft carry mail for the U.S. Postal Service. Some regional carriers have interline agreements with major airlines for cargo feeder service to and from small points, an important public service for these communities.

Foreign airlines with passenger service to the United States also hold the right to carry cargo, whether on passenger flights or by freighters, and many of them offer severe competition to U.S. airlines for cargo traffic over international routes. There are also numerous small, foreign, all-cargo operators and several large ones—for example, Cargolux, based in Luxembourg, and the Japanese carrier Nippon Cargo Airlines.

THE CARGO MIX

The various commodities being carried by air constitute the cargo mix. Identifying them provides a picture of the importance of air cargo in the economy and some clues to the marketing problems that airlines face.

The Air Transport Association lists the "Major Commodities Moving in Air Freight" as follows:

Wearing apparel

Electronic/electric equipment and parts, including appliances

Machinery and parts

Printed matter

Cut flowers, nursery stock

Auto parts and accessories

Fruits and vegetables

Photographic equipment, parts, and film

Edible fish

Tools and hardware

Metal products

Medicines, pharmaceuticals, drugs

Instruments—controlling, measuring, medical, optical

Food preparations, miscellaneous bakery products

Plastic materials and articles

Chemicals, elements and compounds

Footwear

Animals, live

Sporting goods, toys, games[6]

Most traffic that moves by air would be described by transportation economists as "high value." Notice that this means high value *per pound* (or ton or other unit of weight). By contrast, coal, grain, ores, and gravel are low value per unit of weight and typically travel by slow, cheap transportation such as rail and water. Even petroleum, which we think of today as high-priced, is low-value per weight unit and travels by slow, inexpensive modes such as ship and pipeline. But everyday articles of clothing, or small objects like ball-point pens, which we may think of as of low value, are actually high value for transportation purposes—that is, by weight unit—and they will frequently travel by air.

The thought behind this low-value/high-value terminology is that, since weight is a major determinant of transport charges, a high-value (per weight unit) item can bear a high transportation charge. That is to say, a high charge for transportation will cause only a relatively small increase in the price tag on a high-value item but might cause a sizable jump in the price tag on low-value commodities. So, a ton of coal will go by rail but a ton of merchandise will often go by air.

A statistic often shocking to aviation's friends is that less than 1 percent of the nation's cargo moves by air—if measured by the conventional unit, the ton-mile. But to measure the value to society of air cargo, we should more logically use the value of the cargo rather than its weight. A joint study of international air cargo by DOT and the Department of State, presented to Congress in 1987, deals with this point as follows:

Although U.S. airborne trade accounts for only a small portion of total U.S. exports and imports in terms of weight, international air cargo carriage makes a vital and growing contribution to the national economy, particularly U.S. exports. In 1986, airborne exports represented over a quarter of the value of total exports, and airborne imports accounted for 17 percent of the value of total imports. In 1975, such exports and imports accounted for 14 percent and 9 percent, respectively.[7]

More recent figures (1997) show exports by value accounting for 32 percent, imports by value for 24 percent as the airborne proportion of U.S. foreign trade.[8]

The current mix may be divided into three groups, as suggested by Lewis M. Schneider in a book on the air freight industry: emergency traffic, routine perishable traffic, and routine surface-divertible traffic (that is, traffic that an airline has won from the surface modes and must work to keep from returning to surface modes).[9]

Schneider defines emergency traffic as traffic that is not planned in advance and in which time is of the essence. By contrast, routine perishable traffic, while sensitive to time, is unlike emergency traffic in that it is planned. Emergency traffic could mean drugs for a medical emergency or the rather dramatic example of flying a part to repair a machine on an assembly line in a factory where the whole line is shut down until the machine is fixed. Actually only a small proportion of today's air freight falls into that category.

The second group, routine perishable, includes cut flowers going to florists, fresh fruits and vegetables (such as strawberries, cherries, and artichokes traveling east from California), and printed matter (magazines and newspapers whose value perishes quickly). For both categories, speed is the primary consideration and the cost factor is of secondary importance. The demand for air service is relatively inelastic. A rate increase is not likely to scare away much traffic, at least within reasonable limits.

But in the third category we find that the cost factors become primary, while the speed factor becomes only incidental to cost considerations. After all, what is the hurry in moving ordinary merchandise? Why not send cameras, toys, tools, and so on at a much lower transport charge by truck, or across the ocean by ship? The answer is that the shipper, or recipient, may save in many ways that more than cover the step-up in transportation charges. We have previously mentioned several of these: costs of carrying large inventories, costs of warehousing, and the problem of obsolescence. Sometimes another factor, not exactly cost-related, enters the picture: the psychology of customer satisfaction from quick service. The further growth of air cargo depends largely on persuading shippers that it will pay them, overall, under this total cost concept, to divert some more of their traffic from surface to air.

What should be emphasized is that although the public's image of air cargo may still be tied to the emergency and perishable shipments, the greater part of the traffic today consists of the routine surface-divertible variety. Looking once again at the above list of major commodities moving in air freight, we might ask whether there is any industry that is not dependent, at least to some degree, upon air freight.

Mail as Air Cargo

The U.S. Postal Service, which in a sense was the first customer of the infant airlines, is still an important customer today. In 1998, mail accounted for about 11.5 percent of the air cargo ton-miles of the U.S. scheduled airline industry, 13.7 percent of its cargo revenues, and 1.5 percent of *all* its operating revenues, passenger and cargo combined.[10] A customer of this size has much bargaining power, and in past years the CAB had the duty and the power to protect the airlines by regulating the rates the Postal Service had to pay them for carrying the mail. When deregulation came along, however, this authority terminated at the end of 1984 with respect to domestic rates. The Postal Service now negotiates contracts and may employ competitive bidding. DOT, however, still retains authority to regulate the rates for international service.

Certain trends in airline flight scheduling have adversely affected the Postal Service. Hub-and-spoke patterns have replaced many direct flights, thereby slowing daytime service, while many overnight flights (especially freighter services) have been discontinued. As with many other types of cargo, mail tends to accumulate at the end of the business day and requires overnight service. To ease the situation, the Postal Service has considered owning and operating its own fleet of aircraft to supplement the services it receives from scheduled airlines. Instead, however, it now has contracts with cargo carriers whereby specific freighter aircraft are dedicated entirely to carrying the mail, with emphasis on overnight service.

Expedited Small-Package Services

A variety of services are offered today that are limited to small packages and emphasize expedited handling, often next-day delivery. Many of the parcels are extremely small. Some are envelopes containing documents, such as blueprints and payroll or other financial records, weighing a pound or two, although most of the services will take a package up to 50 pounds, and in some cases 70 pounds. (A practical definition of a "small" package is one that can be picked up by one employee without need for mechanical aids.) Typical contents are computer chips, medical supplies, videotapes, merchandise samples, and replacement parts for machinery.

Until the early 1970s, this type of service, also generally known as "air express" as distinguished from "air freight," was a relatively small and somewhat neglected facet of air transportation. As far back as 1927 the airlines had an arrangement with the Railway Express Agency (REA) whereby that nationwide, railroad-connected agency would perform pickup and delivery service for the small parcels that were then the only type of cargo carried on the small aircraft of the day. REA continued this air express service until it went out of business in 1975, but in its later years it was greatly overshadowed by the much more rapidly growing air freight service, which the airlines began in 1944 and which is oriented to larger shipments.

Competition for the small-package trade was offered to REA before its demise by air parcel post and by several air freight forwarders, notably United Parcel Service, which at that time elected to confine its activities to parcels under 50 pounds.

In the early 1970s, a remarkable expansion of expedited small-package traffic began and has continued into the 1990s. Federal Express is the outstanding example of this development. Founded in 1973, it established itself in the small package field by offering a door to door service wherein its own trucks (or occasionally contracted trucks) did the pickup and delivery, and its own small aircraft did the air haul. At the time, Federal Express was classified as an air taxi and had to confine its operations to very small aircraft. Subsequently it obtained certification under sections 401 and 418 of the Federal Aviation Act, which allowed it to use large aircraft. As of 1998, it had a fleet of 333 large aircraft and its services were worldwide.

The initial Federal Express service was a scheduled overnight service hinged on a central distribution center at Memphis, Tennessee. Packages were picked up along specified routes for destinations anywhere in the Federal Express system. Unless the destination happened to be a point right along the same route, the package was brought to Memphis, where it was placed on a flight going out on a route to the destination. This is still the basic mode of operations for this carrier, although it now has additional sorting hubs, including some at foreign points. A package may travel many hundreds of miles out of its way through the sorting center, yet the shipper and recipient will not be concerned so long as a Federal Express truck delivers it the next morning. What appears to be a serious inefficiency—carrying cargo over wasted mileage—seems to be more than compensated for by the savings derived from having a single sorting point.

Many other carriers offer expedited small-package service. One of these, United Parcel Service, operates a large fleet, including some 747s. The U.S. Postal Service has entered the competition for overnight delivery with Express Mail, and found it popular.

The line between small-package service and air freight has become blurred, as the maximum size for a shipment tends to go up due to competitive pressures and perhaps to a growing need to fill space on the large aircraft. Federal Express and United Parcel Service today state no maximum weight limit for their services.

The integrated carriers today will sometimes put cargo on available facilities of the combination carriers, especially for international service, and will contract with trucking firms for some pickup and delivery. Thus, although they are still described as "integrators," they have moved partly away from the characteristic that originally defined them.

The regular passenger carriers are also participating in the small-package boom. Most airlines will accept a small package at an airport passenger counter for a specific flight, which is met at the destination airport by a representative of the recipient. Delta, for example, has a service it calls "Dash," while Continental has one called QUICKPAK. These parcels travel with passenger baggage, and the added cost to the airline is minimal, with the result that the airlines find this a very profitable service. Some airlines now offer pickup and delivery in conjunction with the service.

The remarkable growth of small-package traffic has occurred despite the rather high prices charged, especially for overnight service. The prevailing characteristics seems to be one of highly inelastic demand. According to *Air Cargo World* magazine:

Delivery is *time*-sensitive rather than *price*-sensitive. . . . [C]ustomers are willing to pay for time—especially when the delay of a business day can cost thousands of dollars. (For the same reason, the air express industry doesn't suffer from the destructive price wars that have plagued the airline industry.)[11]

It has been suggested that one factor contributing to the constant increase in the small-parcel market is the "just-in-time" concept developed in recent years whereby manufacturers and retailers keep exceedingly small inventories and rely on swift dependable arrivals of raw materials, components, and finished products.[12] We will consider this topic later in this chapter; it ties in with the total cost concept mentioned earlier, where more expensive modes of transportation are justified by savings in inventory and other costs.

The document portion of air express traffic is subject to serious competition from electronic mail, which includes the facsimile transmission of drawings, charts, graphs, and the like. On the other hand, the express carriers are being helped by a different aspect of electronic media—the use of the Internet by consumers to order merchandise. UPS has predicted a fivefold increase in Internet orders from 1998 to 2001. Some of this, of course, will merely substitute for orders by mail or phone from catalogues. This service, however, raises a problem with respect to carrier profitability, since consumer purchases involve residential deliveries with their relatively high labor costs, rather than "the high-margin businesss traffic the express carriers covet."[13]

A variant of the small package traffic is *courier service*, where a courier travels as a passenger on a flight, taking a shipment along which travels as passenger baggage. The object may be to assure the safety of very valuable cargo or may simply be to speed delivery in such ways as obtaining quick customs clearances at foreign destinations. The term *courier service* is sometimes used where the shipment is taken to the airport by special messenger, travels unaccompanied, then is picked up at the destination airport by another special messenger and hand-carried to the consignee.

The Cargo Mix—Summary

At this point we might break down the term *air cargo* into the following

1. Mail
2. Small packages, carried on an expedited basis and often described as air express.
3. Airfreight
   a. Emergency
   b. Routine perishable
   c. Routine surface-divertible

But keep in mind that on any flight the greater part of the cargo, measured by weight, is likely to fall in the last-named subcategory, routine surface-divertible air freight. Measured, however, in other ways—by the revenue being received by the airlines from each category or by the value of the cargo—the small-package traffic might today predominate on many flights.

CARGO VERSUS PASSENGER CHARACTERISTICS

Certain characteristics of air cargo cause transportation problems quite different from those pertaining to passenger service. Air cargo is nearly always one-way; by contrast, passengers are usually round-trip. Cargo generally prefers to travel by night, passengers by day. Cargo is passive—that is, it must be physically moved, loaded, and unloaded, while the passengers walk about the airport, as well as on and off the aircraft, under their own power. Passengers do not like indirect routings or plane changes (although, as we have seen, they often have to put up with these today), but shippers and recipients of cargo are not concerned with plane changes and indirect routings as long as the cargo arrives when expected. There are large differences in the weight and volume of cargo shipments, whereas in this respect passengers come close to homogeneous. Passengers prefer newer (or at least new-looking) aircraft and are concerned with the decor and cleanliness of the cabin, while cargo can travel on older aircraft with no regard for the aesthetics of the cabin.

TYPES OF AIRCRAFT AND THEIR IMPACT ON CARGO

There are two ways in which the introduction of a new type of passenger aircraft may affect air cargo: through the fact that more than half of all air cargo travels on passenger flights and through the likelihood that later on the new passenger aircraft will be redesigned for use as freighters—for example, the Boeing 727, 737, 757, and 767, and older types such as the McDonnell Douglas DC-8 and DC-10.

Most freighters now flying were either converted from passenger use or were made at the factory as freighters but on the basic designs of passenger aircraft. (For the latter category the letter *F* is usually added to the designation—727F, DC-10F, and so on.) But there have been aircraft designed from the drawing board up as freighters; for these we use the terms *uncompromised* or *dedicated* cargo aircraft.

Uncompromised Cargo Aircraft

We can conceive of an uncompromised (or dedicated) cargo aircraft as being built with huge doors and a floor close to the ground, at truck-bed height. And it should be designed to reflect the usual trade-off between cube and weight of the cargo that travels in major markets. An aircraft whose initial design was premised on the requirements of passenger service will, when used as a freighter, usually become filled to capacity with respect to space well before the maximum permissible pay-load weight is reached. In airline parlance the aircraft will "cube out" before it "weighs out." (Part of the cube problem, of course, derives from the differing shapes of shipments and the fitting of square-cornered shipments into the curved contours of the aircraft fuselage.)

Two examples of uncompromised cargo aircraft are the Lockheed C-5A, which the military uses, and the Lockheed Hercules, a medium-size, medium-range turboprop aircraft with a large rear cargo door at truckbed height. The Boeing 747F could, in a sense, be looked on as an uncompromised cargo aircraft because, although the first sales of the 747 were for passenger use and its predominant use has been in passenger service, the original conception was for a freighter.

The European consortium, Airbus, has proposed a "super-jumbo" freighter aircraft with a capacity somewhat greater than the 747F, but it would have to have extensive purchase commitments from airlines before it could proceed with production and, at a price of $200 million each, the venture remains very much merely a proposal. The development of any such wholly uncompromised cargo aircraft in the near future remains doubtful. Air cargo traffic worldwide remains small by comparison with air passenger traffic; thus, the need for freighters remains small by comparison with the need for passenger aircraft. The number of uncompromised freighters of wholly new design that could be sold would be nowhere nearly great enough to make the development of such a freighter economically justifiable. The great developmental costs would have to be spread over a relatively small number of aircraft, making each plane very expensive when compared with the cost of a freighter derived from a passenger model.

Convertible Aircraft

There are aircraft that can be employed one day for passengers, the next for cargo. Seats must be readily removable, and cargo doors must be provided for the main deck. The manufacturer usually designates these convertible aircraft with the letter C, such as 707C, DC-8C, and DC-10C. They are particularly useful in charter service, adaptable to the needs of potential charterers. The Boeing 727 was, for a time, manufactured in a "quick-change" convertible model, designated by the letters QC and intended for passenger use each day and for cargo use each night. Thus, it would service the peak-load times for each type of traffic. But the quick change twice a day proved to take longer and cost more for labor than expected, and there were other problems such as the extra weight of passenger seating when palletized for daily removal and the wasted space and weight on the cargo leg from such passenger appurtenances as overhead racks and galleys. Most airlines that tried the idea later dropped it. However, more recently the Boeing 737 has been used on a quick-change basis in Alaska and Hawaii, and, in Europe, by the Irish carrier Aer Lingus and the German carrier Lufthansa.

The concept of the quick-change convertible, with its promise of very high utilization of today's expensive aircraft, may yet come into its own.

The "Combi" Aircraft

We use the term *combination aircraft* to mean the usual passenger aircraft, with a belly compartment for cargo. But the term *combi* aircraft has come into use as a nickname not for the usual combination aircraft but for a passenger aircraft where cargo is carried not only in the belly compartment but also in a section of the main deck carved out of what would normally be passenger space. These have been found useful on some international routes where cargo traffic is heavy, but their use has been confined mostly to foreign airlines.

While any make of aircraft can be made into a combi, the 747 has been the prevailing type used. Today, however, the A-340 Airbus, the MD-11, and the Boeing 727 and 757 are available in combi configuration.

The Noise Problem

Noise is a major problem at airports. As noted in Chapter 4, the airlines were required by law to phase out, by the end of 1999, their noisier (so-called Stage 2) aircraft or retrofit their engines to meet the higher (so-called Stage 3) standards.

The noise problem is a particularly difficult one for freighters. Because air cargo typically travels overnight, the peak hours for departure of freighter aircraft are late evening, with arrivals in the very early morning hours, and it is during night hours that airports are most sensitive to noise. Some cities have even established night curfews on operations of noisier aircraft. Also, freighters very often are older aircraft that have been retired from passenger service, and thus have less modern, less quiet engines.

The problems of the freighter operators do not end once all their aircraft meet the U.S. Stage 3 standard. There is now discussion of a Stage 4 standard for even quieter aircraft, to be phased in gradually as with the earlier stages. The European Union is pressing for such a standard and, meanwhile, has proposed barring from the airports of its members any aircraft that have used hush-kitting of engines to meet U.S. Stage 3 requirements. The prohibition would be phased in, to take full effect in the year 2002. Federal Express, which has hush-kitted its 727s, would be especially hard hit. As of the end of 1999, the U.S. government was strongly opposing the proposal and considering taking its complaint to ICAO.[14]

Allied to the noise problem is the question of emissions by aircraft of nitrogen oxide and carbon dioxide, with resulting environmental damage. Pressure to reduce such emissions is particularly strong in Europe. The airlines are working with ICAO and the concerned governments to seek ways to reduce emissions while maintaining engine fuel efficiency and noise standards. Freighter operators are particularly vulnerable if emission standards are raised since older aircraft have higher levels of emissions.[15]

New versus Converted Freighters

In deciding whether to purchase a new freighter or one converted from previous passenger use, an airline often faces a difficult evaluation. A new freighter involves much higher capital costs, and the fact that a freighter is generally not utilized as many hours a day as is a passenger aircraft makes the spread of the capital costs more severe than with a passenger aircraft of the same price. On the other hand, we have seen that a new aircraft will save on fuel and maintenance costs. Moreover, fuel costs figure as a larger percentage of the operating costs of a freighter versus a combination aircraft because labor costs as a fraction of total operating costs are lower on the freighters.

As an example, a new 737 aircraft will cost $30 to $35 million, while a used passenger 737 may cost between $13 million and $24 million (depending on its age and history) with costs of conversion running between $1 million and $5 million.[16] Although the decision is usually in favor of buying the used passenger aircraft and converting it, there are notable exceptions. Thus, in late 1998 United Parcel Service ordered 60 new Airbus A-300-600 freighters, planning to use them for at least 30 years.[17]

Possible Future Cargo Aircraft

From time to time there are proposals for an uncompromised or dedicated cargo aircraft, often intended to fill a particular niche in the industry. In the early 1970s, when it appeared that construction of the Alaska pipeline might not be permitted, Boeing proposed the RC-1 (RC for "Resource Carrier"), with the extraordinary payload of over 1,000 tons, designed to carry petroleum, and also mineral ores, from isolated areas. Later, and perhaps more realistically, Boeing, McDonnell Douglas, and Lockheed jointly proposed the "Spanloader," with a payload of over 300 tons and a wingspan of over 250 feet. As often happens with such proposals, there were not enough airlines willing to make the financial commitments necessary to make production feasible.

Much more recently (1999), Airbus had a pending proposal for a "super-jumbo" freighter, tentatively designated the A3XXX. It would have a 150-ton payload, and Airbus reportedly has projected a market for 60 such aircraft between the years 2004–2016. But prior commitments are needed, and the reported price of $200 to $250 million per aircraft may well cause the whole idea to flounder. One advantage to this proposed freighter would be that its fuselage would be 16 feet taller than that of the largest of the 747s, and thus would be adaptable to outsize cargo that will not fit on the 747F.[18]

The carrying of outsize cargo (defined, as a practical matter, as something too large—but not necessarily too heavy—to fit on a 747 freighter) is a niche market receiving much attention recently. Outsize cargo includes satellites, power generating equipment, construction equipment, drilling rigs, turbines, transformers, etc. Airbus has developed a very large aircraft especially adapted for outsize cargo—the A-300–600ST, nicknamed "The Beluga" because of its whale-like appearance. Much outsize cargo today is being carried on a freighter called the Antonov AN-124, constructed in the 1980s as a Soviet military transport but now being made in the part of the former Soviet Union called Ukrainia. It can carry a payload of 160 tons and, on this basis, may be described as "the world's largest aircraft." It lacks fuel efficiency, however, and requires a large crew to operate it.

Strictly speaking, the honor of being the world's largest aircraft should go to another Antonov freighter, the AN-225, built to carry an astonishing 250 tons of cargo. However, at last report, as of late 1999, there were only two of them still in existence, neither one in operating condition.[19]

On a more modest scale, Boeing has a pending proposal for a freighter to be called the MD-17, limited to about 85 tons payload. According to Boeing's advertising, there would be "no better way to deliver your outsize cargo" and the aircraft could use "some of the world's shortest and most austere air fields." However, as of mid-1999, the MD-17 had not gone into production, possibly handicapped by a price reported as high as $170 million, and Boeing was believed to be rethinking the total economics of the venture.[20]

A most interesting and promising development is the airship, the modern version of the lighter-than-air dirigible, presently the subject of research in several countries, including the United States. Although the airship is often conceived as a rather gracious form of passenger travel, combining the speed of air with the joyful living of a cruise ship, the truth is that it may well prove more suitable to cargo than to passengers. It is slow; the more optimistic predictions say 200 miles per hour. But cargo is not in such a hurry as passengers. It can go overnight. And the airship does not need a long runway and might well be able to operate in and out of a factory yard. However, although there are differing predictions as to the payload a modern airship might carry, the ratio of the volume of helium needed to lift a unit of weight may well limit the practical use of the airship to the small-package traffic rather than to heavy freight.

Nevertheless, as of 1999, a German company established for the purpose was planning an airship about the size of the famed Hindenburg, intended to move outsize cargo and to carry 160 tons. It would travel at a speed of only 65 miles per hour, but would not need the landing facilities required by freighter aircraft. In fact, it could be moored above a delivery site, such as a construction site, and could lower loads using an on-board crane. The company is called CargoLifter, and its airship would have the same name. As of 1999, it was seeking commitments from potential customers which, of course, may or may not develop.[21]

Airships are highly economical on fuel compared with conventional aircraft, a fact that would tend to promote their usefulness as freighters from the twin standpoints of operating costs and national fuel conservation policy. The big cost hurdle would be that of constructing a modern cargo airship, and there is an allied question of how costs of research and development are to be financed.

We have been considering massive aircraft and airships, but there is a niche at the other extreme that has received little attention lately, but where it is possible that some promising technology may develop. This would be a helicopter or similar vehicle, but one far less expensive to operate than current models. It would move containers or even truck vans short distances from factory to airport or from factory to factory. How to accomplish this at low cost has so far proved a discouraging problem.

TERMINAL FACILITIES

We turn now from an overview of air cargo to a consideration of a major problem area—the airline cargo terminal at the airport. Airline management at the terminal must minimize delays to the movement of cargo through terminals, must protect cargo from damage and theft at terminals, must load and unload aircraft swiftly, and must hold down costs. Moreover, the problems of management in achieving these goals are aggravated by the variability factor. The tendency of many shippers to dispatch cargo at the end of the business day for delivery at destination the following morning means that trucks bearing cargo crowd terminals in the early evening between five and seven o'clock. While some of this cargo will go out on evening passenger flights, much will travel on freighters scheduled to depart in late evening for arrival very early in the morning. Another crowding of trucks at terminals occurs between five and seven o'clock in the morning, with the objective of picking up cargo from the freighter arrivals to get goods to the recipients early in the business day. To accentuate this peaking, the Postal Service has desires similar to other shippers; its trucks bring mail in heavy volume to the terminals in early evening and show up to pick up arriving mail in early morning.

In the previously cited book that reports on research on the domestic air freight industry, Schneider says:

The terminal problem confronting air freight is difficult for a variety of reasons. Perhaps most important is that it represents a buffer between a capital-intensive, carefully planned system of aircraft operations and a fragmented, chaotic conglomeration of private and common carriers for the most part delivering mountains of packages in relatively small vehicles.[22]

It is an apt description of the lineup of trucks, large and small, that come to the receiving platform of an airline's terminal. Some are owned by shippers, some are common carriers, while some belong to air freight forwarders (a topic to be addressed shortly). But perhaps Schneider should not have said "mountains of packages"; that sounds like the parcel post system at Christmas. A shipment of 50 pounds is considered small in air freight today, and the largest may run to several tons. Thus, the "packages" in the "mountain" may include some very large ones.

Because of the blurring of the distinction between air freight and small-package service, there is no longer any meaningful comparison of average shipment weights of air freight with such averages in previous years. However, earlier figures, when air freight could still be considered a category clearly apart from small-package service, showed a trend to a reduction in the weight of air freight shipments. A 1985 study put it at about 175 pounds for U.S. scheduled airlines. But international shipments tended to be larger than domestic; a Flying Tiger official in 1988 estimated the average international air freight shipment in the range of 350–500 pounds. Earlier, in 1977, the average weight was reported as over 300 pounds in domestic service, over 600 pounds in international service.[23]

Operations at a terminal are labor-intensive, despite much use of complex sorting and conveying apparatus. It takes labor to receive goods at the loading platform; to handle the paperwork; to compute and collect the charges; to weigh, sort, and allocate each piece to the proper flight; and to provide the proper protection. Even with sophisticated equipment it still requires human effort to load a plane and, at the destination, to unload the cargo, as well as to sort it once again and get it into the hands of the recipients. By contrast, on an aircraft in flight, a great deal of work is being accomplished by the small number of employees on a flight crew.

Wage inflation hits particularly hard on terminal costs. Usually this labor is unionized, and wage demands may at times reflect not only the general inflation in the economy but a substantial excess as well.

An airline will ordinarily hire a labor force to meet peak demand. While in terms of worker output it would be advantageous to employ much of the force on a split-shift system, working four hours at the evening peak and at the morning peak, there is both individual and union resistance to this type of workday. Thus, an eight-hour shift adequate to handle the evening peak will have several hours when work is slack, and likewise with the shift adequate to handle the early morning peak. In a field as speed oriented as air cargo, delay must be minimized even at the cost of much labor efficiency. Part-time employees willing to work at the evening or early morning peaks may help the situation if properly qualified ones can be found and if possible union resistance can be overcome.

The trend to more expensive aircraft adds to the pressure at a terminal, making aircraft depreciation high, and aircraft utilization and turnaround time critical. Cargo, whether on a freighter or combination flight, must be unloaded rapidly when a flight arrives, and outgoing traffic must be ready for quick loading.

Cargo awaiting a flight must be held in a storage area, as must cargo at a destination waiting for the recipient to pick it up or arrange for its delivery. Storage areas, especially when overcrowded, lend themselves to loss, damage, and pilferage. It is difficult to steal goods when they are in the air, a point airline sales personnel make when soliciting traffic. But at terminals air cargo is a special target for thieves, often organized and sophisticated, since it consists largely of high-value merchandise. The airlines have invested much money in round-the-clock security guards, fenced and locked areas, pass controls, and so on, but theft remains a problem.

Another cost is paperwork, which the airlines make more burdensome because they have used as a competitive ploy a promise to tell shippers where their cargo is at any moment. Computerization, however, is well advanced in the industry, reducing the paperwork burden, although at the expense of much capital investment.

The bar code and scanner, familiar to any supermarket patron, form the basis of much of the computerization of air cargo. The coded label affixed to each package contains all the information which would otherwise be contained in a variety of shipping documents, and it is readily available to be read or printed out at any computer station in the system. Employees out on the floor in the terminal can be furnished with handheld bar code readers linked to the central computer. A record is thus available at any moment of the location of every shipment. Functions such as sorting and weighing may be automated through use of this type of system. Automation may even extend to robot-like guided vehicles moving shipments within the terminal. For example, Delta now uses *automated guided vehicles* (AGVs) at Atlanta to pick up and move shipments around its terminal and even to take them to the scales for weighing.[24]

In addition to saving labor, computerization speeds the transit time of cargo. (It is estimated that about 90 percent of the time that an air shipment is in transit is spent on the ground.) And, as noted by the director of security of the Air Transport Association, computerization at terminals has helped to reduce theft "by providing sophisticated systems that help to expedite shipments, improve accountability, and screen out a great deal of insider opportunity."[25]

A promising development known as *electronic data interchange* (EDI), has been defined in the following manner:

EDI means different things to different people. Taking a broad approach, it can be defined as the electronic transfer of standard business documents, such as invoices, shipment status notices, and bills of lading—any standard business document.

EDI is also the standard interchange format that makes all this possible. Following the motor, rail, and ocean freight industries, the air cargo industry is moving toward both U.S. and international electronic translation standards that will enable users to exchange their documents across industries and around the world. . . .

The greatest advantage of EDI is that it moves documents directly from one company's computer to another company's computer.[26]

One use of EDI is to verify the status of a shipment, with the shipper's own office computer directly accessing the system. The shipper is tied into the carrier's system in a manner resembling, in the passenger service, the direct access that a travel agent has through a CRS.

According to one source, EDI gives management improved control over "many of the notorious service bottlenecks in air cargo: airport ground-handling, Customs, gateway transit-points, and inter-carrier transfers of shipments."[27]

One of the greatest delays in international air cargo has been the awaiting of customs clearance. Today, most air cargo entering the United States can be cleared in advance with the Customs Service. Once the aircraft has departed from the foreign point, a copy of the cargo manifest is sent electronically to the Customs Service in the United States, which then informs the airline's office at the destination city which shipments may be considered cleared and which the Customs Service will wish to examine.

One problem with EDI has been the need for standardization of systems among airlines, forwarders, and those truckers that do pickup and delivery. The integrated carriers have an advantage here in that they own or control both the motor and air systems, although, as we have seen, they sometimes put cargo on the combination airlines or contract with outside motor carriers. The airlines and forwarders have been working together, seeking to establish, at a minimum, a common barcode standard. On the international scene, a group called "Cargo 2000," consisting of 19 airlines and 15 forwarders, both U.S. and foreign, has been working toward international standardization. Yet, as of March 1999, an officer of a U.S. air freight forwarder was pointing to a continuing lack of standardization of data communications among truckers, forwarders, airlines, and customs brokers. According to this official, "Each transportation mode relies upon each other, yet there is no current system whereby they easily and smoothly receive and transmit data from one another. Ultimately, all sectors will have to talk with each other, and have status reports automatically issued that inform all parties about a shipment's status."[28]

Shippers who are major users of air cargo facilities are being encouraged to barcode shipments before turning them over to the forwarder or airline. Also, consignees should be enabled to access the system to determine where a particular shipment is in transit.

A parallel development is the use of the Internet by shippers, not only to obtain information about a carrier's services but to actually book cargo for shipment. Federal Express and United Parcel Service already allow such direct bookings, and the practice is expected to spread rapidly.

It will be evident that a terminal is a place where costs can easily get out of hand and where there is room for much constructive managerial cost-control activity. Measured by tons of cargo processed, the costs at an air cargo terminal are much higher than those at a truck terminal, some estimates running to about five times as high. High terminal costs make the task of successfully soliciting short-haul cargo traffic particularly difficult. We have seen in previous chapters that the cost of processing a passenger at a terminal is about the same whether the trip will be short or long and that the spreading of this cost over a relatively short trip results in a relatively high per-mile cost. The same situation obtains for cargo. According to one authority, "Airfreight terminal costs can range from a high of about 80 percent of the total costs of transporting goods a distance of 400 miles to about 30 percent for a range of about 5,000 miles."[29] Moreover, just as with passengers, the demand for short-haul service is more elastic than that for long-haul, and there is the short-haul dilemma: rates must be kept high to cover costs but must be kept low to attract traffic.

Separate Airports for Freighters?

It has sometimes been suggested that, at least in large cities, there should be a separate airport altogether, devoted only to freighters. It could be built far out from the city center, since cargo does not resist long trips to the airport as passengers do. Land would be cheaper, noise problems reduced. Congestion at the regular airports would be reduced, and the passenger service would thus indirectly benefit. Cargo would move unhindered by the congestion at the passenger airports. The two types of traffic would no longer get in each other's way.

But there are disadvantages. Not many cities today have enough air cargo traffic to justify the operating expenses of a freighter-only airport, and even fewer have enough such traffic to justify construction of an entirely new airport for this purpose. And since more than half of air cargo travels on combination flights, there could be confusion, delays, and inefficiencies involved in separating the cargo to travel out of the cargo airport from the cargo to travel on combination flights. Cargo connecting between a combination flight and a freighter flight would also become involved in this two-airport confusion and delay.

Since the late 1980s there has been a growing interest in all-cargo airports, and several have been established. One reason for this trend is the great increase in traffic being carried by integrated carriers, who do not operate combination flights and thus have no problem of interlining with such flights. Another reason is the closing of some military air bases, both in the United States and abroad, which has opened up the possibility of their use as all-cargo fields. Still another reason is that the concept of the development of industrial activities at an airport, while not a new idea, is receiving increased attention.

Under the just-in-time concept we have mentioned earlier, there are now parts warehouses at airports where parts are immediately available to be flown to purchasers. Similarly, a retailer may wish to store goods at warehouses right at an air cargo terminal for ready transportation either to its stores about the country or directly by mail order to the consumers. Moreover, manufacturing processes, particularly those involving assembly of parts purchased from many sources around the country or around the world, can be conveniently located right at the airport where the components arrive. All these activities could be linked around an all-cargo airport, much as warehouses and factories in the past were built at seaports or at rail terminals.

Efforts have been made to develop all-cargo airports, or airports intended primarily for freighters, near such cities as Austin and Fort

Worth, Texas. Two freighter-only airports now operate in California—Mather Field, a former military airport near Sacramento, and March Cargoport, a former military airport thirty miles inland from Los Angeles.[30] In Europe, former military bases are being used as airports specializing in cargo traffic—such as Hahn Airport near Frankfurt. In central France, 90 miles east of Paris, a freighter-only airport is scheduled to open in early 2000, called Europort Vatry.[31]

A more ambitious proposal is proceeding in eastern North Carolina near the city of Kinston, where it is hoped to develop a large industrial area around an all-cargo airport. It has been described by the *Wall Street Journal* as

Global TransPark, a 21st-century industrial metropolis. At its core will be factories, scores of them, that want supplies and want them fast. They will be surrounded by a web of monorails and electronic-vehicle corridors connecting them to an airport with long runways—their gateway to global markets. It will be the epitome of just-in-time manufacturing, with conveyor belts ferrying parts from airplane to factory floor and finished products back to the cargo hold.[32]

The growth of all-cargo airports may be slow and it may be many years before major industrial parks develop around them. It may even be that some airports dedicated primarily to freighters, but not as yet attracting many of them, will fill the void by accepting private or business passenger flights or even commuter or other scheduled passenger services. Still, as the volume of air cargo grows and as congestion at passenger airports gets worse, the case gets ever stronger for the all-freighter airport.

PICKUP AND DELIVERY SERVICE

The airlines use the term *pickup service* for the truck trip *to* the airport of departure, and the term *delivery service* for the truck trip *from* the destination airport to the recipient.

Many shippers use their own trucks to take cargo to the airport, and sometimes the recipient will use its trucks for the delivery haul at the destination. The Postal Service and the air freight forwarders provide pickup and delivery of their traffic, usually with their own vehicles, although they occasionally resort to contract arrangements. The integrated carriers, as an inherent part of what constitutes "integrated" service, use their own vehicles, but even they occasionally contract out the pickup and delivery. With the combination carriers, however, a contract arrangement with a local trucking firm is the typical arrangement.

Air Cargo, Inc.

If a shipper requests a combination airline to arrange pickup and/or delivery, it will do so, but usually not with vehicles of its own. (A few airlines provide service at some points with their own vehicles, but this is not the prevailing practice.) There is a corporation called Air Cargo, Inc. (ACI), which is jointly owned by certain airlines and has as its principal function the negotiating of contracts with local truckers all over North America and in many foreign countries, to provide pickup and delivery service to and from airports. ACI has about 70 members that it serves, including some air freight forwarders and some foreign airlines. It maintains contracts with some 600 to 700 truckers in North America, each of which is at the service of any ACI-member airline or forwarder using the airport or airports in its locality. In this manner these airlines (and forwarders) can furnish shippers door-to-door service without getting into the trucking business themselves. In recent years ACI has been expanding its operations worldwide, and now has contracts with local truckers at many foreign points.[33]

ACI has other services it offers it members, such as the handling and storage of cargo at some terminals, the contracting for some intercity truck hauls, an insurance and claims service, and a computer system linking its member airlines and forwarders with the trucking contractors.

Long-Haul Pickup and Delivery

Air cargo often travels long distances by truck, for example, from a mid-western city to New York City for onward travel by air to Europe. Air Cargo, Inc., negotiates contracts with over-the-road truckers for such hauls. Due to the deregulation of trucking, beginning with the Motor Carrier Act of 1980, the surface haul of air cargo is, for all practical purposes, free from governmental regulation. Accordingly, today a forwarder may develop its own nationwide trucking operation, as may an airline that chooses to do so as an alternative to the Air Cargo, Inc. system.

Even foreign air carriers may own and operate their own trucks within the United States in conjunction with their airline services. They must, however, confine such trucking to a 35-mile radius of the airport unless they have authorization from DOT to extend it nationwide. Such authorizations are granted where the airline's government grants similar rights to U.S. airlines.

AIR FREIGHT FORWARDERS

It is an unusual fact about air cargo that a major portion of it travels through the hands of intermediaries known as air freight forwarders. In Europe the word *consolidator* is often used instead of *forwarder*, and it is really a more accurate term because the essence of a forwarder's function is to consolidate many small shipments into one large shipment and then to offer the large shipment as one entity to the airline. (Thus, the pickup and delivery services arranged by Air Cargo, Inc., do not constitute air freight forwarding as the term is commonly used and legally defined.)

An air freight forwarder is an indirect air carrier—it accomplishes the air haul indirectly by using the facilities of the airlines rather than having aircraft of its own. Put another way, it has the legal responsibilities of a common carrier without actually performing the line haul. Since deregulation, however, a forwarder may readily obtain certification under Sections 41101 or 41103 to operate its own aircraft and thus "graduate" from the status of a forwarder to that of an integrated carrier. Companies such as Emery and UPS, which prior to deregulation held air freight forwarder authority with no right to operate aircraft, have since acquired large aircraft fleets and are considered integrated carriers. If they do any forwarding at all (that is, assembling shipments and sending them on other airlines), it is very much a sideline. In practice today, the term air freight forwarder is used to mean the old-style forwarder that operates no aircraft but merely assembles shipments and sends them via scheduled combination or cargo airlines. We will use the term in this restricted sense.

The forwarder is responsible to the shipper for the safe delivery of the cargo into the hands of the recipient and charges the shipper in accordance with its own set of rates. Formerly each forwarder had to file a tariff with the CAB, but this requirement was abolished in 1979 by a CAB regulation pursuant to the regulatory reform philosophy (Regulation ER-1094, January 24, 1979). Usually the rate offered by a forwarder for door-to-door service is lower than the rate that shippers would pay if they dealt directly with the airline (assuming that we add to the airline's rate the charges for pickup and delivery). It will be lower because the forwarder attracts the shipper's business by offering the lower price and then more than makes up the difference by consolidating the shipment with other people's cargo and obtaining a reduced rate from the airline—that is, a lower rate for the single consolidated shipment than would be charged if each of the smaller shipments were sent separately.

Formerly a forwarder had to obtain an operating authorization from the CAB. While the procedure for obtaining it was much simpler than the certification procedure for an airline, matters were made even easier for a would-be forwarder by CAB Regulation ER-1094. It substituted a simple registration procedure. No longer was a would-be forwarder required to demonstrate fitness or to file evidence of cargo and motor vehicle liability insurance. Reporting of data was still required but was simplified. Subsequently, the board abolished the registration and reporting requirements altogether, so that the air freight forwarding industry really became totally deregulated.

There are times when forwarders do not consolidate but simply send shipments along to the airline and pay the airline the regular rate for each individual shipment. This can happen when a forwarder accepts a shipment and then receives no other cargo that day consigned to the same destination. There is an economic motive for holding the shipment until a consolidation can be made, but there is a countervailing motive to move the shipment without undue delay or lose the customer's future business. If a forwarder sends, without consolidating, a shipment it accepted under its forwarder rate, it may well lose money on the transaction.

But there are other situations where the shipper knows in advance, and agrees, that the forwarder will not consolidate the shipment. In such cases the shipper pays the airline rate plus a charge for the forwarder's pickup and delivery service. This can occur when the shipment is destined for a point not shown in the forwarder's rates, or when the shipper is utilizing one of the special services offered by many forwarders where expedited handling is received at a premium rate.

There were 365 U.S. air freight forwarders in September 1977, shortly before enactment of the cargo reform law, increasing to 505 by March 1979, and then, in the two years following ER-1094, to 1500 by March 1981. The current number is unknown in light of the abolition of the registration requirement, but is generally believed to have dropped in recent years as small and medium-sized forwarders have had financial difficulties and have had to face large capital investments for computerization. There have been mergers even among some of the larger ones. The integrated carriers have won away much traffic that formerly traveled via the forwarders on the combination airlines, and the latter have also made the life of the forwarder more difficult by greatly reducing the number of freighter flights. (The FAA shows a figure of nearly 3,000 forwarders as of 1998, but this figure is apparently based on FAA registrations related to hazardous cargo and would include shippers and cargo agents as well as the true, consolidating forwarders.)

The proportion of cargo tendered to the combination airlines by forwarders can only be estimated in light of the absence of any requirement that they register with or furnish data to DOT, as well as in light of their large number and the blurring of the distinctive forwarder function. However, it is generally agreed that it is around 90 percent in international services, but lower in domestic markets. American Airlines in 1990 estimated that 95 percent of its international cargo was being received from forwarders, but only 50 percent of its domestic cargo.[34]

Weight Breaks and Rate Differentials

Air freight rates are usually stated as so much per pound (above a certain minimum), but the per-pound amount drops when a shipment is above certain so-called weight breaks. For example, at 100 pounds, 500 pounds, and 1,000 pounds, the per-pound rate may drop. The amount of the drop is called the rate differential. (Metric system weights, instead of pounds, will be found in many international rate patterns.) The pattern of an airline's weight breaks, and the size of the rate differentials at these breaks, are a forwarder's bread and butter, since they determine the profit the forwarder may realize on consolidations. Forwarders have sometimes complained that the weight break/rate differential pattern for international traffic tends to be less favorable to them than the domestic pattern.

Cargo Agents

We have seen that forwarders sometimes do not consolidate particular shipments but instead send them at regular airline rates, adding a charge for their services, such as pickup and delivery. When they do this, they are acting as cargo agents. What can be confusing is that some firms are cargo agents without being forwarders. These are particularly prevalent in international air freight. A cargo agent, whether or not a forwarder, will promote its service by advertising that through its knowledge of airlines it can send cargo by the best and most reliable airline services and route traffic around bottlenecks. It may also advertise that, with respect to international service, it is expert at coping with the intricate rules and paperwork of customs authorities.

Justification for Having Forwarders

When air freight forwarders were first authorized by the CAB, in 1949, the airlines generally were opposed. They argued that a forwarder would slow the movement of air freight by holding shipments in hope of large consolidations. They feared a loss of revenue, since the revenue to be received from a consolidated shipment would be less than the gross revenues if each item in the consolidation were to be sent separately.

Yet in time the airlines became supporters of the forwarder system. They have found that any loss in revenue is more than compensated by the cost savings inherent in dealing with one large shipper (that is, the forwarder) with a few large shipments, rather than with a multiplicity of individual customers with numerous smaller shipments. They also recognize that some traffic would not go by air at all were it not for the lower rates made available to the shipper by the forwarder.

A large forwarder may have enough economic leverage to negotiate commissions from the airlines, which give it additional profit on top of the profit it makes from consolidating under the weight break/rate differential system. In turn, part of such commissions may be reflected in lower rates charged the shippers by the forwarder.

Truckers and Railroads as Forwarders

In 1969 the CAB first permitted long-haul motor carriers, including trucking subsidiaries of railroads, to acquire air freight forwarder authorizations. But the air freight forwarding operations of these surface carriers were closely monitored to see that they seriously intended to promote air freight and were not seeking the authority as a device to persuade air freight customers to use motor carriers instead. Then, in 1977 the CAB concluded that there had been no diversion from air to surface, nor any other undesirable effects on the air cargo industry. Today surface carriers not only have the right to be air freight forwarders but, pursuant to regulatory reform, they may become cargo airlines. A company can be multi-modal—being at once a railroad, a motor carrier, an air freight forwarder, and a cargo airline.

Foreign Air Freight Forwarders

So far we have been considering only those air freight forwarders that are U.S. firms. But there are also firms of foreign nationality that have authority to accept and consolidate cargo within the United States for shipment abroad. Foreign firms have never been required to hold authority from the U.S. government if they consolidate shipments at the foreign point and send them *into* the United States. But to consolidate cargo that *originates* in the United States, the forwarder must register with DOT, and the government of its home country must have a policy of granting the equivalent privilege to U.S. forwarders. In fact, DOT will now permit a foreign forwarder to handle domestic shipments if its home government grants the same privilege to U.S. forwarders. As of early 1994, about 250 foreign air freight forwarders had registered with DOT, but it was not known how many of these were actively operating.

Cooperative Shippers Associations

A cooperative shippers association is not, strictly speaking, an air freight forwarder, but operates similarly in the sense that it consolidates smaller shipments into larger ones before turning them over to the airlines, and does so in order to profit from the rate differentials at the weight breaks in the airline rate patterns. As a cooperative, it accepts cargo only from its member firms and returns its earnings to its members. Typically such an association will be formed by shippers of one type of product (cut flowers, tropical fish, etc.) who ship in large volumes in one or a few markets. Although the individual shippers are otherwise in direct competition with each other, they pool their forces with respect to savings on air cargo costs.

It is possible that the cooperative shippers association may become more significant in the future, as the utilization of air freight in our economy increases. A group of manufacturers, such as in the electronics field, or a group of retailers might form an association as a device to hold down their air freight bills by consolidations. In fact, they might even have their association operate its own aircraft, since this is now permitted to a cooperative shippers association.

The Future of Forwarders

Deregulation had broadened the options open to shippers but at the same time has increased the confusion they may often face in seeking the best carriers, routings, and rates for their shipments. The expertise of the forwarder in these matters is needed more than ever. Yet with the strong competition from the integrated carriers and the lack of enthusiasm of most combination airlines for overnight cargo flights, the forwarders are facing difficult times and many may not survive. The larger forwarders may grow larger still through mergers and acquisitions, as well as through their sheer ability to attract shippers. One authority, Professor Nawal K. Taneja, held, in the mid-1980s, that the broad-based, medium-sized forwarders were especially vulnerable, and his opinion appears equally applicable in the late 1990s.

To survive in the current environment, a forwarder has to be either large and computerized, or specialized. Volume has become critical as yields have eroded. Moreover, shippers are demanding computer capabilities, which require resources that can be provided cost-effectively only by the large forwarders. A small forwarder can go around these two requirements (volume and computer capability) if it can maintain a special niche. Medium-sized forwarders are thus caught in the middle.[35]

If this analysis is correct, the forwarder of the future will either be part of an oligopoly of giants or will be a small company tailored perhaps to one locality, one industry, or one type of traffic.

It has been suggested that forwarders should concentrate, at least for domestic shipments, on second-day traffic. Here a shipper turns cargo over to a forwarder on, say, Monday at the end of the business day, with the expectation that it will not take to the air until Tuesday's daytime passenger flights and will not be delivered until Wednesday. In short, give up fighting the integrated carries for the overnight service in which they specialize and give up fighting to get the combination carriers to supply adequate overnight freighter service. A disadvantage is that second-day service is lower revenue service than the overnight.

COMPETITION WITH OTHER MODES

Competition with other modes means, as a practical matter, with ocean vessels and with trucks. While railroads carry more in sheer ton-miles of cargo than trucks, nowadays it is of a sort that is not divertible to air: low-value-per-ton commodities such as coal, ores, and grain. The truck, being substantially more expensive than the train yet offering what is usually a much faster service, is the carrier of the high-value-per-ton traffic, mostly merchandise and other manufactured or partly processed goods, from which air diverts.

Competition between Air and Truck

Truck and air compete with respect to price and service. Air is usually faster, but as the haul gets shorter, the speed advantage of air over truck diminishes. The truck nowadays competes for overnight service for 500-mile hauls, if the shipper has a "truckload," that is, if the shipper has enough freight to warrant *engaging the whole capacity of the truck*. Overnight hauls of this sort are effectively as fast as air cargo, since all that is desired is next-morning delivery. And truck rates for truckload traffic are likely to be much lower than air freight rates. But for hauls in the thousands of miles, such as transcontinental service, air freight clearly has a speed advantage, although the trucker competes on the basis of lower price.

Comparisons of air with truck rates must be made with caution, since there are so many factors to be taken into account. Rates of both air and truck vary by length of haul, type of cargo, whether containerized, and whether (for truck) the shipment is on a truckload or less-than-truckload (LTL) basis. Also, the great expansion in document and small-package traffic in recent years has introduced into air cargo statistics some figures that are not meaningful when considering air-truck competition since much of this traffic is not suitable for truckload transportation. Perhaps the best that can be said is that a shipper engaging the whole capacity of a common carrier truck for a long haul should not be surprised at a rate about one-third that of air.

A shipper that does not have enough freight to engage a truckload must use the less-than-truckload service that offers *slower* speed at a *higher* rate. LTL service means that the trucking company will send a small truck to pick up the shipment and take it to a truck terminal, where it will be off-loaded and subsequently placed on a large truck that will take it to the destination city. There it will be off-loaded at a terminal and subsequently delivered by a small truck, usually on a daily run. Each step of the way there may be delays, so that an LTL trip may well take twice as long as the same trip on a truckload basis.

LTL costs to the trucker are higher than for the truckload, and rates reflect this fact. Moreover, the airlines, perceiving some LTL traffic as especially divertible, may offer that traffic reduced rates by such devices as specific commodity rates and container discounts (to be discussed shortly). Thus the rate gap can be further narrowed. Some shippers even find that for them the difference between air and LTL rates is negligible. But even when the LTL rate remains somewhat cheaper, the nontransportation cost savings that we covered in connection with the total cost concept may come into play enough to swing the traffic to air.

The deregulation of the trucking industry, which began with the Motor Carrier Act of 1980, has resulted in an increased number of firms and also some rate competition that has won some traffic back from the airlines. However, it has also resulted in the concentration of the small-package segment of LTL service into a few dominant nationwide firms. There has also been a blurring of lines of distinction between air freight forwarders and trucking firms, as certain forwarders have developed extensive longhaul trucking networks while some truckers have coordinated their services directly with airlines so as to offer long surface hauls within the United States for international air cargo shipments.

Two developments in the trucking industry might make its competition with air stronger. One is the use of double bottoms or multiple bottoms, where two or more trailers are hitched to one tractor with substantial cost savings in labor and fuel. The hurdles here are state safety laws based on protecting the private automobile, and labor union resistance. The other development is the movement of truck vans and containers on railroad flatcars, the TOFC (trailer on flatcar) or COFC (container on flatcar) service, nicknamed "piggyback." This service offers substantial cost savings, although the service can be slow. Some motor carriers and unions have been dubious about this type of operation because it deprives the trucker of the long-haul portion of the traffic, but TOFC and COFC are well established and expand yearly. To the extent that speed can be further improved while holding costs down, TOFC and COFC may further strengthen truck competition with air. They also serve environmental policies as they reduce oil consumption, air pollution, and highway congestion.

The latter 1990s have seen a trend toward the acceptance by forwarders and integrators of cargo designated as "air cargo" that goes the entire journey by truck. As with regular air cargo, barcoding is used, with a tracing service, and often a "time-definite" guarantee where transportation charges are refunded if arrival time is not met.

While the truck is generally considered to have the time advantage over air in the 500-mile range (though some would extend this to 600 to 800 miles), there is also fast, reliable long-haul truck service, such as three-day transcontinental trips using two-driver equipment. This is competitive with the forwarder's traditional offering of deferred three-day air service and at a much lower cost.[36] The forwarder can see such traffic lost to the motor carriers or can acquire its own long-haul trucks.

Competition between Air and Ocean Vessel

In 1998, 61 percent of the freight and express ton-miles of U.S. scheduled airlines (including the all-cargo carriers) were performed in international services.[37] If we add to this the traffic of the foreign airlines, which carry about two-thirds of the airborne trade in and out of the United States, we see that the larger part of the air cargo commerce of the United States is to or from foreign countries. One reason for this great development of international air cargo is that the geographic position of the United States is such that, with the exception of Canada and Mexico, all international trade must move either by air or by sea. Ship transportation, compared with its land counterpart, the truck, is cheaper but also much slower. The time-and-cost trade-off between air and sea is different from that trade-off between air and truck.

It is possible to find figures showing ocean transport averaging one or two cents a ton-mile, but this extraordinarily low figure is really meaningless when discussing competition with air because it is derived primarily from the carriage by ships of tremendous quantities of commodities in bulk, such as coal, petroleum, and grain. The cost of carrying manufactured goods by sea is well above these figures, even before we add on the cost of moving cargo from factory to port and from the destination port to the inland recipient. Various estimates indicate that transportation of the high-value goods for which air and ocean compete, carried on fast modern container vessels, may cost the shipper anywhere between one-tenth and one-third what it would cost if shipped by air.[38]

The gap between the two modes with respect to time is far greater.

Ship transport may take 10 or 20 days to move cargo where air would take only a day or two. The time advantage by air is so great—so much greater than air's time advantage over truck on domestic hauls—that international air cargo has shown impressive development despite the cheaper rates by sea.

Given the choice between a day or two by air and perhaps two weeks by ship (including the slow process of loading and unloading at piers), the shippers of clothing, radios, binoculars, toys, and so on will choose air, even at much higher transportation costs. Even large, heavier manufactured goods such as machinery, computers, and refrigerators sometimes travel by air across oceans.

The maritime industry has seen some of its most valuable cargo go over to air. But there are developments in the industry that may make it a stronger competitor with air in the future. Principal of these is the container ship, where truck vans are loaded on the ship by a crane and stacked on top of one another. (The vans must be specially constructed to withstand the weight in the stacking process.) The combination of truckload haul to the port city, rapid loading (very rapid compared with old-style loading), and the reverse of the process at the destination all contribute to a great reduction in the total transit time as well as savings on costs (especially the longshoreman labor), damage, and theft. Moreover, the vessels themselves are typically constructed with a view to speed, at least speed by maritime standards. Cargo may move from Ohio to Switzerland, at all times safely stowed in one truck van, in 10 days, instead of 20.

A variant of the container vessel is the LASH system (lighter aboard ship), where the ship anchors in the harbor instead of requiring dock space, and barges called lighters are moved by tug out to it and swung aboard by a crane. The barge is the container. Cargo can be taken down the Mississippi, carried by ship to a European port, carried up the Rhine to an inland destination, all without leaving its container and with swift and simple loading devices.

There is much labor resistance to container ships, since they eliminate many longshoreman jobs. Nevertheless, the use of container vessels grows steadily, and they represent a factor favoring sea in its competition with air. It should be noted that the type of cargo that goes by these ships is often the very type of cargo (merchandise, manufactured goods, and so on) that air cargo solicits.

Data for 1996 on U.S. international commerce (air and ocean vessel only), measured by the *value* of the goods, show that 39.3 percent went by air, 60.7 percent by vessel.[39]

An interesting arrangement in which the airlines cooperate rather than compete with ocean transport has developed with respect to Asian trade. Cargo travels by ship, typically a container ship, from Far Eastern ports to U.S. West Coast ports, especially Seattle, then proceeds by air to other U.S. points, to Latin America, or to Europe. The rate is in-between an all-air or all-sea rate, and the transit time is similarly in-between all-air and all-sea time. For example, the sea/air service Asia-Seattle-Europe takes about 10 to 14 days, while all-sea would take about 30 days and all-air perhaps two days or less. As to rates, data must be used with caution as many elements enter into rate comparisons, but apparently sea/air runs roughly a third less than all-air, but about three times as much as if all by sea.[40] The figures will, of course, vary with the proportion of the haul that is performed by each mode; a developing service from Asia to Latin America, with a long sea haul to Los Angeles, shows sea-air a third less than all-air, but all-sea only one tenth of all-air.[41]

Other sea/air routes are developing around the world, notably Asia-Europe westbound with cargo traveling by sea to the port of Dubai on the Persian Gulf from where it is flown to European cities. Reportedly some cargo from India and Pakistan destined for the United States now travels westbound by sea/air through Dubai. As container ships become even faster and more efficient, sea/air services can be expected to grow.

COMPETITION FOR CARGO BETWEEN U.S. AND FOREIGN AIRLINES

In 1987, the Department of State and the Department of Transportation submitted to Congress the results of a joint study analyzing the reasons why the proportion of air cargo carried in and out of the United States by U.S. airlines had been dropping. By the middle 1980s, foreign airlines were carrying about 69 percent of this traffic, measured by weight. Their findings included the following major points:

1. All the major U.S. combination carriers with international services, with the single exception of Northwest, had ceased operating freighters, nor did these carriers operate combis. (Combis, as earlier explained, are aircraft with cargo carried in a partitioned-off portion of the passenger cabin as well as in the hold.)

2. Many foreign airlines had aggressively pursued cargo traffic, while U.S. airlines, in general, had not.

3. Some countries had discriminatory practices such as the failure to provide proper cargo facilities at their airports or requiring that cargo of U.S. carriers be handled at their airports by the competing home-country airline rather than by the U.S. carrier itself or an agency of its own choice. There are many other problems of this sort, generally described as "doing business" problems. Some countries also limited the number of U.S. airlines that could serve their cities and restricted Fifth Freedom cargo traffic.

The report noted, however, that the integrated carriers, including former air freight forwarders such as Emery that had acquired their own aircraft, were vigorously expanding their services to and from foreign points.

There has been no substantial change in the international air cargo picture since the 1987 study, except that in 1997 United Airlines resumed freighter service on its transpacific routes. Except for Northwest and United, all the U.S. combination carriers still shy away from freighters or combis, being content to carry cargo in the belly holds of passenger flights, while certain foreign airlines aggressively pursue cargo traffic, using freighters and combis extensively. Progress has been made in some areas in reducing discriminatory treatment at foreign airports, but some complaints continue. It also remains true, however, that the U.S. integrated carriers are steadily and vigorously expanding their services at foreign points. As earlier noted, many of them use wide-bodied freighter aircraft and are expanding into accepting ever larger shipments, so that the distinction between small-package service and air freight is breaking down. Thus, the U.S. airline industry, taken as a whole, seems to be holding its own in the cargo field against foreign competitors.

There were, of course, managerial reasons why the major combination carriers ceased operating freighters. Directional imbalance has been cited as one reason. But it seems likely that these airlines simply found freighter operations less profitable than limiting their cargo carriage to the substantial cargo space in the bellies of passenger aircraft where, in a sense, it is being carried on an added-cost basis. Of course, these aircraft fly on schedules attractive to passengers, not the overnight schedules attractive to cargo shippers; thus, much cargo is lost when freighter service is dropped, regardless of how much cargo space is available on the passenger flights.

Meanwhile, the U.S. all-cargo carriers, especially the small-package specialists, are a growing segment of U.S. international air cargo transportation. As we have seen, small-package traffic yields high revenue in proportion to weight; thus, the revenues from the international services of the U.S. airline industry as a whole may rise even while the tonnage is holding level or falling.

THE SELLING OF AIR FREIGHT SERVICE

We have previously used a breakdown of air freight into emergency, routine perishable, and routine surface-divertible. And we have seen that, for the first two, speed is the primary selling point, while for the third the shipper must be convinced of overall cost savings under the total cost concept.

There are certain other selling points. Fast transportation may open up new distant markets for perishables or may enable a manufacturer to compete in distant markets with other manufacturers who are located much nearer those markets. In the latter case, the ability to deliver promptly is essential, and a shipper may switch to air simply to meet this customer requirement, even where the goods are not perishable and no total cost savings accrue to the shipper.

Airlines, aircraft manufacturers, and the Air Transport Association have all from time to time done surveys of the inner workings of manufacturing and retailing establishments, in the hope of showing them that they would benefit from increasing their use of air cargo. Smaller corporations are more likely to permit this sort of survey, since the larger will be more likely to have done their own cost and marketing research.

But such surveys do not always get the desired result. Perhaps no true savings are discovered. Perhaps the firm may utilize the findings not to switch business to the airlines but to improve its inventory and warehousing practices or to reorganize its truck transport arrangements. Or a firm may be sold on cost savings and switch traffic to the air, only to switch back when the competing truckers offer improved service or lower rates.

Both manufacturers and retailers share a concern with costs such as inventory carrying charges and warehousing. But retailers have a particular interest in other total-cost considerations such as lost sales due to stockouts, too much merchandise on hand after a season ends, and merchandise that proves unpopular with the public and can be sold only at sharp discounts. The fact that public taste in clothing styles is hard to predict is one reason why clothing has become a major air freight item. An airline's sales approach to a retailer may emphasize that air freight works to keep inventories small, to keep what is on the store shelves closely tied to what the public is buying.

Earlier in this chapter we mentioned the "just-in-time" concept, where manufacturers keep very small inventories of raw materials and components, and retailers keep very small inventories of goods—relying on swift transportation and reliable deliveries. A variant of the total cost concept, just-in-time (often abbreviated as JIT) puts an unusual burden on the air carriers and forwarders to have shipments arrive on the exact day desired. A manufacturer (of automobiles, for example) may arrange with suppliers of components to have a precisely timed flow from each, with a computerized record of where each shipment is, and an ultimate reliance on the air and truck transportation systems. The objective is minimum inventory, and shipments must not only not arrive late, they must not arrive even one day early. Promotion of the JIT concept is a challenging task for airline and forwarder sales personnel.

Cargo traffic by its nature is far more one-way than passenger traffic.

In some markets this may lead to a directional imbalance. In the early days of airlines, the tendency of cargo to flow more heavily out of industrialized areas than into them caused a heavier cargo flow in the United States from east to west and from north to south. This tendency is much less pronounced today, with the industrialization of the West and the South. In the Pacific there has been an imbalance wherein the development of light industries in Japan, Hong Kong, Korea, China, and Taiwan has caused cargo inbound to the United States to be heavier than the outbound. In the mid-1980s, the strength of the dollar in relation to other currencies had strengthened U.S. imports and weakened U.S. exports, which further accentuated the imbalance in the Pacific. By 1987, however, the dollar had weakened, moving U.S. imports and exports somewhat closer to a balance, and, by mid-1988, the directional air cargo problem in the Pacific had eased greatly. In the years 1990–93 the directions were about in balance, but by the late 1990s the Asian economic downturn caused a large drop in exports to Asia while prosperity in the United States caused imports from Asia to be high—resulting in a major imbalance in the easterly direction.

Air cargo between the United States and Latin America used to favor heavily the southbound, but by the early 1990s the directions were about evenly balanced. One reason was that agricultural development in Latin American countries has caused increased shipments of high-value perishables such as flowers, berries, and fish to the United States and also to Europe and Asia via U.S. airports. Also, economic development in Latin America has increased the northbound air shipments of manufactured goods. Changes in levels of customs duties have also been an influence.[42] As of 1997, the balance between the United States and South America was about 55 percent northbound to 45 percent southbound.

The U.S.–Europe balance that year held to a nearly even 52 to 48 percent, favoring the westbound.[43]

Directional rates favoring traffic in the lighter direction are permitted and often resorted to. But sales policy on the part of the airline, directed specifically to the lighter direction, is also necessary. Otherwise, low cargo load factors in one direction can easily cancel out whatever profits are being made from high cargo load factors in the busy direction.

Sales policy of an airline may also be directed at the cube-out problem of aircraft. Its sales personnel may be directed to refrain from soliciting low-density traffic, but to promote high-density traffic aggressively. The object should be to try to get the best mix for the types of aircraft in the airline's fleet.

Since an airline, under deregulation, is now permitted to negotiate special rates with one shipper, a new type of sales practice has appeared. According to a TWA cargo official, Scott Johnson, much cargo traffic today "comes from corporate deals made with the head offices. . . . [O]perations are tied into corporate-to-corporate deals with contracts of six months to a year in duration. The result is a lot of bargaining."[44]

UNITIZATION—CONTAINERS AND PALLETS

Unitization is a general term that means putting many small pieces of freight into a single physical unit. Two more specific terms referring to types of unitization are:

Palletization—stacking shipments on a simple platform, usually made of wood, which can be readily moved around a terminal, or on or off aircraft, by forklift trucks or by more advanced forms of mechanism called pallet loaders and pallet transporters.

Containerization—the use of certain boxes of a size and shape *standardized by airline agreement*.

The term *unit load device* (frequently abbreviated as ULD) is a general term covering both the container and the pallet.

Airlines use pallets and containers for their own convenience in handling the many miscellaneous shipments that come to them. Many small shipments stacked on a pallet with a protective net or plastic cover can be moved through a terminal and loaded on an aircraft with much lower labor cost than if each shipment were to be handled separately. And standardized containers, many of which are shaped to fit the contours of the aircraft, will make not only for efficient handling but also for protection of the contents from damage and pilferage, as well as more efficient use of the space inside the aircraft.

But the airlines also want shippers (including forwarders) to use pallets and containers that they load at their own place of business, with the airline simply handling the already unitized cargo. When airlines speak of "containerization," they usually mean use of a container *by a shipper*, and to encourage this practice they offer rate discounts when cargo is containerized.

There are two series of standardized containers, one for domestic cargo agreed to by U.S. carriers, originally with CAB approval, the other for international cargo agreed to by IATA carriers with approval of the governments. Many of the containers in the domestic series are compatible with containers in the IATA series, which is important when cargo is to travel in the United States and then be transferred to an international flight. Complete compatibility, however, while it would appear desirable, does not seem to be developing.

While some containers are designed to fit the contours of different aircraft models, some are simply square-cornered boxes of standard di-

mensions. Containers conforming to the required standards may be purchased by shippers, and there are firms that manufacture them to
specifications. Certain types are usually owned by the airlines, which use
them for their own convenience in handling shipments or lend them to
shippers.

The airlines have widely advertised and aggressively promoted the
concept of containerization. The advantages to the airlines may be summarized as cost savings on labor, faster turnaround time on aircraft, better utilization of the space within aircraft, reduction in theft and damage,
space savings at terminals, and resultant lower rates, which, in turn, will
help develop air cargo traffic. Shippers benefit primarily from the rate
discounts but also may benefit from reduced damage and theft.

Yet the disadvantages, though less publicized, are many. Containers
cost money, even those that are made of simple fiberboard (really heavy-
duty cardboard) but especially those made of plywood, fiberglass, or
metal. There are disposable containers for one-time use, but most must
be used repeatedly to cover their cost, and this gives rise to the problem
of empty returns. To keep shippers interested in containerizing, the airlines must offer to return an empty shipper-owned container at an extremely low rate. Also, the airline's own containers must be brought back
on a nonrevenue basis. Ideally, an airline will have enough use for its
containers in both directions on a route so that it will have few empty
returns. It may also use collapsible containers, which minimize the space
required when returning empty. And, of course, the empties are normally returned on a space available basis.

There are other problems, such as the interchangeability (or lack of it)
of containers between different types of aircraft and between the domestic and international series. And for the larger containers, some of
which may, when loaded, weigh six or seven tons (more for the new
types being used on the 747F), an airline must invest in expensive loading equipment at every airport where they are to be loaded or unloaded.
Such investment may be hard to justify at many points where the amount
of cargo traffic (or at least the potential amount using huge containers)
is small.

One serious and growing problem has to do with the airlines' policy
that shippers may lock and seal containers. This is an excellent device to
minimize theft, but it poses the question of how an airline is to assure
itself that the contents qualify for specific commodity rates and that they
do not violate rules concerning hazardous cargo. In the case of international shipments, there is the problem of customs inspection, although
there are various facilitating arrangements such as for shipments in bond
across a country or to an to an inland destination point.

Logically there should be a container the size of a truck van, used
interchangeable by air, truck, rail TOFC, and container ship. However,

a truck or ship van is very large even for a 747 freighter, and it must be constructed to withstand the rigors of highway and especially ocean travel. The resultant extra weight makes it unsuitable for the air mode, with its high fuel consumption per unit of weight. Still, a future time with much larger aircraft and much greater fuel efficiency may see regular use of such a truly intermodal container.

CARGO RATES

The economic principles that underlie cargo rates are basically the same as those underlying passenger rates, as are many of the ratemaking regulatory procedures. Chapter 6 covered such matters as the following:

Cost-of-service and value-of-service factors in determining rates;

Out-of-pocket and fully allocated costs in determining rates;

The common cost problem in determining rates;

Unreasonably high or low rates; unjustly discriminatory rates; predatory rates; the standard foreign rate level;

DOT regulation of international rates; tariffs; the IATA system; new U.S. international rate policies.

Here the various types of air freight rates and some policy questions surrounding them will be examined.

Types of Air Freight Rates

Air freight rates may be divided into three basic types, together with some special discounts: general commodity rates, specific commodity rates, and exception ratings.

There is a *general commodity rate* schedule for every pair of cities an airline serves. The amount the shipper will pay will vary with the weight of the shipment, and the schedule will reflect rate differentials at weight breaks (as earlier described). (The rate differentials at the weight breaks are also sometimes called volume spreads.) The rate may also vary according to the direction in which the cargo is moving. However, a general commodity rate is *not* based on the type of commodity in the shipment.

A *specific commodity rate*, as its name implies, covers a specified commodity. Moreover, it applies to that commodity only when it is moving between two specified points, and it often applies in only one direction. As with the general commodity rates, the amount the shipper will pay will depend on the weight of the shipment, using the weight-break system for heavier shipments. Thus, wristwatches, for example, may have a specific commodity rate from Hartford, Connecticut, to Chicago, Illinois, with the amount the shipper pays depending on the weight and on the weight breaks. Or the commodity may not be quite so specifically described; there may be a rate for printed matter, and, under this heading, a separate rate for newspapers. (The term *class rate* is sometimes used to refer to a specific commodity rate for a specified class of commodities.)

The reason for having a specific commodity rate is to attract and retain traffic. For example, much traffic in a particular item may be moving by truck from city A to city B, yet a total-cost analysis may show that much of it would move to air if the air rates were lowered by, say, 20 or 30 percent from the existing general commodity rate. A specific commodity rate is introduced by a carrier, is usually equaled by competing carriers, and the commodity begins moving by air. The airlines usually find, however, that they must continue offering a specific commodity rate indefinitely, or they will lose much or all of the traffic back to the trucks.

Thus, specific commodity rates are demand oriented, motivated by the value-of-service concept, typically set well below fully allocated costs, and applied where the surface-versus-air decision is marginal. They are found where there is a large amount of traffic in that commodity moving in a particular market and are ordinarily substantially lower than the general commodity rates.

A third type of air freight rate involves an *exception rating* and is higher than the general commodity rate. Some shipments are charged more than the general commodity rate by the device of adding a percentage to that rate, the percentage being called an exception rating. Typically this device is used where there are unusually high costs connected with the air transportation, such as the handling and care necessary with live animal shipments. Very valuable cargo, requiring extra care and guarding, may also have an exception rating.

There is another way in which a shipper may find itself paying more than the general commodity rate—via the *dimensional weight* policy of an airline. For articles of very low density, such as cut flowers and empty plastic bottles, the carriers assume a weight higher than the actual weight and compute the rate on that presumed higher weight. That is, the cube of the shipment is measured, and what is really a fictitious weight is used when looking up the rate in the general commodity rate schedule.

Container Rates

We have already mentioned container discounts, which are discounts from the general commodity or specific commodity rates offered to shippers simply for using containers in the standardized series. Sometimes, however, an airline will offer a flat rate to carry a container (for example,

$120 for an LD-3 container from Chicago to New York); here there is no use of a general or specific rate as a base, and the term *discount* is really not appropriate.

There is also a *density incentive discount*, usually applied as an additional discount on containers when they are filled with cargo above a specified weight. But an airline may offer a density incentive discount for any shipment, even if not containerized. This discount is, of course, related to the cube-out problem previously discussed.

The *daylight container discount* is offered, in addition to the regular container discount, when a shipper arranges for a shipment to arrive at the airline terminal during slack hours and agrees that its delivery at the destination city may be delayed until slack hours. As we have seen, early morning and early evening are the peak congestion times at terminals. Accepting the conditions of the daylight discount may mean midday delivery the following day but in some markets may stretch the total transit time to two or three days. (Sometimes the daylight privilege is extended in the form of a flat rate rather than a discount.)

A shipment may qualify for all three discounts. Containerized, high-density, daylight freight consisting of a commodity for which there is a specific commodity rate may travel at a very low rate, in some cases even below the truck rate.

Air Freight Forwarder Rates

So far we have been considering the rates that an airline charges shippers (including forwarders). But, as we know, a shipper who takes cargo to a forwarder is charged in accordance with the forwarder's own set of rates. These are usually based on the same pattern as an airline's rates— that is, general and specific commodity rates and the several discounts. The rate level will usually be lower than the airline rate for the same service (allowing for pickup and delivery comparability), which, as we have seen, may be one reason why a shipper uses a forwarder.

Desirability of Specific Commodity Rates

The desirability of the specific commodity rate is often questioned. It is criticized as moving the airlines, under competitive pressures, steadily further away from cost-based pricing. The elimination of specific commodity rates, it is argued, would result in a lowering of the general commodity rate.

Proposals to phase down or phase out specific commodity rates meet strong opposition from the affected shippers. Yet there seems a rather strong economic argument for at least limiting the use of such rates. The issues resemble those surrounding the special, demand-oriented passenger discount fares. There are two tests for the short-run justification of these special rates. First, does the airline realize more revenue by use of the rate? Or does the loss of revenue from traffic that would have traveled at the regular rate exceed the revenue gained from new traffic that the special rate attracts? Second, does the added revenue (if any) exceed the out-of-pocket costs of carrying the extra traffic?

But the critical consideration for the long run is the capacity that the airline possesses. If the new traffic due to the special rate is filling space that would otherwise be carried empty, the continuation of the special rate may be justified both with respect to the airline's profitability and with respect to equitable treatment of the regular traffic. The latter is not being burdened if the low-rated traffic is only filling otherwise empty space. But the real test comes when the airline begins making capacity decisions (such as fleet purchases or the expansion of terminal facilities) premised on traffic that includes the low-rate traffic. Once the airline begins to look upon this traffic as normal and to expand to accommodate it, the justification behind the special rates diminishes. Thus, where much freight in a market is moving at specific commodity rates, the airlines may slide gradually into basing capacity decisions on this traffic.

Justification for Directional Rates

Directional rates are quite common in air cargo because of the directional traffic flows that we have previously discussed. The complaint is sometimes heard that they tend to persist after the directionality has disappeared. If directional traffic flows in a market have been equalized by directional rates, some experimentation may become desirable after a time to see how much traffic will be lost in the favored direction if the gap between the two rates is slowly reduced.

Perhaps the best advice respecting both the directional and the specific commodity rates is that they should be looked upon as temporary, and the justification for each of them should be reviewed periodically.

Negotiated Cargo Rates

The foregoing discussion of cargo rates must be conditioned, much as our discussion of passenger rates was conditioned, by pointing out that large-volume shippers and air freight forwarders may readily negotiate reduced rates with the airlines, just as large corporations negotiate lower passenger fares. With respect to domestic rates, there is no regulatory barrier to such negotiated rates. DOT has authority to regulate cargo rates if they are international—and thus could require that tariffs for such rates be filed and adhered to. This would make negotiated cargo rates (if international) a tariff violation. In practice, however, DOT does not exercise this authority and, as of 1996, has exempted both U.S. and foreign carriers from having to file tariffs for international cargo rates.[45] A shipper or forwarder with a steady volume of business is in a good position to negotiate a favored rate, although the airline, in return for granting the rate, may require a guaranteed minimum amount of traffic over a specified period of time.

In arranging a contract with a shipper or forwarder for carrying cargo at a favored reduced rate, an airline must be careful not to obligate itself to carry so much of such low-revenue traffic that some of its higher-yield cargo is displaced. The situation resembles the yield management system for passenger bookings, whereby space is carefully controlled in the computer reservation system so that deeply discounted passenger tickets will be sold only to the extent that they do not displace full-fare passengers on any specific flight. The negotiated rate is apparently becoming the rule rather than the exception in air cargo movements.

CARGO CHARTERS

There is an increasing trend toward the use of chartered freighters by shippers and forwarders, as well as by one airline from another. This has given rise to a type of carrier that specializes in operating freighter charters—leading examples being Atlas Air and Gemini Air Cargo. Sometimes a charter is used temporarily where demand has exceeded available capacity, but there is a strong trend toward charters under long-term contracts.

From a forwarder's standpoint, one advantage to a charter is the ability to select a late cutoff time (for example, 11 P.M. or midnight), instead of having to meet a cutoff time in the early evening when using space on a combination carrier that tailors its schedules to its passenger service. Given the propensity of shippers to deliver cargo to the forwarder at the end of the business day, meeting an early evening departure may be very difficult. But there are also disadvantages to chartering. The forwarder may be charged for an empty backhaul on a charter flight and, even if this does not occur, may find the charter more expensive than the belly transport on a combination carrier. Perhaps the forwarder cannot fill the chartered plane or, even if it does, may find the carriage more expensive than belly transport on a combination flight, given that the latter is often priced on an added-cost basis. Of course, if a forwarder is facing a decision to purchase its own aircraft and begin performing the air haul itself, it may decide that chartering is a preferable alternative since charters, especially on a long-term basis, give a forwarder needed capacity without the high costs of owning and operating its own aircraft fleet.

There has been a definite trend in recent years for combination airlines, particularly foreign air carriers, to put some of their cargo on chartered freighters, usually on a long-term contract basis. Traditionally, a charter by one airline from another has been called a *wet lease*. More recently, the acronym ACMI (aircraft, crew, maintenance, insurance) has come into use, meaning a type of charter where the operating carrier provides the four elements just mentioned, but the charterer pays for the fuel. Although particularly popular for the foreign air carriers, U.S. combination airlines and integrators also use ACMI services. They are really part of the trend to outsourcing found generally in industries today.[46]

CONTRACT AND PRIVATE CARRIAGE OF CARGO

Carriage of passengers or cargo by air may be common carriage, open to the public; contract carriage, open only to a limited list of clients solicited without public advertising and usually operated under a long-term contract with each client; or private carriage, where a firm (or person) carries its own personnel or property. This book is concerned almost entirely with common carriage, but contract and private operations have a particular significance with respect to cargo.

Contract and private carriers, while subject to safety regulation by the FAA, are not, and have never been, under entry, rate, or other economic regulation, either by DOT or, earlier, by the CAB.

Private Carriage of Cargo

Although there is much private carriage of passengers in aviation, counting both pleasure flying and corporation aircraft, which fly executives and other company personnel, there is relatively little private carriage of cargo. (An example of such carriage would be an oil company carrying drilling equipment or other company supplies in its own aircraft.) But in the future it is distinctly possible that there will be much more of it, as firms become aware of its advantages. It is even conceivable that someday there will be private cargo aircraft fleets much as there are now fleets of private trucks, each carrying the goods of its owner corporation.

The advantages to a manufacturer or retailer in owning its own cargo aircraft include availability of lift when needed, tailoring to the company's needs, faster service, better control over loss and damage, and perhaps lower costs. Disadvantages include empty or light backhauls and the idle time on the aircraft.

Private carriage need not be limited to carriage of traffic belonging to the one owner and operator of the aircraft. There are other possible arrangements, some of which involve a hybrid of private and contract carriage and raise a controversial legal question as to their true status. Some examples are the following:

Joint ownership of a private fleet by more than one shipper;

Ownership of the fleet by a subsidiary corporation set up by several manufacturers or retailers, with the sole function of carrying the cargo of these firms;

Ownership of the fleet by one shipper, using it for its own cargo and also accepting cargo from a limited group of clients as in contract carriage.

Contract Carriage of Cargo

Figures on the amount of contract carriage of cargo by air are hard to find, since contract carriers, never having been subject to economic regulation by the CAB or DOT, have never had to file traffic statistics with either of these agencies. It is generally believed, however, that contract carriage is relatively minor compared to common carriage. Yet, if airline freight rates should rise rapidly or if service speed should decline, there could be a rise in the number of contract carriers and perhaps a sharp increase in the amount of traffic they carry. There is nothing in present law to prevent a contract operation with the largest and most modern aircraft, such as the 747F. However, a contract carrier contemplating a major investment in large aircraft might opt to become a common carrier of cargo, at least for domestic operations, considering the ease of entry under Section 418 and the negligible regulatory burdens.

Foreign Authorization for Private and Contract Carriage

When private and contract operators wish to conduct flights between the United States and foreign countries, they may run into problems in obtaining the permission of the foreign governments. The bilateral agreements that cover scheduled airline services do not apply to private or contract carriage.

Private carriage is generally permitted by most governments. But if such carriage should expand greatly, to a point where it cut seriously into the scheduled service of a country's airline, the government of that country might become more restrictive, especially if the operation were of the hybrid type just discussed. If U.S. electronics manufacturers, for example, should arrange joint ownership of a private fleet and send most of their previous airline cargo on this private facility, the injured airlines might urge their governments to question the private status of the operation.

Contract carriers are more likely than private carriers to run into difficulties when they operate to foreign countries. The common versus contract concepts are not part of the legal thinking in some countries, and thus a contract carrier may be looked upon merely as an unauthorized airline.

SOME CURRENT PROBLEMS

Certain problems in the air cargo field deserve special notice, such as inflation, multilateral cargo agreements, the impact of trade agreements, fuel policy, hazardous cargo, and cargo alliances.

Impact of Inflation

Although inflation remained moderate through the 1990s, a resumption of a higher inflation rate through the whole economy, particularly with respect to fuel and wages, could have consequences for the cargo services of the airlines, as with their passenger services. Inflation, however, can have a favorable effect on the growth of air cargo to the extent that it makes some commodities higher in value per weight unit and causes high interest rates, which make inventories even more costly to hold.

Multilateral Cargo Agreements

Although obtaining multilateral regional air cargo agreements of the open skies variety has been advocated as a U.S. policy, negotiations for cargo routes have remained largely on a bilateral basis, with the United States seeking the most liberal terms. Should efforts ever succeed in obtaining a regional agreement, it would probably be first with Western Europe, with efforts then turning to the countries of the Pacific Rim and then to Latin America.

The Impact of Trade Agreements

The worldwide trend toward freer trade, by increasing the flow of world commerce, should increase international air cargo traffic. There may be individual exceptions, however, as where a regional free trade bloc is formed and seeks to protect cargo traffic within the bloc from penetration by U.S. carriers. The North American Free Trade Agreement (NAFTA) should increase trade with Mexico and thus increase air cargo movements to and from that country, but a countervailing factor is that NAFTA facilitates U.S. truck traffic into Mexico and may thus reduce the need for air cargo to and from some Mexican points.

The World Trade Organization (WTO) has entered the air cargo picture by planning international talks looking toward a worldwide liberalization of restrictions on airline services. Its intervention in airline matters has been resisted in some parts of the airline industry, but the WTO may provide at least a forum for working on a broadening of air cargo rights.[47] The WTO could have an impact of another sort on air cargo. By pursuing its mandate to obtain reductions of customs duties and other barriers to trade, it could increase the flow of goods internationally, with an obvious growth impact on air cargo.

National Fuel Policy

If, as now appears to be the case, a general national shortage of energy is to be an increasing problem in future years, the impact could fall heavily on air cargo, since even the most fuel-efficient freighter (as an optimally loaded 747F) uses up much more fuel per ton-mile of payload than any other mode. Figures vary—and are controversial, in light of the strong industry interests involved—but some past studies indicated that air freighters might require about 15 times as much fuel per ton-mile as trucks and about 50 or 60 times as much as railroads and ships.[48] (The figures would not be as extreme today in light of improved airline fuel efficiency.) It is not inconceivable that in a severe petroleum shortage the law might compel some air cargo to shift to truck or ship, and some truck cargo to shift to rail piggyback.

To save air cargo from such a fate, we must look to technology. The history of aircraft development has been in the direction of greater fuel efficiency. A future aircraft may find itself judged heavily by the payload it can deliver per gallon. And the case for the airship as a cargo carrier, and for government funds to advance its development, may become even stronger, since it would be remarkably fuel-efficient.

Government fuel policy could take another form: a prohibition or limitation on freighter flights, so that all or most cargo would have to travel on passenger flights. This would be disruptive to the development of air cargo, to the airlines, and to industries depending on air movement of freight. Yet if fuel conservation had to be placed above all other considerations, it could be argued that a ton of cargo on a passenger flight uses very little fuel—a type of added-cost thinking. So drastic a policy, of course, presupposes a truly critical fuel shortage.

The Hazardous Cargo Problem

The problem of cargo that poses a potential safety hazard has received much attention lately. The scope of the problem may be sensed from the list of dangers; cargo can be radioactive, explosive, combustible, corrosive, poisonous, or magnetic (and thus affecting navigation instruments).

Airlines have "restricted articles" tariffs that contain rules carrying out DOT and ICAO regulations as to articles excluded from all flights, articles excluded from passenger flights, articles acceptable only when packaged in a prescribed manner, and proper labeling.

The airline's most difficult problem in connection with hazardous cargo is that of shipper compliance. The airlines ordinarily do not open shipments to verify the contents. They could scarcely run their busy systems if they did. Thus, if a shipper, either inadvertently or purposely, fails to identify and clearly label a restricted shipment, the airline is not alerted to check it for proper packing and to segregate those shipments that must not go on passenger flights. Matters are made more acute by the desire of the airlines to promote shipper-loaded, shipper-locked containers.

The problem is being met by revisions in regulations, by the tightening of penalties for false labeling, and particularly by airline programs of shipper education. There are now worldwide regulations promulgated by ICAO, with the assistance of IATA, and similar U.S. regulations prepared and enforced by DOT. In 1993, DOT issued new regulations bringing U.S. standards into line with the ICAO standards.

Cargo Alliances

The alliances among U.S. and foreign airlines discussed in Chapter 3 are built around the passenger service and may or may not include cargo in their scope. The Northwest–KLM alliance initially involved a desire by KLM to buy into the large freighter fleet of Northwest as well as its transpacific traffic rights, although in practice it has been merely a sharing of capacity. The Star Alliance mentioned in Chapter 3 was, as of mid-1999, considering extending its alliance-style operations to cargo. This would involve joint marketing, shared facilities and sales staff, and a sharing of capacity both on the ground and on the members' aircraft. The member airlines would be motivated by a desire to reduce costs, which would allow them better to compete with the integrators.[49]

As explained in Chapter 3, the term "alliance," while often meaning a broad range of joint operations, may be limited to nothing more than code sharing. For example, United Parcel Service has a cargo code sharing agreement with the Japanese carrier, Nippon Cargo Airlines. Also, it is possible for a carrier in a passenger alliance to form a cargo alliance with members of a rival passenger alliance.

An advantage to shippers and forwarders from cargo alliances is improved service through dealing with a large system offering a great number of destinations, with coordinated connections. Given the sensitivity of air cargo to speedy and reliable delivery, especially in an era of JIT, shippers and forwarders have a motive for favoring cargo alliances. On the other hand, they must consider the impact on rates, since alliances effectively reduce the number of competitors with whom they deal. Still, it can be argued that the cost savings to the airlines deriving from an alliance may be passed on to their customers in the form of lower rates. And, as we have seen, the big shippers and forwarders, far from being helpless in the matter of airline rates, characteristically negotiate reduced rates from the carriers. They could do the same with respect to an alliance, always provided that the alliance does not monopolize a market, which authorities such as the EU and DOT will presumably prevent.[50]

Other Continuing Problems

Other problems, which we have already discussed, seem to be inherent in the air cargo business. Among these are directional imbalance, the absence of new dedicated freighter aircraft, airport noise regulations, and the dependence in many domestic markets on belly cargo and thus on schedules tailored to please passengers.

Despite these chronic problems, air freight continues to grow, and small-package traffic continues to grow rapidly.

NOTES

1. Will Durant and Ariel Durant, *The Lessons of History* (New York: Simon and Schuster, 1968), p. 16.

2. U.S. Civil Aeronautics Board, *Report to Congress, Fiscal Year 1971*, pp. 89–90; and *Report to Congress, Fiscal Year 1972*, p. 89.

3. Author's calculations from Air Transport Association, *Annual Report-1999*, p. 5.

4. Ibid.

5. *Air Cargo World*, October 1999, p. 94.

6. *Air Freight Speakers Kit* (Washington, D.C.: Air Transport Association, 1972); and Nawal K. Taneja, *The U.S. Airfreight Industry* (Lexington, Mass.: D.C. Heath, 1979), p. 85.

7. House Committee on Public Works and Transportation, *U.S. International Aviation Policy*, p. 44.

8. *Air Cargo World*, February 1999, p. 54.

9. Lewis M. Schneider, *The Future of The U.S. Domestic Air Freight Industry* (Boston: Harvard Graduate School of Business Administration, 1973), pp. 26–29.

10. Author's calculations from Air Transport Association, *Annual Report-1999*, p. 4.

11. *Air Cargo World*, February 1984, p. 35.

12. *Air Cargo World*, July 1988, p. 42.

13. *Air Cargo World*, February 1999, p. 11.

14. *Air Cargo World*, March 1999, pp. 2, 4–5; and *Aviation Week and Space Technology*, January 1, 2000, p. 30.

15. James Jones, "Can Airlines Live With Clean Air?," *Air Cargo World*, May 1997, pp. 46–50.

16. *Air Cargo World*, July 1995, p. 32.

17. Robert Dahl, "Medium is the Freighter Message," *Air Cargo World*, November 1998, pp. 27, 30–32.

18. *Air Cargo World*, April 1998, pp. 5–6.

19. Sean S. Kilcarr, "Oversized, Overfilled?," *Air Cargo World*, December 1998, p. 39.

20. *Air Cargo World*, May 1998, pp. 59 and 68; July 1999, p. 8.

21. Michael A. Taverna, "Heavy-Lift Dirigible Demo Nears First Flight," *Aviation Week and Space Technology*, July 19, 1999, p. 41.

22. Schneider, *Future of the U.S. Domestic Air Freight Industry*, p. 46.

23. Nawal K. Taneja, *Introduction to Civil Aviation* (Lexington, Mass.: D.C. Heath, 1987), p. 185; *Air Cargo World*, August 1988, p. 27; Taneja, *U.S. Airfreight Industry*, p. 23.

24. *Air Cargo World*, June 1993, p. 20.

25. *Air Cargo World*, May 1987, pp. 22–23.

26. Laura Lang, "EDI Systems Work Well," *Air Cargo World*, December 1991, pp. 24–25.

27. *Air Cargo World*, April 1994, p. 8.

28. Gary Downey, Towne Air Freight, quoted in *Air Cargo World*, March 1999, p. 36.

29. Taneja, *Introduction to Civil Aviation*, p. 194.

30. *Air Cargo World*, February 1998, p. 36; May 1998, p. 76.

31. *Air Cargo World*, February 1999, p. 20; April 1999, pp. 14 and 18.

32. Daniel Pearl, "Fields of Dreams," *Wall Street Journal*, December 2, 1992, p. A–1.

33. John Gorsuch, "Taking the High Road," *Air Cargo World*, November 1996, pp. 44–48; Sean S. Kilcarr, "Ground Assault," *Air Cargo World*, August 1997, pp. 34–35.

34. *Air Cargo World*, January 1990, p. 22.

35. Taneja, *Introduction to Civil Aviation*, p. 186.

36. Sean S. Kilcarr, "Gaining Ground," *Air Cargo World*, February 1999, pp. 38–43.

37. Author's calculations from Air Transport Association, *Annual Report—1999*, p. 13.

38. *Air Cargo World*, October 1996, p. 20; April 1998, p. 26; December 1998, p. 11; and May 1999, p. 30.

39. U.S. Bureau of the Census, *Statistical Abstract of the United States*, 117th ed., 1997, p. 656, Table 1065; Author's calculations.

40. Sean S. Kilcarr, "Smooth Sailing by Air," *Air Cargo World*, August 1998, pp. 24–27.

41. Michael Fabey, "By Sea, Si?," *Air Cargo World*, July 1999, pp. 18–19.

42. *Air Cargo World*, April 1991, pp. 18–19; December 1993, p. 17.

43. Brian Clancy and David Hoppin, "The 1998 Merge Global Air Cargo Forecast," *Air Cargo World*, May 1998, pp. 35 and 38.

44. Quoted in *Aviation Week and Space Technology*, May 14, 1984, p. 29.

45. *Air Cargo World*, February 1996, p. 4.

46. Paul Page, "Not Plane Simple Anymore," *Air Cargo World*, November 1996, pp. 22–30; Paul Page, "Chartering New Routes," *Air Cargo World*, June 1998, pp. 36–39.

47. *Air Cargo World*, July 1998, p. 2.

48. Eric Hirst, *Energy Intensiveness of Passenger and Freight Transport Modes* (Oak Ridge, Tenn.: Oak Ridge National Laboratory, 1973), p. 27; "The Railroad Paradox," *Business Week*, September 8, 1973, p. 63; and William H. Jones, "Railroads," in *Transportation in America*, ed. Donald Altschiller (New York: H. W. Wilson, 1982), p. 71.

49. Dave Wirsing, "Alliances," *Air Cargo World*, June 1999, p. 64.

50. Sean S. Kilcarr, "The Price of Alliances," *Air Cargo World*, September 1997, pp. 38–47; Brendan Sobie, "The Alliance Dance," *Air Cargo World*, April 1999, pp. 26–34.

SELECTED REFERENCES

Air Cargo World (called *Cargo Airlift* until October 1976, *Air Cargo* until January 1983) is the only trade magazine of general national circulation that is confined to the cargo aspects of airlines. Appearing monthly, it contains readable, brief articles and news items and is an excellent means for keeping informed on current air cargo matters.

Air Transport Association of America, *Air Cargo from A to Z* (Washington, D.C.: Air Transport Association of America, undated). This booklet, revised periodically, defines and explains the terminology of air cargo in simple, clear language.

Lewis M. Schneider, *The Future of the U.S. Domestic Air Freight Industry* (Boston: Harvard Graduate School of Business Administration, 1973). Intended as a research project involving three trunk lines and an all cargo carrier, this book is an excellent study of the economics, managerial strategy, and problems of the U.S. domestic air freight industry. Some students may find it difficult reading, since it presupposes much background in economics and statistics.

Nawal K. Taneja, *The U.S. Airfreight Industry* (Lexington, Mass.: D.C. Heath, 1979). This thorough and scholarly study of the economics and managerial problems of the air freight industry takes us through the first year of cargo regulatory reform.

Relationships between integrated carriers and air freight forwarders are discussed in *Air Cargo World*, August 1992, pp. 20–26. The article covers cooperation and competitive rivalries as well as the blurring of the respective roles.

An excellent analysis of the pros and cons, the hopes and pitfalls, of all-cargo airports can be found in Daniel Pearl, "Fields of Dreams," *Wall Street Journal*, December 2, 1992, p. A–1. The article deals with the all-cargo airport as an engine of economic development and describes plans for industrial cities built around such airports.

Sea/air intermodal transport is described in *Air Cargo World*, March 1989, pp. 25–26; August 1989, pp. 18–21; and January 1994, p. 8.

The first three years following the cargo deregulation legislation are studied in Andrew S. Carron, *Transition to a Free Market: Deregulation of the Air Cargo Industry* (Washington, D.C.: Brookings Institution, 1981).

A detailed analysis of air cargo as a factor in U.S. foreign trade, as well as a discussion of various airport problems related to cargo, can be found in *Handbook of Airline Economics*, ed. Darryl Jenkins (Washington, D.C.: McGraw-Hill, 1995), chaps. 54–57.

An analysis of the wide-body freighter fleet, worldwide, including economic characteristics of each model, is set forth in Rick Hatton, "Complexities of Air Cargo vis-à-vis Finance," in *Handbook of Airline Finance*, ed. Gail F. Butler and Martin R. Keller (Washington, D.C.: McGraw-Hill, 1999), pp. 535–42.

The problems and possibilities related to future freighter aircraft are outlined in Brendan Sobie, "The Future: Bigger, Faster?," *Air Cargo World*, January 2000, pp. 42–48.

8

Current Problem Areas

We shall conclude our survey of the economic side of airline operations by examining one specific problem area not previously covered—airport-airline relations—and by briefly summarizing the more significant current problems considered in previous chapters, phrasing them as questions to be resolved in the future.

AIRPORT-AIRLINE RELATIONS

As of 1997, DOT data showed that 207 airports in the United States accounted for 97 percent of all passenger enplanements. (The remainder took place at several hundred small points with limited regional or commuter air carrier service.)[1] Nearly all are owned and operated by state governments or subdivisions of state governments such as cities, counties, or airport authorities. Airport management has varying degrees of independence from elected officials such as mayors and county commissioners, In some instances an airport is simply a subordinate division of a city, county, or state government. In other it has a degree of independence, but is generally accountable to an airport commission that sets policies but does not make day-to-day decisions.

State legislatures will sometimes establish an "authority" independent of local elected officials. This authority may exist simply to run the airport, or it may be a port authority or transit authority where the airport is one activity operated along with others, such as docking facilities for ships or subways or bus lines.

Unlike railroads, motor freight carriers, and bus lines, which must own their terminals, the airlines do not own the airports. This has the advantage of holding down the capital investment necessary to operate, but the disadvantage that the airlines must cope with the policies, practices, and charges of hundreds of separate airport-operating entities. An airport is a monopoly in the sense that it is nearly always the only place from which an airline can operate if it wishes to serve a city. Even in instances such as New York, where there are several airports, the airline usually finds that they are under one authority.

Fees for takeoff and landing (usually just called landing fees), premised typically on the weight of the aircraft, are set by the airport unilaterally. The airlines may be consulted about these fees, and there is often an avenue of protest to political bodies such as a county commission, but the airlines do not possess much bargaining strength, since they cannot very realistically threaten to take their business to another airport. It is possible for an airline to take an airport management into court and try to show that fees are unreasonably high. The airport must then demonstrate to the court the relationship of the fees to the cost of service. Courts, however, are reluctant to intervene except in notorious cases of overcharging. Much the same situation prevails with respect to other airport charges such as rentals for counter and hangar space.

Since the 1930s the federal government has been furnishing financial assistance for the construction and expansion of airports. Since 1970 the funds for this purpose have come from a trust fund made up of the proceeds from sources such as taxes on passenger tickets, on air freight charges, on fuel, and on each international passenger departure. The money to construct and expand airports, however, comes from many other sources. The local governmental units (state, county, and city) may put up some of it out of general tax revenues. Sometimes the airport is initially surplus military property given or leased for a nominal consideration to the local government. Thus, it may be said that the original capital costs of many airports have been furnished by local or federal taxpayers. Moreover, the localities may be said to be subsidizing the airport indirectly through exemption from the usual local real estate property taxes, while the federal taxpayers indirectly assist through the income tax exemption on the interest on the bonds that airports sell when they need capital above the public sources that we have already mentioned.

Bond issues have become widespread in airport financing today. There are general obligation bonds, where the credit of the state, county, or city is pledged as security. More likely the revenues of the airport from landing fees, hangar and counter rentals, concessions such as parking and restaurants, and so on are pledged as security for the bonds. These are called revenue bonds and may pay a higher interest rate than the general obligation bonds because they are often considered somewhat riskier.

The distinction between these two types of bonds is not always clear-cut. Sometimes a revenue bond is guaranteed through what is called a secondary pledge by the governmental unit, which means that if the revenues fall short of covering both interest and amortization on the bonds, the state, county, or city will have to make good out of its general tax revenues. It could be said that, in effect, such revenue bonds are really general obligation bonds in disguise.

Of more concern to the airlines, and more troubling to airline economists, is the practice of having airlines, rather than the governmental units, give the secondary pledge, which they do, at least in effect, through such devices as guaranteeing to pay higher rental and other charges if revenues do not prove adequate to meet the interest and amortization on the bonds. The airlines, which are properly merely tenants at the airport, thus become enmeshed in the financial problems of the airport.

Another matter of concern to the airlines is airport capacity. As used in this context, *capacity* means the maximum number of landings and takeoffs possible at peak hours, within safety standards. When capacity becomes critical at an airport, agreements among the airlines to space their peak-hour flights become necessary and must be worked out with airport management and with the FAA since the latter agency is in charge of air traffic control.

There is a growing capacity problem at the busiest U.S. airports. Deregulation, as previously noted, stimulated a trend toward smaller aircraft (reversing a long trend of earlier years), which increased the number of flights needed to serve a given number of passengers. Deregulation has also tended to encourage hub-and-spoke operations, as mentioned earlier, where a carrier selects an airport as a hub and tries to time a number of inbound flights to feed traffic to an outbound flight. The resultant bunching of operations, moreover, tends to occur at peak hours. Aggravating these factors, the long-term growth of traffic continues.

The airlines tend to blame the government for the problem of congestion and delays at the busiest airports, alleging that the air traffic control system, which is operated by the FAA, has lagged in introducing the most modern technology, and that there has been insufficient funding for needed airport improvements. The government has been criticized for allowing monies to accumulate in the trust fund while airport expansion needs are unmet. Yet the airlines themselves have to some extent generated the very problem of which they complain by the vigorous pursuit of hubbing as well as by their use of smaller aircraft as a consequence of hubbing.

There is pressure for the building of complete additional airports at some major U.S. cities. Denver opened a new airport 26 miles out of the city center in 1994, but this was the first major airport built since the Dallas–Fort Worth Airport, which opened in 1974. The objections to building any large airport are many. Because of environmental considerations, notably the noise problem, a modern airport must own a vast area of land beyond its runways, and the runways themselves should be over two miles long. The huge cost of real estate acquisition tends to force the location to a rural area which, for most large cities, places it an inconveniently long distance away from the city center.

Solutions to the capacity problem other than building new airports are being pursued. The swing to smaller aircraft seems to have leveled off and perhaps reversed. Indeed, the trend of the 1990s was somewhat away from hubbing as the airlines perceived the costs of congestion and looked at the financially successful point-to-point services of Southwest Airlines. Additional runways are being built at some airports. Aircraft could take off and land closer together if more modern technology were employed by air traffic control. Terminal buildings can be enlarged, and the number of gates increased, with "people movers" to take passengers over the otherwise long walking distances within the terminal. Economic penalties can be placed on peak-hour operations, such as much higher landing fees during those hours, higher passenger fares for peak-hour flights, and the sale of peak-hour slots to the highest bidder. (The latter would help to resolve the difficult administrative task of allocating slots equitably.)

The most significant of the foregoing measures might well be a reduction in hub-and-spoke operations. A practice that forces passengers to change planes when they would prefer single-plane service, and that also foments peak-hour congestion at the busiest airports, would appear open to question from a public interest standpoint. To the extent that the need for a massive, expensive new airport may derive from hubbing, the project may be hard to justify.

Two developments of the 1990s may have a bearing on airport capacity problems. One is the proposal of the Clinton administration in 1994 to take the air traffic control function out of the FAA and make it a government corporation, somewhat along the lines of the Postal Service. Should this be approved by Congress, its proponents hold that it would encourage recruitment of the best technical personnel, more effective decision making, more efficient long-range planning, and a speeding up of technological advances. The other development is the abandonment of military airfields or their reduced use by the military, allowing use as reliever airports by the airlines.

A different airport problem is that of *adequacy*, a term which should be distinguished clearly from *capacity*. It refers to the ability of an airport to meet the economic needs of the community and its hinterland, present and future. To measure the adequacy of an airport, we must consider the population, income level, and character of the city and its hinterland, as well as the location of the airport within the metropolitan area and the ease of access to it from various parts of the area. Adequacy studies are particularly pertinent when the question is whether a city needs an additional airport or perhaps whether an airport has become obsolete and should be replaced by a new one in a different location. The airlines participate actively in such studies.

Another type of airport problem in which airlines are deeply involved comes under the general heading of environmental interactions. An airport can cause noise, air, and water pollution, as well as automobile traffic congestion. Environmentalists will insist, with some logic, that the true costs of an airport should include the social costs of such pollution and congestion—that is, the losses to society in its quality of living.

Noise problems due to aircraft operations are the most serious of the environmental charges against the airports and in many ways the hardest to resolve. In a few instances it has been possible to acquire huge tracts of land around the airport so that the aircraft flight paths are over airport property when they are at low levels. Dulles Airport outside Washington, D.C., is an example, and an even better example is the Dallas–Fort Worth Airport, which has a site of nearly 18,000 acres. But most existing airports are so located that the acquisition of such vast parcels of land is out of the question.

Proposals have been made to locate new airports at sea or, for Chicago and other lake ports, out in the lakes. So many large U.S. cities are located on the oceans or the Great Lakes that such projects are at least conceivable for the next century, although they would present their own technological and environmental difficulties. An airport on pilings or even below sea level on land protected by dikes, Netherlands-style, could move from fantasy to reality in future years. Such airports would be connected by cause-ways with port cities and might often be more accessible than present airports.

A current example is a new airport at Osaka, Japan, which opened in 1994, built "on a man-made island in Osaka Bay" and designed to have "sea access as well as road and rail links."[2] The cost is reported to be about $14 billion. Two other new airports in the Pacific Rim involve land partly reclaimed from the sea—at Hong Kong, which opened in 1998, and at Seoul, South Korea, scheduled to open in 2001.[3]

The noise problem has also been tackled by finding ways to make aircraft engines more quiet. We noted in Chapters 4 and 7 that the airlines were required by law to replace their older aircraft with quieter modern versions, put new, quieter engines on the older aircraft, or modify the older engines with hush kits. This program was essentially completed for U.S. scheduled airlines by the end of 1999, the deadline set by law for bringing all aircraft to Stage 3 standards. Completion of conversion to Stage 3 may weaken the case for future large-area airports such as Dulles, Denver, or Dallas–Fort Worth. But it should be kept in mind that even a Stage 3 engine makes a great deal of noise, and, given the nature of a jet engine, it is not likely that we will ever see a truly quiet jet airliner.

Just as the airlines were completing their expensive program of meeting Stage 3 standards, there was a movement (as noted in Chapter 7) toward establishing a new, even quieter standard, Stage 4, to be phased in gradually as with the other standards. The EU was especially pressing for such a standard, even as it was resisting acceptance of those Stage 3 aircraft that had been hush-kitted.

Regulatory reform has resulted in certain other problems for the airports. The increased number of airlines serving many cities has meant severe competition for gate and counter space, with airport management having to be arbiter between the newcomers seeking desirable locations and the established airlines seeking to retain their space, which is often at the most advantageous locations. The extent to which airport financing may rest upon long-term guarantees by specific airlines has also been affected by the new freedom of airlines to drop points and the increased possibility that an airline may be forced out of a point through competition from new entrants into its markets.

As will be seen from the foregoing, airport economics and airline economics are closely intertwined.

Airway Efficiency

Allied to the airport capacity problem is the question of the capacity of the airways—the flight paths that airlines are required to follow. Proposals are pending to revise the method of aircraft travel through the airways into a system called *free flight*. As described by professors Dempsey and Gesell: "The existing air traffic control system funnels flights into circuitous, narrow and crowded flight corridors. The alternative is 'free flight,' allowing pilots to choose the best route, taking advantage of favorable winds and avoiding storms. . . . Free flight would cut fuel costs, and allow passengers to reach their destinations more expeditiously."[4]

The "free flight" concept has general support in both the government and industry, although there are many problems with the technology. As the 1990s ended, the FAA was working on a plan to adapt the airways for "free flight."

The new concept, however, is not without problems beyond the technological. One such problem has been described as follows: "There are, of course, a limited number of airports with a limited number of run-

ways. Unless the airlines are willing to adjust and coordinate their schedules, aircraft will reach the same destinations at the same time, and any
fuel and time savings will be lost in holding patterns."[5]

QUESTIONS FOR THE FUTURE

The future of the airlines might be best delineated by posing some
questions on the various problems that have been discussed in this book.
What will be the long-run results of the regulatory reform legislation
and philosophy? Will the U.S. airline industry continue to be dominated
by a few large airlines? Will the merger trend resume, shrinking further
the number of major airlines, and, if so, what should public policy be
toward such a development? Will the pattern of the future be dominance
by a few majors and a feeder network of regional and commuter air
carriers, or will a time come once again when new carriers enter the field
and challenge the majors?

We may also ask what the future structure of passenger fares is likely
to be. Will discounting continue its present dominance? Do the frequent
flyer programs place an unhealthy competitive advantage in the hands
of the largest carriers? Are they likely to become a permanent feature of
airline service? Can a deregulated industry give the public lower fares
without impairing the safety of flight and the reliability of service?

We have seen improvements in labor productivity, but will union demands remain moderate at a time of airline prosperity? Will the potential
for small, new-entrant, nonunion carriers keep a pressure on airline labor
with respect to both wage and work-rule demands?

Have small communities become adjusted to regional and commuter
air carrier services with small aircraft in place of the large-aircraft services that many of them once knew? Will regional jet aircraft alleviate
complaints? Is the essential air service program resulting in permanent
dependence on federal subsidy for many of these services, or will they
all achieve profitability on their own after a transition period?

Has bias been removed from CRSs or does a case still exist for divestiture of airline ownership or some other, less drastic, governmental action? Three of the four major CRSs now have multiple airline ownership,
and a travel agent may now access the internal reservations system of
all the carriers participating in the CRS to which it subscribes. Have these
two developments, together with DOT's existing regulations, resolved
the bias problem?

What will the role of the travel agent be in the future? The airlines
have cut commissions and are encouraging direct bookings. Is the public
helped or hurt by these developments?

Can the industry maintain a level of earnings that will not only sustain
good service but also attract the capital needed to finance new aircraft?

While the debt/equity ratios of the airlines improved in the latter 1990s, they are still rather high. The industry would be vulnerable in the event of a recession or a leap in fuel prices, or both together.

We have seen that the scarcity of peak-hour flight slots and gates at the busiest airports puts a practical limitation on the freedom of entry for domestic service granted under regulatory reform laws. While the moderating of hub-and-spoke operations and the possible trend back to larger aircraft should give some relief, airport and airway overcrowding will very likely continue to be a critical problem if the volume of traffic continues its historical pattern of increase. Can improvements in the air traffic control system, bringing it up to a higher level of technology, be speeded up to alleviate the overcrowding?

Will the practice spread of having employees hold equity stakes in the airlines, even to controlling positions? How can union contracts be negotiated when labor is, in effect, on both sides of the table? Can labor costs, in the long run, be held to reasonable levels with labor as the owner?

On the international scene, we may ask to what extent the United States will succeed in obtaining the consent of additional foreign governments to its policies of multiple designation, absence of frequency/capacity controls, and liberal rate arrangements. And will the United States continue its current limited participation in a modified IATA rate-making system, or will it again consider leaving the system altogether? A swing of U.S. policy back toward somewhat tighter control of international airline service could occur if the share of U.S. international traffic carried by the U.S. airlines should drop seriously.

What will be the impact of alliances among U.S. and foreign airlines? Will Congress amend the transportation statute to raise from 25 percent to 49 percent the limit on foreign ownership of U.S. airlines? Will Congress legalize the grant of cabotage rights for foreign carriers? Is a multilateral agreement between the United States and the nations of Western Europe, intended to replace the numerous bilateral agreements, desirable?

Returning to the domestic sphere, the possibility must be considered that if the results of regulatory reform prove to be contrary to the public interest—to what the public wants from its airlines—then the political pendulum that swung so far in the direction of reducing regulation may swing back the other way. The term *reregulation* is being heard nowadays. Such a movement might be supported by small communities or might get impetus from public concern about perceived safety problems or the quality of airline service. There appears to be a high level of public dissatisfaction with the airlines today. The complaints include delayed flights and consequent missed connections, canceled flights, overbooking and resultant "bumping," delayed or lost baggage, poor food, narrow seat width and pitch, and even long delays in making ticket refunds and in compensating for lost baggage. Complaints are also heard about harsh discount fare restrictions such as no-refund policies, and about the extreme discrepancy between full fare and advance purchase fares. To the extent that deregulation is seen as the cause of these deficiencies, there may be rising public sentiment in favor of a governmental solution.

In 1993, a presidential commission entitled The National Commission to Ensure a Strong, Competitive Airline Industry was established to study the industry's financial plight and make recommendations. Among its many recommendations were: making the air traffic control system a government corporation, raising the limit for foreign ownership of voting stock in a U.S. airline to 49 percent, tightening merger policy, using fitness provisions to control overleveraging, reducing ticket and airbill taxes, amending bankruptcy laws to shorten the time gates and international routes can be tied up, and establishing a permanent commission to advise DOT on airline financial problems. The commission emphasized that it was not in favor of reregulation or any increase in DOT's statutory powers. Thus, it pointedly did not focus on such matters as market concentration, rate controls, CRSs, commission overrides, or frequent flyer programs.[6]

The Clinton administration had earlier indicated that it favored better enforcement of merger and fitness standards. It subsequently announced that it favored the reconstituting of the air traffic control system and the increase to 49 percent for the foreign voting stock limit.

Turning to the cargo field, we may ask whether the small-package business will continue to grow at a fast rate, and how well the industry will cope with its chronic problems of directional imbalance, a lack of domestic freighter service, a lack of a dedicated new freighter aircraft, and airport noise curfews.

Certain other problems can be expected to haunt the airlines in the future. The price leaps that fuel has taken in the recent past could occur again, and the possibility exists of future fuel shortages and governmental restrictions on the amount of fuel an airline may use. Security is likely to remain a concern, involving balancing the dangers from such acts as hijacking against the costs of prevention.

For the more distant future, we may look to technological developments to improve airline service. New types of aircraft with lower seat-mile costs might produce lower-fare services more effectively than mere deregulation. For cargo service, as we have earlier noted, the airship might furnish quiet, fuel-efficient, low-cost transportation and be able to operate from areas other than conventional airports. Very short hauls, between nearby city centers or from downtown to the airport, require a quiet machine with low operating costs; the helicopter has thus far proved a disappointment. At the other extreme, for long-distance flights the SST may yet come into its own if it can overcome severe environmental objections as well as prohibitively high fuel utilization and seat-mile costs. Similar difficulties, as well as many technological hurdles, will face the developers of the even faster hypersonic vehicle.

In 1993, the secretary of transportation stated as one of several "simple truths" that "more air travel is better than less."[7] Yet in Chapter 2 we noted the environmental strains and the drain on the world's finite supply of petroleum caused by the airlines. We suggested that there are those who would say that perhaps countries with a high per capita drain on the earth's finite resources should seek to level off the seemingly endless rise in such consumption activities as air travel. This thought runs contrary to much in our culture and is rarely indeed even mentioned by airline economists or government officials. Nonetheless, the new century may see environmental groups first, then governments and international agencies, urging the maximum use of such techniques as videotelephones as substitutes for both business and much personal air travel. A conservation slogan of World War II suggests itself: "Is this trip really necessary?" A study of airline economics should not neglect this conceivable future direction of public policy.

As these problem areas demonstrate, airline economics is closely interrelated not only with other parts of the economic system but also very much with the social, technological, and political arenas. The problems are many and severe, but challenging.

NOTES

1. *Airport Activity Statistics of Certificated Carriers—Summary Tables, Twelve Months Ending December 31, 1997* (Washington, D.C.: U.S. Department of Transportation, 1998), p. iv.

2. *Air Cargo World*, July 1993, p. 31.

3. *Air Cargo World*, March 1997, p. 38; Bob James, "A Lap of Cargo Luxury," *Air Cargo World*, June 1998, pp. 28–30.

4. Paul S. Dempsey and Laurence E. Gesell, *Airline Management: Strategies for the 21st Century* (Chandler, Ariz.: Coast Aire Publications, 1997), p. 404.

5. Kathleen M. Goodman and Scott Davis, "Free Flight and the Pilot-in-Command Concept," *Journal of Air Law and Commerce* 62 (February-March 1997): 660.

6. Amy K. Bock, "How to Restore the Airline Industry to Its Full Upright Position," *Journal of Air Law and Commerce* 59 (February-March 1994): 674–78, 682–88, and 692–94; *Aviation Week and Space Technology*, August 9, 1993, pp. 31–33.

7. U.S. Department of Transportation News Release, November 1, 1993, p. 5.

SELECTED REFERENCES

Laurence E. Gesell, *The Administration of Public Airports,* 4th ed. (Chandler, Ariz.: Coast Aire Publications, 1999), covers the whole range of airport economics and problems of airport management.

Airport and airway congestion, the effects of hubbing, and passenger complaints as to the quality of airline service are covered in "Air Travel in Crisis," *Aviation Week and Space Technology,* October 25, 1999, pp. 42–98.

The "free flight" proposal for the airways is analyzed in Bill Elder, "Free Flight: The Future of Air Transportation Entering the Twenty-First Century," *Journal of Air Law and Commerce* 62 (February–March 1997):871–914, and in the same issue Allison K. Lawter, "Free Flight or Free Fall?," pp. 915–56.

The trend toward regional jet aircraft and its implications for future airline service are the subject of Paul Proctor, "Regionals Strain to Keep Pace with Growth Surge," *Aviation Week and Space Technology,* May 1, 2000, pp. 44–46.

Self-Testing Questions

CHAPTER 1

Terminology

Be able to explain the following terms:

Air carrier, air transportation, and *foreign air carrier*, as defined in the transportation statute.

Cabotage traffic

Common carrier

Undifferentiated product

Questions

Describe the four special economic characteristics of airlines spelled out in this chapter.

Under the terms of the Airline Deregulation Act, the cargo reform act, and the Sunset Act, which functions of the CAB, relative to entry and rates, terminated and which went over to DOT? Distinguish between domestic and international services.

Explain the workings of the International Air Transport Association with respect to international rates, noting the respective roles of the airlines and the governments.

What are the aircraft size limits for the purpose of being classified as an air taxi or commuter air carrier?

Describe the system of classifying airlines established by the CAB in 1981 and in use today by DOT. Name and define each category.

Explain the term *debt/equity ratio* and show how a high ratio could affect the future of an airline.

CHAPTER 2

Terminology

Be able to explain the following terms:

Merchant airline
Natural monopoly
Public utility
Technological density

Questions

The gist of this chapter can be covered by three broad essay questions:

Describe the importance of the U.S. domestic airline system, dividing your answer into three parts—defense, postal service, and commerce—and concentrating largely on the last one.

Describe the various objectives that the governments of the world have with respect to their international airline services. Note which objectives especially pertain to technologically advanced countries, to technologically backward countries, to politically powerful countries, to countries with large aircraft manufacturing industries, and so on.

Describe, and discuss the significance of, the revisions made in the declaration of policy of the Federal Aviation Act by the ADA and the IATCA.

CHAPTER 3

Terminology

Be able to explain the following terms:

"Beyond" rights
Capacity and frequency (and how they overlap)
Contestability theory
Country-of-origin charter provisions
Economies of scale, scope, and *density*
Failing business doctrine

Fill-up (consecutive) *cabotage* versus *full* (unrestricted) *cabotage*

Freighter aircraft

Grandfather certificates

Hub-and-spoke route systems

Market power

Multiple designation

Open skies agreements (as defined by DOT)

Predetermination of capacity

Quid pro quo

Split charter

Questions

Discuss the development of airlines in the 1925–38 era, covering such items as the role of the Post Office Department, the use of mail subsidies, and the effect of the Kelly Act.

What reasons might an airline have for wanting to enter a new market? Why might an airline decide to exit from a market?

Contrast the language of the Federal Aviation Act concerning competition before and after it was amended by the ADA.

Some defenders of regulation of entry have contended that the consumer derives little or no benefit from increasing the number of competing airlines in a market above two. Do you agree or disagree, and why?

Describe the role of the federal courts with respect to orders of government agencies on airline matters. Show the types of actions the courts may take and the grounds for these actions.

Describe the role of the president with respect to issuance of international certificates to U.S. airlines and of foreign air carrier permits to foreign airlines.

Trace the development of the former category known as "local service carriers" from their original mission to their disappearance as a separate class of carrier.

Explain what is meant by a "hub-and-spoke" network, show how one works in practice, and give some examples. What would motivate an airline to develop such networks?

Explain *economies of scale, of scope,* and of *density* in the airline business.

What are the advantages and disadvantages to a community that loses jet service but receives small aircraft service by a commuter air carrier in its place?

Describe the essential air service program, including the criteria for determining an eligible point and for payment of subsidy. Do you think some small isolated points should receive subsidy indefinitely?

Under what circumstances might the DOT suspend or revoke a U.S. airline's international certificate? Under what circumstances might similar action be taken with respect to the permit of a foreign air carrier? What is the role of the president in each of these instances?

What reasons might an airline have for wishing to merge with, or acquire, another airline?

What changes did the ADA make in the guidelines that the CAB, and later DOT, were to follow in deciding whether to approve or disapprove a merger? Do you think that DOT properly applied these guidelines in approving the series of mergers that took place between 1985 and 1988?

What does DOT look for in determining the fitness of a carrier?

The relaxation of government barriers to domestic entry seems to have been succeeded by a process by which a large, well-established airline can prevent the entry, or limit the degree of entry, of a competitor into its markets. Describe the process, and give your opinion as to how effectively it works.

What criticisms can be made of the bilateral agreement system as a method for determining entry into international markets?

Contrast the two Bermuda Agreements (the old and the new) with respect to (a) capacity provisions and (b) multiple designation.

Define each of the *Five Freedoms*. Be able to classify a passenger in a Freedom. What is meant by the so-called Sixth Freedom, and how does the United States construe it?

For what reasons might a foreign government wish to privatize its government-owned airline?

Would you favor a change in U.S. cabotage laws to permit a foreign airline to carry U.S. domestic traffic on flights that originate at, or are destined for, foreign points? Why, or why not?

Why would a foreign airline (as distinguished from other potential investors) wish to buy voting stock in a U.S. airline? List and evaluate the objections that have been raised to foreign airline investments in U.S. airlines. Do you think the limit on such voting stock should be raised to 49 percent?

Distinguish between a code-sharing agreement and the older practice of interlining? What advantages or disadvantages to the public do you see in code-sharing arrangements?

Name the four principal global alliances, as of early 1999, and name the major U.S. carrier(s) involved in each.

What provisions may be found in an alliance as to joint, coordinated, or cooperative activities? What benefits or disadvantages to the public do you see in these big alliances?

CHAPTER 4

Terminology

Be able to explain the following terms:

Available ton-miles
Breakeven load factor

Cost taper

Load factor

Rate taper

Revenue passenger-miles

Revenue ton-miles

Seat-miles (available)

Questions

Define and give examples of *common* and *separable costs*. Also, give an example of a decision where airline management would use these concepts.

Define and give examples of *out-of-pocket, constant,* and *fully allocated costs*. Give an example of a decision where airline management would use these concepts.

Define and give examples of *line-haul* and *terminal costs*. Give an example of a decision where airline management would use these concepts.

Give all the reasons why seat-mile costs are higher for short hauls than for long hauls.

Explain the term *production function*. What is meant by the statement that the production function for most airline services is "homogeneous"? How do airlines of high-wage countries compete on international routes with airlines of low-wage countries? (Include discussion of aircraft and personnel utilization.)

In order to obtain the best utilization of an airline's resources, what factors does a flight scheduler have to take into account?

What was the impact on seat-mile costs of the introduction of new types of aircraft, such as jets and wide-bodies? How has the general inflation in the economy affected this trend? How would the SST fit into this pattern?

What steps are the airlines taking to improve their passenger miles per gallon of fuel?

Describe the changes that have occurred in the labor cost situation as a result of deregulation covering such points as wages, work rules, the two-tier system, and the impact of the hub-and-spoke network on productivity. What factors are shifting the bargaining balance back toward labor's advantage?

In your opinion, is deregulation likely to result in higher or lower employee productivity in the long run, and why?

Describe the steps established by the Railway Labor Act to assist in resolving *major* airline labor-management disputes. Also separately explain the steps to resolve *minor* disputes.

Why are airlines (and other transportation modes) particularly subject to injury by a strike?

Explain how the Mutual Aid Pact worked. What justification did the airlines give for having it? What reasons did labor give for opposing it?

What measures short of a strike can labor use to pressure airline management?

What is meant by "an airline-within-an-airline"? How would its operations differ from the other operations of the airline?

What motivates airlines to be willing to sell substantial, or even majority, equity shares to their employees? Discuss the details of the United Airlines employee ownership arrangement.

Why did deregulation lead to a trend to smaller aircraft? What factors may be inducing a trend back to larger aircraft?

Name the one major U.S. manufacturer of commercial airliners today and the one major European manufacturer. List the basic models now in use, identifying them by such general categories as wide-bodied and medium-range.

From the standpoint of the public interest, should high-speed rail service between large cities in the 150 to 300 mile range be encouraged? Should it be subsidized? What effects, good or bad, will it have on the airlines?

What impact is the introduction of regional jet aircraft having on service at smaller points? If such aircraft begin to be used by major airlines on routes previously served with larger aircraft such as the 737, what effect may this have on discounted traffic?

What factors must airline management consider in selecting a type of aircraft to purchase?

Discuss the noise problem, including the methods and costs to the airlines in bringing their fleets up to Stage 3 standards.

What are the advantages and disadvantages to an airline of leasing versus purchasing aircraft?

CHAPTER 5

Terminology

Be able to explain the following terms:

Computer reservations systems
Cross-section analysis
Off-peak pricing
Override commissions
Secular increase in demand

Questions

What is meant by the statement that airline service is an "intermediate good," and the demand for it a "derived demand"? What problems does this fact present for airline marketing managers?

Explain the term *income elasticity of demand* (and Engel's Law), as it applies to airline service. Why is this concept especially pertinent to airline travel by tourists?

Explain the term *variability* and describe its impact on utilization (and thus on the costs of airline service).

How has the deregulation of domestic entry and rates affected the ability of an airline to deal with the problem of seasonality?

Name the several factors affecting demand for airline passenger service and divide them into three categories: (a) those over which airline management has great control, (b) those over which airline management has no control, and (c) those over which airline management has limited control.

Of the factors in the previous question, which attract passengers to air travel as such, which merely attract a passenger to a particular airline, and which may do both?

What are the four methods shown in the text for estimating passenger demand for airline service? What are the advantages and disadvantages of each?

What is meant by the term *S-curve* as used in airline economics? How was the concept used to explain (or rationalize) the severe overcapacity of the airlines in the early 1970s? Do you believe the concept is a valid one? Valid to some extent or in some circumstances? Not valid at all? Give your opinion and defend it.

What is meant by the term *price/quality options*, and what is the complaint against the airlines on this score made by deregulation proponents? Describe the approach to the "price/quality option" concept whereby the "quality" of the service is related to the passenger's time. Give your opinion of this approach with your reasons.

Give some examples of "quality" options that have arisen since the deregulation of domestic airline service.

To what extent do you think that such developments as electronic mail, video-conferences, and videotelephones will affect airline travel in the future? Focus separately on business travel, tourist travel and family visits.

How do the operations of Southwest Airlines differ from those of the other major passenger carriers?

Name four CRSs now used by the U.S. scheduled airlines, and show the ownership of each.

In what ways might a host carrier try to bias its CRS to favor its flights over those of its competitors? What technological developments limit the ability of a host carrier to do this?

Do you think airlines should be required to divest themselves of ownership of CRSs, putting ownership in the hands of an impartial nonairline company? What are the arguments in favor and what practical considerations are against?

What provision has DOT put in its definition of "open skies" bilateral agreements with respect to CRSs?

What does "ticketless travel" mean?

Why have the airlines cut commissions to travel agents and sought to encourage direct bookings? In what ways is the public benefited or hurt by this development? How might competition be reduced by the reduced role of the agents?

In what sense can the relationship between airlines and agents today be described as "ambivalent"?

CHAPTER 6

Terminology

Be able to explain the following terms:

Capacity-controlled fares
Cost-of-service and *value-of-service factors*
Country-of-origin rate clause
Cross-subsidization
Double-disapproval rate clause
Off-peak fares and peak-load pricing
Yield
Yield management

Questions

In the text is the following statement: "Rates are determined by a complex interaction of both cost-of-service and value-of-service factors." Discuss with respect to airline policy in setting discount fares. Discuss with respect to the tapering of fares with distance.

What is meant by the "zone of reasonableness" concept? Describe the standard foreign fare level concept, which applies to international passenger fares. Why does it have so narrow an upward zone and so wide a downward zone?

Trace the historical development of the passenger rate structure, for example, early one-class service; introduction of coach service; the era of family, youth, and standby fares; the DPFI decision; the impact of deregulation; the current structure.

How may the yield for the coach section drop without there having been any reduction in fares?

What is a predatory rate? Under what circumstances might the concept of a predatory rate be used by DOT or DOJ in future years?

Describe the role of the president with respect to the international rates of U.S. and foreign airlines.

Describe how frequent flyer programs work. What is the primary motive of an airline for establishing such a program?

What problems do the frequent flyer programs raise from an airline's standpoint? What problems from the standpoint of the companies whose employees earn free trips? What problems from a public interest standpoint?

How may the hub-and-spoke system distort the significance of comparative yields per passenger mile?

Describe the various proposals to partly reregulate domestic fares, and analyze the reasoning in support of each. Do you agree with any of them, and why or why not?

IATA: Who may belong? Describe the "conference" system, the role of governments in ratemaking, and the various functions besides ratemaking. In what respects does IATA *not* behave like a cartel?

Do you believe that the United States should remove its carriers altogether from the IATA ratemaking system, as was proposed in the CAB's show-cause order and has recently been advocated by the Department of Justice? Why, or why not?

What are the three types of rate articles found in bilateral agreements? With respect to each type, indicate to what extent (if any) DOT, in reviewing rates, is guided by IATA rates and/or the SFFL?

In international airline service, what methods do airlines and travel agencies often use to evade tariffs? In your opinion, why does DOT take a lenient view of such evasions?

A statutory requirement exists that carriers file tariffs with DOT for their international services. Why has this requirement lost much of its significance?

CHAPTER 7

Terminology

Be able to explain the following terms:

Air freight forwarder

Combination airline (combination carrier)

Combination aircraft

Convertible aircraft (and *"quick change" convertible aircraft)*

Cooperative shippers association

Cube-out problem

Density incentives

Dimensional weights

Double bottoms and *multiple bottoms*

Electronic data interchange

Exception ratings

General commodity rates

Integrated carriers

LASH

Specific commodity rates

Truckload and *LTL*

TOFC (piggyback)

Uncompromised (dedicated) *cargo aircraft*

Unitization, palletization, and *containerization*

Weight breaks and *rate differentials*

Questions

Discuss the "total cost concept" justification for using a more expensive mode of transportation. (Include each element in physical distribution.)

Describe the just-in-time concept. What special responsibility does it place on the transportation system?

Why is it unlikely that we will see a new uncompromised freighter aircraft designed and produced in the near future?

Why might the lighter-than-air airship be a good cargo carrier? What are its limitations as a cargo carrier?

Give examples of commodities that would fall in each of the three air freight categories (emergency, routine perishable, and routine surface-divertible). Which categories are primarily speed oriented? Which are primarily cost oriented?

What is the cube-out problem, and what measures are taken to cope with it? (Your answer should include discussion of uncompromised cargo aircraft, density incentives, cube-based rates, and sales efforts directed to the cube problem.)

What factors make costs at airline cargo terminals high, and what steps can be taken to control them?

What are the advantages and disadvantages of creating separate airports for freighters?

Who are the owners of Air Cargo, Inc., and what is its role in pickup and delivery service?

Explain how an air freight forwarder makes a profit out of consolidation, including an explanation of rate differentials and weight breaks.

What is the justification for having air freight forwarders, from the shipper's standpoint and from the airline's standpoint?

Why are railroads today of little significance competitively to air freight, whereas trucks are of great significance?

Distinguish between truckload and LTL traffic, as used in the trucking industry. Why is LTL traffic more susceptible to being diverted to air?

Two developments that may lower truck costs relative to air are double bottoms (or multiple bottoms) and TOFC service. Describe both and state what obstacles are preventing or discouraging their development.

Describe the operations of a container ship (including the variant called LASH), and explain why this development offers strong competition with air freight.

In their joint report, the Departments of State and Transportation have given reasons why the proportion of U.S. international air cargo carried by U.S. carriers has dropped in recent years. What reasons do they give? In light of all the facts, do you think this is a serious problem? Consider in your answer whether figures reflect tonnage or revenue or the value of the cargo.

What are the advantages and disadvantages of containerization from the shipper's standpoint and from the airline's standpoint?

Explain the following terms: *general commodity rate, specific commodity rate,* and *exception rating.* Why do the airlines have specific commodity rates? To what extent is each of the three oriented to cost of service? To value of service?

Explain the three types of discount: density incentive, container discount, and daylight container discount. What are the airlines' reasons for offering each?

Describe the operations of Federal Express, past and present.

If fuel conservation should become more critical, how might air cargo be adversely affected?

Name the different categories of hazardous cargo. What steps are being taken to improve shipper compliance?

Describe the major changes in entry and rate regulation made by the regulatory reform law for domestic air cargo.

What are the advantages to a manufacturer or retailer of owning and operating its own cargo aircraft instead of using common carriers? What are the disadvantages? How does this private carriage differ from contract carriage? Describe some possible hybrid arrangements that would have some aspects of private and some aspects of contract carriage.

Trace the development of the expedited small-package service ("air express"). Include the types of traffic carried and the varieties of service. Why has this traffic developed rapidly despite high rates?

Explain *electronic data interchange.* What functions can it perform in the air cargo business and what are its advantages?

What functions can be performed at an air cargo terminal by automated guided vehicles?

What developments in foreign countries can influence the directional flow of air cargo?

How does the concept of yield management get involved in negotiated cargo rates?

What might motivate airlines to form cargo alliances? What advantages and disadvantages are there to cargo alliances from the standpoint of forwarders and shippers?

CHAPTER 8

Terminology

Be able to explain the following terms:

Adequacy of an airport
Capacity of an airport

General obligation bonds
Revenue bonds
Secondary pledge

Questions

How have hub-and-spoke networks aggravated congestion at airports? Should airlines reduce hubbing at the most crowded airports? Would you favor governmental action requiring this?

Aside from building new airports, what steps can be taken to alleviate congestion at the busiest airports?

Describe the "free flight" concept. What advantages would it offer to airlines and to passengers?

Describe the aircraft noise reduction program, the three stages, and airline efforts to comply.

The funds to construct and expand airports come from many sources. Name these sources. Would you favor denying further federal aid to large airports that have substantial revenue sources?

Bus lines, truckers, and railroads usually own their own terminals, but airlines do not own airports. What is the advantage to the airlines in this, and what are the disadvantages?

Distinguish between *general obligation bonds* and *revenue bonds* in airport financing. What is meant by a *secondary pledge* and how may it sometimes involve airlines?

Define the terms *adequacy* and *capacity* as applied to airports. What elements enter into a study of the adequacy of an airport?

What do you think the future structure of the U.S. airline industry will be, and why? Dominance by a few large carriers? A stable (or unstable) fringe of specialists? A thriving or shrinking regional sector?

Technological advances in the future may involve improved versions of conventional jet aircraft, airships, helicopters (or other short-takeoff-and-landing vehicles), and SSTs. What are the desirable characteristics of each? For what types of service would each be used?

What were some of the recommendations of the National Commission to Ensure a Strong, Competitive Airline Industry? Where did it stand on reregulation?

What is your opinion, overall, of the regulatory reform movement? Consider both the legislation and the underlying economic philosophy, both the domestic and the international services. Do you think there will be further shrinking of the scope of regulation, or a swing back to increased regulation? Do you think the public interest is well or badly served by the movement, and why?

Appendix: Transportation Statute—Digest of Selected Portions

This is a digest of certain portions of the transportation statue (Title 49, United States Code) pertinent to airline economics, as enacted by P.L. 103–272—July 5, 1994. The full text of the statute covers a wide variety of aviation and other transportation matters not within the scope of this book.

TABLE OF CONTENTS

SECTION 40101 DECLARATIONS OF POLICY

This section sets forth numerous guidelines that DOT, in conducting the economic regulation of airlines, is to consider as "being in the public interest and consistent with public convenience and necessity." They include: "the availability of a variety of adequate, economic, efficient, and low-priced services"; "placing maximum reliance on competitive market forces and on actual and potential competition"; "preventing unfair, deceptive, predatory, or anticompetitive practices"; "avoiding unreasonable industry concentration"; "encouraging entry into air transportation markets by new and existing air carriers and the continued strengthening of small air carriers"; and "strengthening the competitive position of air carriers to at least ensure equality with foreign air carriers."

The section also provides separate guidelines for all-cargo carriers, including: "encouraging and developing an integrated transportation system relying on competitive market forces to decide the extent, variety, quality, and price of services provided."

Another portion of this section adds some guidelines for international air transportation. It includes provisions such as: "freedom of air carriers and foreign air carriers to offer prices that respond to consumer demand"; "eliminating discrimination and unfair competitive practices faced by United States airlines in foreign air transportation"; and "opportunities for carriers of foreign countries to increase their access to places in the United States if exchanged for benefits of similar magnitude for air carriers or the traveling public."

SECTION 40102 DEFINITIONS

This section defines 41 terms as they are used in the statute. They include the following:

"Air carrier" means a citizen of the United States undertaking by any means, directly or indirectly, to provide air transportation.

"Air transportation" means foreign air transportation, interstate air transportation, or the transportation of mail by aircraft.

"All-cargo air transportation" means the transportation by aircraft in interstate air transportation of only property or only mail, or both.

"Citizen of the United States" means—

(A) an individual who is a citizen of the United States;

(B) a partnership each of whose partners is an individual who is a citizen of the United States; or

(C) a corporation or association organized under the laws of the United States or a State, the District of Columbia, or a territory or possession of the United States, of which the president and at least two-thirds of the board of directors and other managing officers are citizens of the United States, and in which at least 75 percent of the voting interest is owned or controlled by persons that are citizens of the United States.

"Foreign air carrier" means a person, not a citizen of the United States, undertaking by any means, directly or indirectly, to provide foreign air transportation.

"Foreign air transportation" means the transportation of passengers or property by aircraft as a common carrier for compensation, or the transportation of mail by aircraft, between a place in the United States and a place outside the United States when any part of the transportation is by aircraft.

"Interstate air transportation" means the transportation of passengers or property by aircraft as a common carrier for compensation, or the transportation of mail by aircraft—

(A) between a place in—

(i) a State, territory, or possession of the United States and a place in the District of Columbia or another State, territory, or possession of the United States;

(ii) Hawaii and another place in Hawaii through the airspace over a place outside Hawaii;

(iii) the District of Columbia and another place in the District of Columbia;

(iv) a territory or possession of the United States and another place in the same territory or possession; and

(B) when any part of the transportation is by aircraft.

"Predatory" means a practice that violates the antitrust laws as defined in the first section of the Clayton Act (15 U.S.C. 12).

SECTION 40109 EXEMPTIONS

This section grants broad power to DOT to exempt "a person or class of persons" from the economic regulation provisions of the statute or from its own regulations, if it finds "that the exemption is consistent with the public interest." The word "person" includes a corporation, whether U.S. or foreign.

This section also grants a specific exemption to air taxis (including commuter air carriers) that serves as their basic operating authority. It defines the class as any air carrier that "provides passenger transportation only with aircraft having a maximum capacity of 55 passengers" or "provides the transportation of cargo only with aircraft having a maximum payload of less than 18,000 pounds." DOT (and, earlier, the CAB) is then empowered to raise the passenger or cargo capacities "when the public interest requires." In 1978, the CAB raised the passenger limit to 60, and DOT has left it there.

Another part of this section authorizes DOT to grant exemptions to foreign air carriers to carry cabotage traffic for temporary periods in emergency situations.

SECTION 41101 CERTIFICATE REQUIREMENT

This section requires an air carrier to obtain a certificate in order to furnish air transportation. As noted in the definitions, "air carrier" means a U.S. citizen, but "air transportation" covers both domestic and foreign operations of U.S. airlines.

SECTION 41102 CERTIFICATION POLICY

This section spells out the fitness requirement and, for certificates for international service, makes the further stipulation that the proposed service be "consistent with the public convenience and necessity." It also notes that any certificate for international service must be submitted for review by the president, in accordance with Section 41307.

SECTION 41103 ALL-CARGO CERTIFICATES

This section allows for the issuance of certificates limited to domestic all-cargo service, subject only to a fitness test. It forbids DOT to "restrict the places served or prices charged by the holder of the certificate."

SECTION 41108 APPLICATIONS FOR CERTIFICATES

This section spells out the procedure for applying for a certificate and the processing requirements for DOT.

SECTION 41109 TERMS OF CERTIFICATES

This section authorizes DOT to prescribe terms for certificates, but forbids DOT to prescribe "a term preventing an air carrier from adding or changing schedules, equipment, accommodations, and facilities for providing the authorized transportation to satisfy business development and public demand." With respect to international certificates, it is left up to DOT whether to specify the points to be served or merely to "specify each general route to be followed." (Domestic certificates do not specify points to be served or even the general route to be followed.)

SECTION 41302 FOREIGN AIR CARRIER PERMITS

This section authorizes DOT to issue a foreign air carrier permit to a foreign citizen and sets forth the guidelines. Besides a fitness finding, the airline must have been designated by its government, or else DOT must find that the transportation covered by the permit "will be in the public interest."

SECTION 41304 SUSPENSIONS OF PERMITS

This section authorizes DOT, after a hearing, to "amend, modify, suspend, or revoke" a foreign air carrier permit if it finds such action "to be in the public interest." A separate part of the section authorizes DOT "without a hearing but subject to the approval of the President," to suspend or modify a foreign air carrier permit where there is a dispute with the foreign country over operations by a U.S. carrier or other "unfair, discriminatory, or restrictive practices."

SECTION 41307 PRESIDENTIAL REVIEW

A decision by DOT "to issue, deny, amend, modify, suspend, revoke, or transfer" either a foreign air carrier permit or an international certificate of a U.S. carrier must be submitted to the president. Within a 60-day period, the president may disapprove the order, but "only if the reason for disapproval is based on foreign relations or national defense considerations" and not "if the reason is economic or related to carrier selection."

SECTION 41308 EXEMPTION FROM ANTITRUST LAWS

This section grants DOT authority to include an exemption from antitrust laws in any order issued under Section 41309.

SECTION 41309 COOPERATIVE AGREEMENTS

Agreements among U.S. and foreign carriers may be filed with DOT, seeking approval of cooperative working arrangements such as IATA agreements and carrier alliances involving foreign air transportation. DOT is supposed to approve if the agreement is "not adverse to the public interest," but should disapprove if the agreement would reduce substantially, or eliminate, competition, unless there is a need that cannot be met by less anticompetitive means. In making the latter finding, DOT may consider "international comity and foreign policy considerations."

SECTION 41310 DISCRIMINATORY PRACTICES

This section begins: "An air carrier or foreign air carrier may not subject a person, place, port, or type of traffic in foreign air transportation to unreasonable discrimination." It then spells out elaborate procedural steps by which complaints of unreasonable discrimination are to be handled.

SECTION 41501 REASONABLENESS OF INTERNATIONAL RATES

This section requires both U.S. and foreign airlines to establish "reasonable prices, classifications, rules, and practices related to foreign air transportation."

SECTION 41504 TARIFFS FOR INTERNATIONAL RATES

This section states the formal requirement for both U.S. and foreign airlines to keep tariffs on file with DOT for international services, showing rates and rules.

SECTION 41509 SUSPENSION OR CANCELLATION OF TARIFFS

This section gives DOT authority to cancel or reject the tariff of a U.S. or foreign airline for international services if it finds the price or practice "unreasonable or unreasonably discriminatory." With respect to foreign airlines, DOT may cancel or reject a tariff if it finds simply that such action is "in the public interest." The section also sets forth the rules for maintaining by DOT of a standard foreign fare level, and provides that DOT may not find a fare unreasonable if it is within the zone set by the foreign fare level.

Orders to be issued under this section must be submitted for presidential review. The president has ten days in which to disapprove an order "on finding disapproval is necessary for United States foreign policy or national defense reasons."

SECTION 41708 FILING OF REPORTS

This section empowers DOT to require both U.S. and foreign airlines to file reports in a manner prescribed by DOT.

SECTION 41709 RECORD-KEEPING REQUIREMENTS

This section empowers DOT to require the U.S. airlines to keep their records and accounts in a manner prescribed by DOT, and permits DOT to inspect these records and accounts.

SECTION 41712 UNFAIR PRACTICES AND METHODS OF COMPETITION

Under this section, DOT may "investigate and decide whether an air carrier, foreign air carrier, or ticket agent has been or is engaged in an unfair method of competition." On making such a finding, DOT may order the practice or method to be stopped.

SECTION 41732 BASIC ESSENTIAL AIR SERVICE

This section defines a minimum essential service in such terms as number of flights per week to a hub airport, size of aircraft, reasonable flight times, and "prices that are not excessive compared to the generally prevailing prices of other air carriers for like service between similar places." Different standards are established for services within Alaska.

SECTION 41733 SUBSIDIES FOR ESSENTIAL AIR SERVICE

This section provides that if a minimum level of service will not be maintained without a subsidy, then DOT may establish and pay such a subsidy.

The section also lists the guidelines DOT should follow in selecting a carrier to perform the subsidized service. These include the applicant's reliability, the arrangements it has made for interlining with majors at the hub airport, and the view of local officials.

SECTION 41737 SUBSIDY GUIDELINES FOR ESSENTIAL AIR SERVICE

This section authorizes DOT to establish guidelines for determining the proper amounts of subsidies, and requires DOT to assure that the services are being carried out, and in a reliable fashion. It describes the procedure for filing and processing and paying subsidy claims.

SECTION 42111 MUTUAL AID AGREEMENTS

This section permits agreements whereby, when an airline is on strike, other airlines benefiting from carrying its struck traffic may compensate it. The agreement must be approved by DOT. There are severe limitations. It is limited to foreign air transportation; benefits cannot be paid for the first 30 days of the strike, nor extend beyond eight weeks; benefits cannot exceed 60 percent of what the struck carrier's operating expenses would have been; and, if the striking employees request, the dispute must be submitted to binding arbitration. These conditions are such that there have been no mutual aid agreements since this language was adopted by the ADA.

Selected Bibliography

BOOKS

Air Transport Association of America. *Air Cargo from A to Z*. Washington, D.C.: Air Transport Association of America, undated.

Bailey, Elizabeth E., David R. Graham, and Daniel P. Kaplan. *Deregulating the Airlines*. Cambridge, Mass.: The MIT Press, 1985.

Biederman, Paul. *The U.S. Airline Industry: End of an Era*. New York: Praeger, 1982.

Brancker, J. W. S. *IATA and What It Does*. Leiden: A. W. Sijthoff, 1977.

Butler, Gail F., and Martin R. Keller, eds. *Handbook of Airline Finance*. Washington, D.C.: McGraw-Hill, 1999.

———. *Handbook of Airline Marketing*. Washington, D.C.: McGraw-Hill, 1998.

Carron, Andrew S. *Transition to a Free Market: Deregulation of the Air Cargo Industry*. Washington, D.C.: Brookings Institution, 1981.

Caves, Richard E. *Air Transport and Its Regulators*. Cambridge, Mass.: Harvard University Press, 1962.

Cherington, Paul W. *Airline Price Policy*. Cambridge, Mass.: Harvard University Press, 1958.

Chuang, Richard Y. *The International Air Transport Association*. Leiden: A. W. Sijthoff, 1972.

Dempsey, Paul Stephen. *The Social and Economic Consequences of Deregulation*. Westport, Conn.: Quorum Books, 1989.

Dempsey, Paul S., and Laurence E. Gesell. *Airline Management: Strategies for the 21st Century*. Chandler, Ariz.: Coast Aire Publications, 1997.

———. *Air Transportation: Foundations for the 21st Century*. Chandler, Ariz.: Coast Aire Publications, 1997.

de Murias, Ramon. *The Economic Regulation of International Air Transport*. Jefferson, N.C.: McFarland, 1989.

Dobson, Alan P. *Peaceful Air Warfare: The United States, Britain and the Politics of International Aviation*. Oxford, England: Clarendon Press, 1991.

Douglas, George W., and James C. Miller III. *The CAB's Domestic Passenger Fare Investigation*. Washington, D.C.: Brookings Institution, 1974.

———. *Economic Regulation of Domestic Air Transport*. Washington, D.C.: Brookings Institution, 1974.

Durant, Will, and Ariel Durant. *The Lessons of History*. New York: Simon and Schuster, 1968.

Eads, George C. *The Local Service Airline Experiment*. Washington, D.C.: Brookings Institution, 1972.

Fredrick, John H. *Commercial Air Transportation*. 5th ed. Homewood, Ill.: Richard D. Irwin, 1961.

Fruhan, William E., Jr. *The Fight for Competitive Advantage: A Study of the United States Domestic Trunk Air Carriers*. Boston: Harvard Graduate School of Business Administration, 1972.

Gesell, Laurence E. *The Administration of Public Airports*. 4th ed. Chandler, Ariz.: Coast Aire Publications, 1999.

———. *Airline Re-Regulation*. Chandler, Ariz.: Coast Aire Publications, 1990.

Holloway, Stephen. *Straight and Level: Practical Airline Economics*. Brookfield, Vt.: Ashgate Publishing, 1997.

James, George W., ed. *Airline Economics*. Lexington, Mass.: D. C. Heath, 1982.

Jenkins, Darryl, ed. *Handbook of Airline Economics*. Washington, D.C.: McGraw-Hill, 1995.

Jordan, William A. *Airline Regulation in America*. Baltimore: Johns Hopkins University Press, 1970.

Kaps, Robert W. *Air Transport Labor Relations*. Carbondale: Southern Illinois University Press, 1997.

Little, Arthur D., Inc. *Civil Aviation Development: A Policy and Operations Analysis*. New York: Praeger, 1972.

Meyer, John R., and Clinton V. Oster Jr. eds. *Airline Deregulation: The Early Experience*. Boston: Auburn House, 1981.

Meyer, John R., and Clinton V. Oster Jr. *Deregulation and the Future of Intercity Passenger Travel*. Cambridge, Mass.: The MIT Press, 1987.

———. *Deregulation and the New Airline Entrepreneurs*. Cambridge, Mass.: The MIT Press, 1984.

Miller, John Andrew. *Air Diplomacy: The Chicago Civil Aviation Conference of 1944*. Ann Arbor, Mich.: University Microfilms, 1971.

Morrison, Steven, and Clifford Winston. *The Economic Effects of Airline Deregulation*. Washington, D.C.: Brookings Institution, 1986.

O'Connor, William E. *Economic Regulation of the World's Airlines: A Political Analysis*. New York: Praeger, 1971.

Schneider, Lewis M. *The Future of the U.S. Domestic Air Freight Industry: An Analysis of Management Strategies*. Boston: Harvard Graduate School of Business Administration, 1973.

Sochor, Eugene. *The Politics of International Aviation*. Iowa City: University of Iowa Press, 1991.

Spencer, Frank A., and Frank H. Cassell. *Eight Years of U.S. Airline Deregulation: Management and Labor Adaptations; Re-Emergence of Oligopoly.* Evanston, Ill.: Northwestern University Transportation Center, 1987.

Straszheim, Mahlon R. *The International Airline Industry.* Washington, D.C.: Brookings Institution, 1969.

Taneja, Nawal K. *Airlines in Transition.* Lexington, Mass.: D. C. Heath, 1981.

———. *The Commercial Airline Industry.* Lexington, Mass.: D. C. Heath, 1976.

———. *The International Airline Industry: Trends, Issues, and Challenges.* Lexington, Mass.: D. C. Heath, 1988.

———. *Introduction to Civil Aviation.* 2nd ed. Lexington, Mass.: D. C. Heath, 1989.

———. *The U.S. Airfreight Industry.* Lexington, Mass.: D. C. Heath, 1979.

———. *U.S. International Aviation Policy.* Lexington, Mass.: D. C. Heath, 1980.

Thayer, Frederick C. Jr. *Air Transport Policy and National Security.* Chapel Hill: University of North Carolina Press, 1965.

Thornton, Robert L. *International Airlines and Politics.* Ann Arbor: University of Michigan Press, 1970.

Transportation Research Board. *Winds of Change: Domestic Air Transport Since Deregulation.* Washington, D.C.: National Research Council, 1991.

Tretheway, Michael W., and Tae H. Oum. *Airline Economics: Foundations for Strategy and Policy.* Vancouver, Canada: Centre for Transportation Studies, 1992.

Wells, Alexander T. *Air Transportation: A Management Perspective.* 4th ed. Belmont, Calif.: Wadsworth Publishing Company, 1999.

Wheatcroft, Stephen. *Air Transport Policy.* London: Michael Joseph, 1964.

ARTICLES

Abeyratne, Ruwantissa I. R. "Would Competition in Commercial Aviation Ever Fit Into the World Trade Organization?" *Journal of Air Law and Commerce* 61 (May–June 1996): 793–857.

Arlington, David T. "Liberalization of Restrictions on Foreign Ownership in U.S. Air Carriers." *Journal of Air Law and Commerce* 59 (1993): 133–92.

Baur, Uli, and David Kistner. "Airline Privatization: Principles and Lessons Learned." In *Handbook of Airline Finance*, pp. 71–81. Edited by Gail F. Butler and Martin R. Keller. Washington, D.C.: McGraw-Hill, 1999.

Bender, Alan R. "Allied Airlines: The New Robber Barons?" *Aviation Week and Space Technology*, June 22, 1998, p. 70.

———. "Battle 2000: The New Jet Entrants Versus the Regional Partners?" *Journal of Aviation/Aerospace Education and Research* 6 (1995): 7–16.

Berardino, Frank. "Integrating Airline Strategy and Marketing." In *Handbook of Airline Marketing*, pp. 105–16. Edited by Gail F. Butler and Martin R. Keller. Washington, D.C.: McGraw-Hill, 1998.

Caver, Paul. "Employee-Owned Airlines: The Cure for an Ailing Industry?" *Journal of Air Law and Commerce* 61 (February–March 1996): 639–81.

Coddington, Peter B. "A Cost Analysis: Re-engining a Boeing 727-200 (Advanced) versus Buying a New Boeing 757-200." *Journal of Aviation/Aerospace Education and Research* 4 (1993): 25–32.

Cross, Robert G. "Trends in Airline Revenue Management." In *Handbook of Airline Marketing*, pp. 303–18. Edited by Gail F. Butler and Martin R. Keller. Washington, D.C.: McGraw-Hill, 1998.

Dempsey, Paul Stephen. "Airline Deregulation and Laissez-Faire Mythology." *Journal of Air Law and Commerce* 56 (1990): 305–412.

Durham, Michael J. "The Future of Sabre." In *Handbook of Airline Economics*, pp. 485–91. Edited by Darryl Jenkins. Washington, D.C.: McGraw-Hill, 1995.

Elder, Bill. "Free Flight: The Future of Air Transportation Entering the Twenty-First Century." *Journal of Air Law and Commerce* 62 (February-March 1997): 871–914.

Elliott, G. Porter. "Learning to Fly: The European Commission Enters Unfamiliar Skies." *Journal of Air Law and Commerce* 64 (Winter 1998): 157–93.

Elsworthy, Lewis E. "The CRS: A Global Electronic Marketplace." In *Handbook of Airline Economics*, pp. 493–97. Edited by Darryl Jenkins. Washington, D.C.: McGraw-Hill, 1995.

Fahy, Richard J., Jr. "The Cutting Edge of Technology and Regulation." In *Handbook of Airline Economics*, pp. 499–506. Edited by Darryl Jenkins. Washington, D.C.: McGraw-Hill, 1995.

Feldman, Joan M. "Empty Gesture." *Air Transport World* (May 1999): 47–52.

Frainey, William M. "Network Profitability Analysis." In *Handbook of Airline Finance*, pp. 161–72. Edited by Gail F. Butler and Martin R. Keller. Washington, D.C.: McGraw-Hill, 1999.

Garvett, Donald S., and Alex Avery. "Frequent Traveler Programs: Moving Targets." In *Handbook of Airline Marketing*, pp. 567–76. Edited by Gail F. Butler and Martin R. Keller. Washington, D.C.: McGraw-Hill, 1998.

Garvett, Donald S., and Kyle J. Hilton. "What Drives Airline Profits?" In *Handbook of Airline Finance*, pp. 173–85. Edited by Gail F. Butler and Martin R. Keller. Washington, D.C.: McGraw-Hill, 1999.

Garvett, Donald S., and Laurence Michaels. "Price Parrying: A Direction for Quick, Decisive, and Profit-Maximizing Pricing." In *Handbook of Airline Marketing*, pp. 333–48. Edited by Gail F. Butler and Martin R. Keller. Washington, D.C.: McGraw-Hill, 1998.

Gesell, Laurence E., and Martin T. Farris. "Airline Deregulation: An Evaluation of Goals and Objectives." *Transportation Law Journal* 21 (1992): 105–27.

Ghobrial, Atef. "Competition for Hub Dominance: Some Implications for Airline Profitability and Enplanement Share." *Journal of Aviation/Aerospace Education and Research* 2 (1991): 20–29.

Gillick, John E. "The Impact of Citizenship Considerations on Aviation Financing." In *Handbook of Airline Finance*, pp. 41–50. Edited by Gail F. Butler and Martin R. Keller. Washington, D.C.: McGraw-Hill, 1999.

Goodman, Kathleen M., and Scott Davis. "Free Flight and the Pilot-in-Command Concept." *Journal of Air Law and Commerce* 62 (February-March 1997): 653–73.

Gordon, Jeffrey N. "Employee Stock Ownership as a Transitional Device." In *Handbook of Airline Economics*, pp. 575–92. Edited by Darryl Jenkins. Washington, D.C.: McGraw-Hill, 1995.

Hardaway, Robert M., and Paul Stephen Dempsey. "Airlines, Airports, and Antitrust: A Proposed Strategy for Enhanced Competition." *Journal of Air Law and Commerce* 58 (1992): 455–507.

Hatton, Rick. "Complexities of Air Cargo vis-à-vis Finance: The Economics of Wide-Body Freighter Aircraft." In *Handbook of Airline Finance*, pp. 535–42. Edited by Gail F. Butler and Martin R. Keller. Washington, D.C.: McGraw-Hill, 1999.

Herlehy, William F., and Tracy Ingalls-Ashbaugh. "Airline Employee Slowdowns and Sickouts as Unlawful Self Help: A Statistical Analysis." *Journal of Aviation/Aerospace Education and Research* 3 (1993): 18–28.

Irrgang, Michael E. "Fuel Conservation." In *Handbook of Airline Economics*, pp. 367–78. Edited by Darryl Jenkins. Washington, D.C.: McGraw-Hill, 1995.

Jansonius, John V., and Kenneth E. Broughton. "Coping with Deregulation: Reduction of Labor Costs in the Airline Industry." *Journal of Air Law and Commerce* 49 (1984): 501–53.

Jonsson, Christer. "Sphere of Flying: The Politics of International Aviation." *International Organization* 35 (1981): 273–302.

Keyes, Lucile S. "The Regulation of Airline Mergers by the Department of Transportation." *Journal of Air and Law and Commerce* 53 (1988): 737–64.

Kotaite, Assad. "Investment and Training Needs among Key Challenges Facing Developing Countries." *ICAO Journal* 48 (1993): 24–26.

Lang, Laura. "EDI Systems Work Well, But Not With Each Other." *Air Cargo World*, December 1991, pp. 24–31.

Lawter, Allison K. "Free Flight or Free Fall?" *Journal of Air Law and Commerce* 62 (February-March 1997): 915–56.

Lewis, Ira. "United States–Canada Air Services: The Role of Alliances in a Future Bilateral Agreement." *Transportation Journal* 34 (Spring 1995): 5–12.

Lyle, Chris. "Computer-Age Vulnerability in the International Airline Industry." *Journal of Air Law and Commerce* 54 (1988): 161–78.

Margo, Rod D. "Aspects of Insurance in Aviation Finance." *Journal of Air Law and Commerce* 62 (November-December 1996): 423–78.

Mendes de Leon, Pablo M. J., and Steven A. Mirmina. "Protecting the Environment by use of Fiscal Measures: Legality and Propriety." *Journal of Air Law and Commerce* 62 (February-March 1997): 791–821.

Mendes de Leon, Pablo M. J. "Nationality and Privatization of Airlines in Light of Globalization." In *Handbook of Airline Finance*, pp. 51–70. Edited by Gail F. Butler and Martin R. Keller. Washington, D.C.: McGraw-Hill, 1999.

Mosteller, Jeff. "The Current and Future Climate of Airline Consolidation: The Possible Impact of an Alliance of Two Large Airlines and an Examination of the Proposed American Airlines–British Airways Alliance." *Journal of Air Law and Commerce* 64 (Spring 1999): 575–603.

Neidl, Raymond E. "Current Financial and Operational Trends in the Airline Industry." In *Handbook of Airline Finance*, pp. 611–25. Edited by Gail F. Butler and Martin R. Keller. Washington, D.C.: McGraw-Hill, 1999.

Papaioannou, Athanassios. "The Employer's Duty to Bargain Over Layoffs in the Airline Industry: How the Courts Have Distorted the Railway Labor Act." *Journal of Air Law and Commerce* 55 (1990): 939–1008.

Pate, Ian E. "In Re Travel Agency Commission Antitrust Litigation." *Journal of Air Law and Commerce* 64 (Summer 1999): 941–76.

Pearl, Daniel. "Fields of Dreams." *Wall Street Journal,* December 2, 1992, pp. A1–A2.

Perry, Linda J. "The Financial Implications of Regional Jet Service at Selected Airports." In *Handbook of Airline Finance,* pp. 543–55. Edited by Gail F. Butler and Martin R. Keller. Washington, D.C.: McGraw-Hill, 1999.

Shearman, Philip. "Airline Marketing: A Great Future but Different." In *Handbook of Airline Marketing,* pp. 131–39. Edited by Gail F. Butler and Martin R. Keller. Washington, D.C.: McGraw-Hill, 1998.

Sobie, Brendan. "The Future: Bigger, Faster?" *Air Cargo World* (January 2000): 42–48.

Spencer, Frank A., and Frank H. Cassell. "Emergence of Policy Bargaining." In *Handbook of Airline Economics,* pp. 549–61. Edited by Darryl Jenkins. Washington, D.C.: McGraw-Hill, 1995.

Swinnen, Benoit M. J. "An Opportunity for Transatlantic Civil Aviation: From Open Skies to Open Markets?" *Journal of Air Law and Commerce* 63 (August-September 1997): 249–85.

Taylor, John H. "Fasten Seat Belts, Please." *Forbes,* April 2, 1990, pp. 84–88.

Zuelsdorf, Robert J., and Eric B. McLellan. "The Economic Impact of Civil Aviation on the U.S. Economy." In *Handbook of Airline Economics,* pp. 267–84. Edited by Darryl Jenkins. Washington, D.C.: McGraw-Hill, 1995.

PERIODICALS

Air Cargo World
Air Transport World
Annual Report, Air Transport Association
Aviation Week and Space Technology
Forbes
ICAO Journal
Journal of Air Law and Commerce
Journal of Aviation/Aerospace Education and Research
Modern Maturity
Transportation Journal
Transportation Law Journal
Wall Street Journal

PUBLIC DOCUMENTS

U.S. Civil Aeronautics Board. *Handbook of Airline Statistics.* 1974.

———. *Implementation of the Provisions of the Airline Deregulation Act of 1978.* 1984.

———. *Report to Congress* (by fiscal year).

———. "TWA, North-South California Service." *CAB Reports* 4 (1943): 373.

U.S. Congress, House Committee on Public Works and Transportation. *U.S. International Aviation Policy: The International Air Cargo Study.* 1988.

———. *U.S. International Aviation Trade Policy.* 1987.

U.S. Department of Commerce. Bureau of the Census. *Statistical Abstract of the United States.* 1997.

U.S. Department of Energy. Oak Ridge National Laboratory. *Energy Intensiveness of Passenger and Freight Transport Modes: 1950–1970.* 1973.

U.S. Department of State. *Protocol Relating to U.S.-Netherlands Air Transport Agreement of 1957.* T.I.A.S. no. 8998, 1978.

U.S. Department of Transportation. *Airport Activity Statistics of Certificated Carriers, 1998.*

———. *Secretary's Task Force on Competition in the U.S. Domestic Airline Industry.* 1990.

———. *U.S. Subsidized Essential Air Service—July 1999.*

U.S. General Accounting Office. *Airline Competition: Impact of Changing Foreign Investment and Control Limits on U.S. Airlines.* 1992.

———. *International Aviation: Measures by European Community Could Limit U.S. Airlines' Ability to Compete Abroad.* 1993

Index

About the Author

WILLIAM E. O'CONNOR is professor emeritus of Embry-Riddle Aeronautical University in Daytona Beach, Florida, where he taught courses in airline economics, air cargo management, government-aviation relations, and transportation principles. His earlier career was with the federal government in Washington, D.C., where he served first with the Department of State and then, for 18 years, with the Civil Aeronautics Board. He holds a doctorate from the School of International Service, American University in Washington.

Dr. O'Connor is the author of *Economic Regulation of the World's Airlines: A Political Analysis* (Praeger, 1971) and articles published in *Air Law* and the *Aviation Research Journal*.